D0282611

WISER, Charlotte Melina Viall. Four families of Karimpur. Maxwell School of Citizenship and Public Affairs, Syracuse University, 1978. 229p ill maps (Foreign and comparative studies: South Asian series, 3) bibl 78-1557. 6.50 ISBN 0-915984-78-4

There can be very few Westerners (and perhaps no Western anthropologists) who know any Indian village more intimately than Charlotte Wiser knows the North Indian village of Karimpur. She and her late husband, William, first went to live there in 1925. Much of Wiser's life since then has been spent in the village and its vicinity. The Wisers described Karimpur in *Behind mud walls* (1930); later, Charlotte reissued that volume (1963) with an extended postscript recording the changes and continuities of the intervening decades. Here Wiser tells again of Karimpur's people, chronicling three generations of four families whose members she has known closely over the past half century. She writes of them warmly and yet objectively as well-loved friends and neighbors. Susan Wadley of Syracuse University did her own field research in Karimpur and adds a useful introduction to both author and subject. This is a relaxed, readable, and pleasantly personal book. It would make a fine introduction to Indian village life for a high school library; yet graduate students and their teachers will also find it freshly informative. The faintly irksome reminders of a missionary perspective, which some readers thought they

Continued

WISER

detected in *Behind mud walls,* are absent, and Wiser emerges here as a skillful storyteller in the best tradition of rural reminiscence. The book makes a fine complement to two others recalling personal sojourns in village India, Prakash Tandon's *Punjabi century* (1961) and M. N. Srinivas's *The remembered village* (CHOICE, Jul.-Aug. 1977). Attractive typescript paperback format.

LARRY A. JACKSON LIBRARY
LANDER COLLEGE
GREENWOOD, SC 29646

FOUR FAMILIES OF KARIMPUR

by

CHARLOTTE V. WISER

226491

Foreign and Comparative Studies / South Asian Series, No. 3

Maxwell School of Citizenship and Public Affairs

Syracuse University

1978

LARRY A. JACKSON LIBRARY
LANDER COLLEGE
GREENWOOD, SC 29646

Copyright

1978

by

MAXWELL SCHOOL OF CITIZENSHIP AND PUBLIC AFFAIRS

SYRACUSE UNIVERSITY, SYRACUSE, NEW YORK, U.S.A.

Library of Congress Cataloging in Publication Data

Wiser, Charlotte Melina Viall

   Four families of Karimpur.

   (Foreign and comparative studies : South Asian
series ; no. 3)
   Bibliography: p.
   1. Karimpur, India--Rural conditions.
2. Villages--India--Karimpur. 3. Family--India--
Karimpur. 4. Karimpur, India--Social life and
customs. I. Title. II. Series.
HN690.K293W57   954   78-1557

TO MY FRIENDS IN KARIMPUR;
ESPECIALLY PARBAT, BALRAM,
DINESH AND RAMESH LAL

CONTENTS

LIST OF ILLUSTRATIONS

LIST OF MAPS

LIST OF TABLES

FOREWORD

One October day in 1925, two young Americans,
William and Charlotte Wiser, set up two tents in a mango
grove on the outskirts of the Indian village of Karimpur.
Here they lived with their two sons for most of the following five years while they continued their search for
deeper understanding of village men and women, a search
that had begun soon after their arrival in India.

The Wisers first went to North India in the second
decade of the twentieth century under the auspices of the
Presbyterian Mission to work in an Agricultural Institute
in Allahabad. When the extension program in which they
had hoped to work did not materialize, they found employment teaching at a nearby college. At the same time,
they began their lifelong study of the languages and customs of India. Later they worked with factory workers
in Kanpur and, after a year's study-leave in the States,
returned to advise a cooperative loan society in Mainpuri
District. It was their experience with the loan society
that convinced them that they must pursue their goal of
learning about Indian rural society by living in a village for an extended period of time. Finally, their
superiors in the Mission gave them permission to try the
experiment for one year. One year in the mango grove was
extended to five, followed by three years of study at
Cornell University and some years of teaching. Eventually Bill founded India Village Service, an experimental
program in rural development which became one of the mod-
els for independent India's Community Development Program.
In 1959, when they could finally retire, they chose to
build a house in Karimpur. It was their first real home,
built on land donated by Prakash, Bill's assistant from
the 1920's.

Unfortunately their enjoyment of their home was
brief, for immediately after the all-village housewarming,

Bill was ordered to a hospital for surgery. Three years
later, after Bill's death in the United States, Charlotte
returned to Karimpur alone. She intended to live by herself in her village home, but found that her neighbors
had occupied it during her absence, following a village
maxim that no housing space should be left untenanted.
Hence she settled in with Prakash's family and continued
to live with them many months each year for the next decade. Prakash's family became her family and Karimpur's
residents her friends. While in Karimpur she utilized
her long acquaintance with the village and its inhabitants to chronicle their history and the changes that
were occurring. Some of her observations appeared in
the second and third editions of <u>Behind Mud Walls</u>, her
and Bill's first portrayal of an Indian village for
outsiders.[1]

But the few additional chapters in <u>Behind Mud Walls</u>
were not sufficient for depicting the magnitude of fifty
years of change, particularly as it affected individuals.
So, Charlotte began to study four families, representing
different social and economic categories of Karimpur
society. This book is the result: a three-generational
study of a Farmer, a Carpenter, an Oil Presser, and a
Brahmin family. It reflects the kind and sympathetic
observations of a woman who knows India and Indian villagers well. It could only have been written by someone
who personally knew members of all three generations.

Although Charlotte may still sometimes be referred
to in Karimpur as "mem sahib," she is often called
"babenji," a respectful term for older sister, or, more
common among the young, "Dadi," grandmother. It is as
"Dadi" that I know Charlotte. In 1967, as a young and
naive anthropologist I too pursued my study of Indian
villages, while living with Prakash's family. Ten years
later, I find myself finally able to repay some of my

---

[1].For a listing of publications on Karimpur, see
the Bibliography.

xi

debts to Dadi by having the honor of editing and supervising the publishing of Four Families of Karimpur. I
only hope that at some future time I will have the wisdom to deal with later generations as perceptively and
humanly as she does here.

Many people contributed to the completion of this
book. Photographs were provided by Donald and Jean
Johnson, Bruce Derr, Mrs. Wiser and myself. Bruce Derr,
and David E. Sopher, with the aid of D. Michael Kirchoff
of the Syracuse University Cartographic Lab, provided
the maps. Mr. Derr also aided me in editing the manu-
script and writing the Introduction. Madge Bowie and
Mildred Marchiante deserve our gratitude for ably typing
it. Special thanks are due to the Johnsons who worked
with us at every stage. Most importantly, Dadi and I
both express our deepest gratitude to the residents of
Karimpur, particularly to Prakash's family and the
families of Parbat, Balram, Dinesh and Panditji whose
stories are told here. This is really their book. I
only hope that we do them justice.

Susan S. Wadley

Syracuse, New York
December, 1977

INTRODUCTION
by Susan S. Wadley and Bruce W. Derr

In their first book, Behind Mud Walls, William and
Charlotte Wiser introduced the village of Karimpur to
the world. In later additions to that work, Mrs. Wiser
has kept us informed of the changes and continuities in
Karimpur over the intervening years. During the fifty
years that she has known the village and its inhabitants
much has occurred in India. In the present volume we
are introduced to four families of Karimpur, to the
people, to their lifestyles, to their differences and
similarities as they exist in this one Indian village.
These families represent four different castes and sta-
tuses: the family of Parbat, Farmer by caste; the family of Balram, Carpenter by caste; the family of Dinesh,
Oil Presser by caste; and the family of Panditji, Brahmin by caste. The situations and intricacies of each
family's story vary. Yet certain themes predominate:
land and food, education, family relationships, government policies, and--more than anything--the changes
wrought by a modernizing India. The pull of urban life
and new modes of behavior are ever present. Sons leave
to pursue non-traditional occupations in faraway places;
daughters-in-law begin to revolt against their secluded
lifestyles, and machines replace men and oxen on certain
jobs. Mrs. Wiser presents us with a vivid portrayal of
these families' joys, sorrows, hopes, and fears as they
are drawn out of their sheltered village existence into
the modern world. We see how they react not only to
mundane household problems but also to crises imposed
upon them by a government and an economy of which they
suddenly and irrecoverably have become a part.

In order to more fully understand the wider context
in which the members of these families were, and are
today, existing it is necessary briefly to set the stage.

Karimpur is located in the state of Uttar Pradesh, in north-central India (see Map 1). It lies in the fertile basin between the mighty Ganges and Jamuna Rivers, 150 miles southeast of New Delhi, India's capital, and eighty miles east of Agra, site of the Taj Mahal. This area is frequently referred to as the "Hindu heartland" of India, and was the site of many battles as emperors, kings, and princes attempted to gain control of its rich farmland and strategic waterways.

The people of Karimpur live in three housing clusters: Karimpur khas, the largest residence area; kachhi ka nagla, located some 200 yards from the main part of the village between the ruins of an old fort called the khera and the main road; and chamar nagariya, also located on the main road some seventy-five yards south of the kachhi settlement. A fourth small grouping of houses and shops has grown up around the bus stop on the main road. These four groupings of buildings together constitute what is called the village of Karimpur (see Map 2).

Little is known of the origins of Karimpur beyond the village legend that a Muslim raja (king) from a nearby city granted what is now the dominant group in the village the right to live there and supervise the lands of the village sometime in the early eighteenth century. In 1802, the area in which Karimpur is located was ceded to the British East India Company by the raja in whose domain it then was. Under the system of landholding and revenue the British maintained in this part of India at that time, a person who held control over an estate had to collect revenue from his tenants and pass it on to the British collectors. However, the British severely over-estimated the level of revenue that could be paid and, in consequence, many landlords were unable to meet the demand. This resulted in some lands frequently changing hands as one landlord replaced another. This was the situation in Karimpur, where the Brahmins, those people given residency rights by the Muslim raja, were originally held responsible for the payment of revenue.

xv

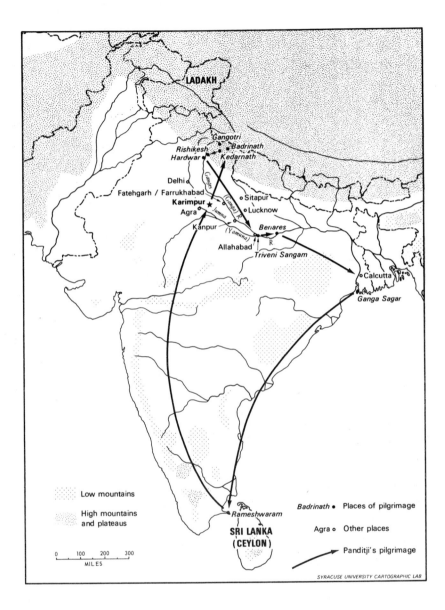

Map 1.   India: Reference Map

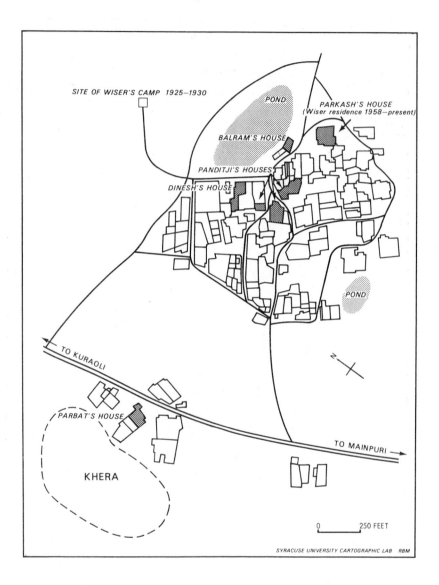

Map 2.   Village of Karimpur

When they could not pay it, the village was sold to
another, and over time passed through the hands of five
different landlords and their descendents until 1950,
none of whom ever lived in the village. It was the
agent of the last landlord who altered the land records
so that Balram, the Carpenter, could claim his rightful
inheritance.

After India was granted Independence from the British in 1947, one of the new Government's first goals was
to reform the traditional land system. This was done in
1950 by abolishing absentee landlordism and granting individual rights of ownership to those people who were
actually tilling the soil. When the Wisers first went
to Karimpur the farmers of the village were tenants of
and subject to the demands of the two landlords then
controlling the area. Twenty-five years later they saw
these farmers granted legal possession of their fields,
and twenty-five years after that, while writing about
these four families, Mrs. Wiser could look back on further changes in land and farming that had come about as
a result of the Consolidation of Holdings act and the
institution of what is generally called the "Green
Revolution."

In a country where 80 percent of the population
lives in rural villages, land and farming are the basis
of life. Many centuries had to pass before the individual Indian peasant farmer could actually claim legal
ownership of his land. But in a very short period of
time thereafter the farmer was to see many innovations
introduced and further adjustments made in his traditional scheme of production. The Consolidation of Holdings had a great effect on the farmer's life, as the
concern shown by Parbat and his sons clearly demon-
strates. No longer did his holding constitute a plethora
of scattered plots, some a mile or more apart. No longer
did he have to waste valuable time in simply moving his
draft animals and implements from one plot to another.
Consolidation provided him with incentives to develop

his holdings, possibly to add his own irrigation facility, and certainly to reap a better harvest. At the time the Consolidation of Holdings was completed in Karimpur in 1971, the farmers of the village had been exposed to new agricultural implements and techniques. Some farmers had already installed diesel or electrically powered pump-sets; others such as Ganesh, Panditji's grandson, had been using the new "miracle" seeds for four years, and the advantages of both were readily visible. Once a new implement or technique was seen to be advantageous, the farmers were quick to adopt it. The first privately owned and operated pump-set was installed in Karimpur in January 1969; by May 1975 there were fifteen privately owned pumps in use.

After centuries of dependence on the monsoon rains as their source of irrigation water, the farmers now had insurance against the late arrival or total failure of the rains. For the most part, it is thus guaranteed that some crops will survive even in the driest of years. Having outright ownership of their land and a relatively reliable source of water with which to irrigate their fields, the farmers of Karimpur in the early 1970's felt quite secure. But they were soon to know that the contact with the outside world which brought them this measure of security could also cause them serious problems. With the spiraling costs of oil and petroleum products brought on by the Arab oil embargo of 1973, the costs of fertilizers, pesticides, fuel oil, and electricity--all necessary for growing the new varieties of seeds--rose dramatically and threateningly. In one year, the cost to the farmers of fertilizer and pumped irrigation water more than doubled. The farmers were faced with the problems of living in the modern world. But they quickly learned how to cope with such a situation. The miracle seeds gave much greater yields than did the traditional varieties. The contact now established with regional and international markets put a high value on crops which fifty years before were considered worthless and

uneconomic--that is, crops which were not foodgrains.
These spices and condiments are now valued and can be
sold for a substantial cash profit. So the farmers began
planting these cash crops on some of their land to earn
for themselves the cash now needed to pay the costs of
growing the foodgrains used for subsistence. The farmers
had applied their instincts and wiles to the problems of
the modern world and, to however small a degree, have
become businessmen. Their primary aim is still to produce enough grain for their families, but now in addition
to weighing factors such as the monsoon, their labor
force, and their soil conditions, they recognize the
importance to themselves of market demands and prices.

But while the farmers are, in a sense, the most important villagers, not all villagers are farmers. Farmers need more than food in order to live: they need
carpenters such as Balram to build houses and fix plows;
barbers to shave them and act as matchmakers; potters to
supply their storage jars, pots, and vessels; laborers
to assist in their fields; shopkeepers to supply goods
which cannot be made in the village; tailors to make
their clothes; and others to provide required life-
support services. When the Wisers first arrived in
Karimpur it was a small village of 754 people. These
people were divided into twenty-four distinct, named
social groups. Each group represented an occupational
category and their name was derived from that occupation.
In English such groups are referred to by the term "caste"
but in Hindi, the language of north-central India, they
are called jati. The members of each jati followed the
occupation which their fathers and grandfathers had followed before them. Taking into account religious be-
liefs about levels of purity, impurity, as well as economic and ritual power, associated with each occupation
the jatis in any one village are ranked hierarchically
in relation to one another. Thus the Brahmins, traditionally acting as priests, are thought to embody the
highest level of innate purity and are normally ranked

1. A lane in Karimpur

2. Dadi in her courtyard with Prakash's family

at or near the top of the hierarchy in most villages. In
Karimpur they occupy the highest ranking not only because
of this inherent purity but also because they are the
largest of the jatis and the most powerful politically
and economically, owning more land than all the other
villagers combined. The jatis of Karimpur, their Hindi
names, traditional occupations, and populations in both
1925 and 1968 are presented in Table I.

It should be mentioned that it is not necessarily
the case that every single member of any one jati follows
that group's traditional occupation. In fact, it is becoming more and more unusual to find even a majority of
the members of a jati following that line of work, as
illustrated by these four families. Many traditional
occupations serve to provide the other villagers with
services or goods which they could not obtain elsewhere.
But today many of these goods and services are available
outside the village: in markets, as ready-made factory
produced goods, or from mechanized plants and mills.
For these reasons, many of the traditional village services have been outmoded and replaced by modern processes
of production and manufacture, as the story of Dinesh,
the Oil Presser, (found in Part III) so poignantly illus-
trates. Many people now must find employment in fields
other than those which they learned from their fathers.
Yet other groups simply encompass too many people for
all of them to be needed in the performance of their
traditional occupation. The Brahmins, as exemplified by
Panditji's family in Part IV, are a case in point. In
1925, there were 188 Brahmins residing in Karimpur, 105
of them eligible to become priests by the fact that they
were males. But in that year only three village Brahmins
were acting as priests, for they were all the village
needed. Thus, while any Brahmin could theoretically act
as a priest, only three did so on a regular basis while
the remainder lived by some other means, usually farming.
This problem of having more workers than are needed has
become even more acute in recent years, as the population

Table I

Castes of Karimpur, 1925 and 1968

Jati Name	Traditional Occupation	Primary Real Occuaption(s)	Number of families 1925	Number of families 1968	Total population 1925	Total population 1968
BRAHMAN	Priest	Farmer	41	41	188	315
RAY	Bard	Farmer	2	2	15	12
SUNAR	Goldsmith	"Businessman"	2	2	10	8
KAYASTHA	Accountant	Accountant	1	2	6	17
BARHAI	Carpenter	Carpenter/Farmer	8	8	42	56
GARARIYA	Shepherd	Milkseller/Farmer	6	19	26	88
LODHI RAJPUT	Rice Grower	Farmer	1	3	6	18
KACHHI	Farmer	Farmer	26	43	152	253
MAHAJAN	Shopkeeper	Shopkeeper/Money Lender	3	3	15	19
KAHAR	Water Carrier	Laborer/Farmer	19	29	83	173
KUMHAR	Potter	Potter	3	2	9	6
BHURJI	Grain Parcher	Grain Parcher	1	3	10	19
DARZI	Tailor	Tailor	5	3	21	15
MALI	Gardener	Farmer	1	3	17	17
DHOBI	Washerman	Washerman	1	3	6	13
TELI	Oil Presser	Laborer	4	5	10	36
DHANUK	Midwife/Mat Maker	Laborer/Midwife	7	16	28	103
CHAMAR	Leatherworker	Laborer/Farmer	8	9	29	55
BHANGI	Sweeper	Laborer/Sweeper	8	14	35	87
FAQIR	Beggar	Laborer/Rickshaw Driver	8	12	22	44
MANIHAR	Bangle Seller	Bangle Seller	2	3	10	11
DHUNA	Cotton Carder	Laborer	1	4	9	20
TAWAIF	Dancing Girl	(not resident)	2	--	3	--
NAI	Barber	(not resident)	1	--	2	--
TOTALS			161	229	754	1385

Note: 1925 Data from Census of Karimpur, taken by W. and C. Wiser, December 26, 1925.
1968 Data from Census of Karimpur, 1968, taken by Susan S. Wadley.

of the village has continued to increase. For example, Panditji's family of two brothers and their children, comprising twelve members in the 1920's, now forms more than four separate households with a total of thirty-five members.

Over half of Karimpur's families continue to live in extended family households--that is, families formed by more than one conjugal couple living together with all their children. Yet, as is typical, the composition of the households frequently changes as economic and other stresses impinge upon family harmony. All four of the families whose stories are told here underwent divisions of some sort over the past fifty years. Parbat, the Farmer, was first separated from his half-brothers, then from his own brother because of a supposed inequality in the sharing of resources. Meanwhile, his sons had married and their families continued to live with him and his wife. Balram's household was split from his nephews as a result of their court case over the land that they had inherited. Dinesh's immediate family was separated from those of his two brothers, most probably because of very limited food and cash resources and his brothers' desire to expend their meager incomes on their own offspring. Panditji's third son moved his parents and wife into a newly built house because of the turmoil created by his older brother's wife. Personality clashes also contributed to Raju's separating from his brother. Thus the cyclical and ever-changing nature of extended family organization is well-documented in these four histories.

Most houses in Karimpur are built of mud and adobe, while brick houses are limited to those who can afford them. The most common house design consists of an outer verandah where the men relax in the daytime and sleep on the hot summer nights. A room usually separates the verandah from the high walled courtyard, the domain of the women. Here the women prepare food stuffs, cook, sleep, and entertain their guests. Attached to the courtyard

are one or more rooms used for storage and sleeping on
cold winter nights. None of the rooms have windows and
consequently they are dark and dreary. The facades of
the houses are unrelieved, with the mud or mud-plastered
walls clearly demarcating the women's world within and
the men's and strangers' world without.

Even today the practice of purdah (seclusion of
women) is strictly enforced. Wives of the village are
hidden from the gazes of strange men as well as their
husband's elders through physical seclusion in the courtyards as well as by dhotis and shawls during their few
opportunities to go outside the house. Contact between
men and women is minimal and it is more important for a
bride to be well-received by her mother-in-law than by
her husband. Even Panditain admits that she had little
conversation with her husband, while Usha's first years
of marriage to Ganesh were made all the worse by her
mother-in-law's disapproval of her.

As the modern world and western values become known,
pressures are being developed which will surely affect
purdah and male-female relationships. Ganesh built a
separate room for Usha and himself in their new house,
something previously unknown in Karimpur. Bhalai took
his wife with him to Delhi, much to his parents' dismay.
As the young women travel more and increasing numbers of
them live in urban areas, even for short periods, the
total seclusion of the upper caste women is subjected
to pressures for change. Young women who have enjoyed
the mobility allowed in cities and the absence of veil-
ing as well as the companionship of their husbands are
beginning to rebel against the strictures of Karimpur
purdah. So far there is mostly wishful talk and a few
gestures such as Ganesh's room. But other changes will
surely follow soon.

Educational advances are important to both men and
women in Karimpur. In 1925, the sole school in the
village was a boy's primary school (grades one through
five) from which untouchables were banned, although a

few Sweepers learned to read under Mrs. Wiser's tutelage.
Schooling beyond grade five could only be obtained in
Mainpuri. Few non-Brahmin boys were able to attend because of time, expense, and community attitudes towards
advanced schooling, as is shown by the pressures put on
Parbat's father when he attempted to send his son to
Mainpuri. Now there are three schools: the boys' primary school, a girls' primary school, and a coeducational
middle school (grades six through eight). At present,
all but Sweepers attend school, though few lower caste
boys go beyond the first few grades and lower caste girls
do not attend at all. Ganesh, Panditji's grandson, was
the first Karimpur recipient of a college degree, but
others have followed him, though jobs are difficult to
obtain. Girls are still limited to eighth grade educa-
tions, both because of early marriages and because the
high school in Mainpuri is felt to be too distant for
sending daughters to attend. However, in 1975 one girl
was studying "privately" for her high school degree and
a few wives, such as Usha, have advanced past the eighth
grade. Nevertheless, as Table II shows, literacy rates
are still very low, especially among women and lower
caste males.

Although farming, land, education, and family concerns dominate the histories of these four families,
changes in the political climate, both nationally and
locally, are critical to their total environment. In
1925, Karimpur was ruled by the British and Panditji as
mukhiya was the local representatives of the government.
He was appointed to this position by the District Magistrate, although his effectiveness derived from his
stature in the community. After Independence in 1947,
the Indian government established local elected govern-
ing bodies called gram panchayats. Each gram panchayat
(village council, literally "council of five") was headed
by a pradhan, also elected. In Karimpur, as elsewhere,
panchayat elections are fiercely contested and the various factions of the village work arduously to have their

Table II

Literacy in Karimpur in 1925 and 1968

| | Literacy percent (number) | | | |
| | 1925 | | 1968 | |
Caste	Male	Female	Male	Female
Brahmin	41.9(44)	20.4(17)	78.6(125)	29.9(44)
Bard	66.6(6)	16.6(1)	71.4(5)	60.0(3)
Goldsmith	80.0(4)	--	100.0(5)	33.3(1)
Accountant	100.0(2)	--	100.0(10)	25.0(3)
Carpenter	33.3(6)	--	42.9(12)	7.1(2)
Shepherd	--	--	23.4(11)	2.4(1)
Rice Grower	25.0(1)	--	50.0(6)	--
Farmer	11.9(10)	--	36.6(52)	1.9(2)
Shopkeeper	44.4(4)	20.0(1)	66.6(6)	14.2(1)
Water Carrier	--	--	4.9(4)	--
Potter	--	--	20.0(1)	--
Grain Parcher	16.6(1)	--	27.3(3)	--
Tailor	10.0(1)	--	62.5(5)	--
Gardener	12.5(1)	--	10.0(1)	--
Washerman	--	--	--	--
Oil Presser	20.0(1)	--	47.6(8)	--
Mat-maker	--	--	13.8(8)	2.1(1)
Leatherworker	--	--	20.0(6)	--
Sweeper	22.2(4)	5.8(1)	2.0(1)	--
Beggar	6.6(1)	--	4.2(1)	--
Bangle Seller	50.0(2)	--	83.3(5)	--
Cotton Carder	20.0(1)	--	33.3(3)	10.0(1)
Dancing Girls	--	--	not resident	
Barber	--	--	not resident	
TOTAL	21.9(89)	5.7(20)	36.9(278)	9.4(59)

Note: Figures for 1925 are taken from W. Wiser 1933:282.
Literacy is defined as ability to read and write
a simple letter.
Figures for 1968 are taken from Wadley 1975:25.
Literacy is defined as having two or more years
of schooling.

candidate elected <u>pradhan</u>. All of the <u>pradhans</u> elected
in Karimpur have been Brahmins. The Brahmins, who own
over half of the land, are economically powerful enough
to control village politics, although the competition
between the various Brahmin lineages is strong enough
to often render the <u>pradhan</u> and <u>panchayat</u> ineffective.

National and state elections are less important in
Karimpur, although the level of voting participation is
high. Yet, because the personalities and planks of these
officials are not well-known and their functions are less
understood, voting often takes place along caste lines.

One major government institution which is important
to Karimpur is the Community Development Program. Under
this program, a series of Village Level Workers (VLW's)
have been assigned to live in Karimpur and to instruct
its residents through experimental plots, posters, advice, and so forth on agricultural and community development projects. The VLW is also, at times, able to aid
farmers in obtaining loans for new equipment and other
farm-related services. In addition, a government-
sponsored cooperative seed store and bank are located
in the village. These are the primary outlets for the
new fertilizers and seeds of the Green Revolution. Unfortunately, both the VLW and the cooperative socities
work primarily with the wealthier upper-caste farmers,
and thus do not reach the more needy majority of the
population.

Probably the most important factor of life in Karimpur today is a rapidly growing population. Between
1925 and 1968, the population increased by 84 percent.
In the following seven years, from 1968 to 1975, it increased by an additional 20 percent. By 1990, the population could easily reach 2,400, more than three times
the population of 1925. But the acreage remains the
same and even the miracle seeds cannot increase production forever. The residents of Karimpur are aware of
the problems of increasing family size--from an average
of 4.68 individuals in 1925 to 6.05 individuals in 1968.

Better medical care has increased longevity and cut
maternal and infant mortality rates (though both remain
high). The family planning programs of the government
are known, and sometimes used. Like many other places,
Karimpur was visited by a family planning camp during
the 1975 Emergency. Even before then, a few women had
had the "operation" (tubal ligation). To them, this was
one viable alternative to having more children: intra-
uterine devices ("loop" is now a Hindi word) were known
for causing bleeding and other problems. Pills are not
available to the poor, as they have never been sanction-
ed by the government. Vasectomies and condoms were unpopular with the men, who are less concerned than their
wives about contolling family size. However, the oper-
ations require both substantial sums of money and a long
period of convalescence. Few can afford either. So,
more children are born and the land must be forced to
feed them. And all the while, aspirations for a more
luxurious life style and better education grow. Either
the children will be fed or radios will be bought. The
land cannot provide for both forever. It is this conflict, more than any other, which must be faced by the
younger generation.

The following pages recapture the travails of these
families when faced with a changing world and changing
circumstances. Land is gained and lost, new forms of
earning a living are found as old ones are outmoded,
children are born and the old die, families divide and
brides arrive to form new ones. Certainly life in
Karimpur is neither "stagnant" nor "traditional."
Rather, we have here a picture of continual change and
adaptation as circumstances allow or require. And although beset by erratic weather, inflated prices, in-
comprehensible government regulations, and more numerous mouths to feed, the people of Karimpur continue to
survive and, in some sense, to prosper. Though the
Karimpur of 1990 will most probably be very different
from the Karimpur of today, the sons and daughters of

the present generation will be raising their sons and
daughters. Their problems will be different from those
of their fathers, just as the generation of the 1920's
faced issues different from those of the 1960's. Some
patterns are developing in the following pages, yet
only time can give us their final form. While waiting
for the future, we have here the story of the past.

PART I

THE FAMILY OF PARBAT, FARMER

PARBAT'S FAMILY TREE

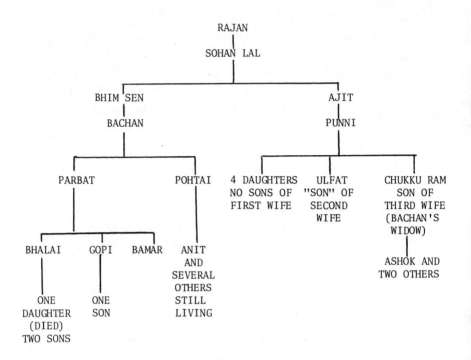

CHARACTERS

RAM LAL - our first Farmer friend, operated on for a cataract.

BACHAN - more progressive than his Farmer neighbors, head of
his family.

PUNNI - Bachan's (cousin) brother.

PARBAT - eldest son of Bachan.

POHTAI - Bachan's second son.

ULFAT - Punni's foster son, treated as a legitimate son.

CHAKKU RAM - Punni's own son, born after his marriage to
Bachan's widow.

BHALAI - Parbat's eldest son.

GOPI - Parbat's second son.

BAMAR - Parbat's youngest son, still in school.

SHANTI - Parbat's wife.

Two of Parbat's daughters-in-law.

Mahajan brothers living in the Farmer colony.

In Karimpur life revolves around farming. Survival
depends on it. Holidays are associated with it, from
the season of sowing to that of reaping. And when men
gather in small neighborly circles after the evening
chores, they rarely argue over politics. Instead, they
discuss crops, fertilizer, the latest variety of seed
offered by the seed store, market prices of grain, the
possibility of early rain.

In the autumn when I see men bound for the fields,
each with a plough over his shoulder and a pair of oxen
trailing behind, I know that the sowing of wheat and
barley, of mustard and winter legumes has begun. Soon
after that the green shoots appear, and as winter passes
the plants grow taller and a darker green. Lines of
bright yellow appear where mustard has been sown between
several rows of wheat or barley. There are bushes of
chick peas with their tiny yellow blossoms, paler than
the mustard. And close to the ground is the light green
of pea vines and other low growing legumes. This is the
season of greatest beauty and promise--and suspense.
Fear of drought has been reduced by the digging of deep
wells; but there is still the possibility of unseasonal
rain or heavy winds, hail or pests. Farmers have learned from experience that any one of these can destroy
part or all of their crops. Only when spring comes and
the grain is cut and safely stacked beside their threshing floors do they relax. If the harvest is abundant,
the whole village rejoices with them. If it is meager
everyone prepares for hunger or near-hunger. This is
the rabi or spring harvest, the high point of the year.
After the grain has been threshed and winnowed and
stored, the fields lie bare under the blazing sun, until
the ground becomes hard and cracked. Then in late June
or July come the showers that herald the monsoon; and
again I see the farmers carrying their ploughs, while
their oxen come trailing behind. They are preparing to
sow corn and millet, sorghum and summer varieties of legumes, and perhaps rice. Except for the rice which may

be harvested earlier, these crops will be ready for the
kharif or autumn harvest, in September or October. It is
less sensational than the rabi but almost as important.
If it proves to be ample, it restocks the almost empty
storerooms with enough food to tide families over the
coming months, until spring. They live from harvest to
harvest, not only the families of farmers but others on
whom the farmers depend, many of whom are without land
of their own. Such people are Carpenters, the Washerman,
the Barber, the Potter, the Tailor and others who are
field hands or are working on shares.[1]

In land ownership, Brahmins rank highest, with the
Farmers second. There is a distinct difference between
the two. Although a Brahmin is born into a caste whose
traditional occupation is that of Priest, he cultivates
the fields which he has inherited while a Farmer (Kachhi)
is born into a group whose traditional occupation is
farming. When asked about his caste by a stranger--a
familiar question in a gathering in the town or when on
a journey--a Brahmin's immediate reply is "brahmin." If
questioned further as to his occupation, he explains that
he is a kisan, one who farms. If a Farmer is asked the
same question he has only one answer, "kachhi," "Farmer."
The pride of Farmers comes not only from their birth but
from their reputation as genuine farmers. They are
nearer to the soil than the Brahmins and are more
acutely aware of its needs and demands.

When we came to Karimpur--Bill and I and our two
sons, aged five and one and a half--we made our home in
a Swiss-style family tent in a mango grove, half a furlong from the village proper. Not far from us was the
partially paved main road leading from Mainpuri, headquarters of the district, to Kuraoli, six miles in the

---

[1]Generally caste names are given in English. A few,
such as Brahmin, which are widely known, are given in
Hindi, without diacritics. A capital letter denotes a
caste (as in Farmer), while a lower case letter denotes
"doing the work" (as in farmer).

opposite direction. Spread along both sides of the road was an offshoot of the village, known as the khera, and here the Farmers lived. They were hard working, thrifty, and while they were members of the village, they tended to remain somewhat aloof.

By tradition they were vegetable growers. However, by the time we arrived, they were raising the usual cereal and legume crops. The few vegetables they grew were primarily for their own use and were rarely sold. Their caste standing is unclear: by some, they are listed as sudras, a varna division of menials, but they consider themselves kshatriyas, the second major varna division, traditionally of warriors. They have proof of this in their freedom to accept certain foods from Brahmins and their right to serve certain foods to Brahmins. When we first knew them, not one of them was literate.

The Family of Parbat

By the end of our first year in the village, we had been accepted by the various caste communities of the village, with the exceptions of the Farmers. Then a new boy appeared in our grove. Other village boys had been with us for months, making use of the red wagon and the tricycle and other play equipment of our sons. Our old friends called the new boy "Parbat" and explained that he was a Farmer, the only Farmer boy to attend the village school. We hoped that perhaps Parbat could help us establish contact with the Farmers. Yet when Bill tried greeting Farmers he met on the road or in a lane their response was as guarded as ever.

Later we learned more about Parbat's father, Bachan. He was more liberal than his relatives and had dared to send his son to school. Men of his caste reminded Bachan that Farmer boys were supposed to work in the fields with their fathers, as Tailor boys and Carpenter boys worked under their fathers as apprentices. Books were for Brahmins and for people in cities. Bachan was unmoved, and took a further, more radical step by allowing Parbat to come to our grove. This the elders would not countenance. They resorted to the customary punishment for such misdemeanors and denied him the right to smoke the hookah (hubble-bubble pipe) with any circle of Farmers, a painful ostracism which was usually effective. Bachan bowed to the verdict but continued to allow Parbat to attend school and to play with our sons.

Eventually contact was made with the Farmers through a call for help from an elder named Ram Lal. He was highly respected, but he was pitied because he was becoming blind. A member of the village council had recommended that he consult Bill. When Bill arrived on Ram Lal's verandah, he found not only Ram Lal and his sons but an audience. He knew from experience that most of the men were simply inquisitive as we were still a novelty. Others, he discovered later, were there to test the Sahib. If he had come to the village representing the British government, as they suspected, he would be concerned only with taxes and would make no effort to help a frail old man. Bill found that Ram Lal had cataracts in both eyes and offered to take him to an eye specialist working in a hospital seventy miles away. After days of discussion with relatives and friends, Ram Lal agreed to go. The doctor operated, successfully, and sent the patient home, able to see with the aid of a pair of spectacles. People came flocking to hear more about the miracle. Too old for manual labor, Ram Lal spent his days sitting on his verandah watching all that went on, directing morning and evening chores and talking with anyone who would join him. With his spectables he looked so much like pictures of Gandhiji that people commented on the likeness, which delighted him. Bill went to see him often, and it was on Ram Lal's verandah that he had his first normal contact with the Farmers. Among them was Parbat's father, Bachan, whom he had most wanted to know. Bachan was the first to invite him to his home.

It was from Bachan that we learned how it came about
that their family, along with other Farmers, were living
in the khera apart from the main village. Originally
their home had been in the center of the village. In the
19th century, the zamindar who at that time owned the
land in and around the village decided that it would be
to his advantage to have a settlement of village families
between the road and a hillock to the west known as the
khera, on which a legendary fortress once had stood. He
chose Rajan, Bachan's great grandfather, as a likely
leader of the new community and offered him a wooded lot
with space for a large house beside it. Rajan accepted
gladly. He already had a joint family too numerous for
the house they occupied and felt the need for more space.
Other Farmers were given the same opportunity but were
afraid to move from the security of close neighbors. Only
two or three families joined him. Those who remained
still occupy a few houses crowded between a Brahmin colony and what we called Humble Lane. Gradually others of
Farmer caste had come from scattered hamlets to join
Rajan. And when it had become a considerable community,
it was given the name of the hillock, becoming known as
the khera. By 1960 there were at least thirty families,
each with its own chulha, or hearth-fire, living in the
khera.

Because Parbat was a good student, Bachan decided
that when the boy had completed the sixth class in the
village school he should go to town to attend school
there until passing the high school examinations. He
could walk the six miles. As for expenses, he had arranged for Parbat's marriage and there would be money
saved from the dowry he had claimed from the family of
the bride. If the plan succeeded, Parbat could get a
good post in some government office and help the family
with badly needed cash. When Bachan informed his relatives they were angry. How dared he send a Farmer boy
to school in town? It was unheard of. Only two or
three from the whole village were going, and they were

Brahmins. Besides, they needed Parbat's strong arms for field work.

Before the plan could materialize, Bachan died and a stern relative succeeded him. Parbat was immediately taken from school and given full-time work in the fields.

When I returned in 1961 and had settled in our own house, I was free to visit old friends. From among them I had made a tentative choice of three of the four families I should study more closely. I had known most of the men in the main village who were now heads of large families; if I did not recognize them at once, they reminded me of their pranks with my sons. With their wives I had to make a fresh start. Everyone of them now forty-five years of age or younger had come to live here as a wife after we had departed in 1930. However, some of them I had come to know on our visits, and others accepted me because of the tales their husbands had repeated about us, our sons, and our life in a tent.

This was not true of families in the khera. When we had come to Karimpur to visit, we passed their houses along the main road and paused there to greet the men who came to the car to welcome us, but we rarely went into their homes. After some time I finally went to the khera with the intention of renewing acquaintance with a Farmer family. It was basant, supposedly the first day of spring; but mornings and evenings were still cold. Going at noon when the sun was warmer, I walked along the narrow tops of low ridges that marked the boundaries of fields which separated the khera from the main village. I hoped that housewives would be free from work long enough to visit. My first stop was to be at Ram Lal's, the man whose successful cataract operation had drawn us dearer to the Farmer community.

When the fields ended I passed between the feeding troughs where animals would be fed on their return home in the evening. This was what had been Ram Lal's cattle yard, now apparently used by his sons. His house was beside it, and there on the verandah sat a group of women.

Farmer women are less restricted than the Brahmin women
of my neighborhood, at least to the extent that they may
spend their leisure hour on the outer verandah which the
men reserve for themselves in the evening. The women
there all turned to gape at me, making me feel very much
as I had feared I would--an intruder. Suddenly a middle-
aged woman broke away from the group and rushed towards
me. To my surprise she embraced me, village fashion.
She was Ram Lal's own daughter, home for a fortnight's
visit. She must have been quite small when we lived
here but she remembered our family. Now she led me to
the other women. To an expanding audience she related
her father's story with details I had forgotten. I could
not have wanted a warmer welcome than his daughter and
her neighbors now gave me.

Soon several of the women asked me to come next door
into the courtyard they shared to look at their ailing
children. There were boils and sore eyes, colds and
scabies. Saddest of all were the babies from 18 months
to two years old, suffering from under-nutrition in homes
where there was plenty of milk and nourishing food.
Mothers in the village still think that their own milk
is sufficient, and do not make the effort to teach their
children to accept anything else.

The women around me were not as robust as I had expected. They were very thin, as were the men who drifted
in and out while we were talking, but the men looked
healthier than the women. The older women had only one
or two teeth left, and even some of the younger women had
already lost several front teeth or had teeth which were
alarmingly loose and painful. Several of the women asked
me to examine their badly inflamed eyes. Those of the
older women were red-rimmed and blurred, almost void of
color--the result of many years of leaning over smoky
fires of sticks and dung cakes. Yet not one was stooped
from the heavy work that I know they were obliged to do,
and they were far from listless. But I missed the

sturdiness one associates with good health.

The older women had clung to the colorful long full skirts of thirty years ago, with the long-sleeved blouse and bright head covering, larger than a stole, smaller than a mantle. The younger women, like most other women in the village, had adopted dhotis, about the same length as those worn by the men, but covering the whole body. All these were white with black, red, green or blue borders. Their dhotis were soiled as garments are bound to be when worn for every kind of work in fields, courtyards and kitchen and were all threadbare and wrinkled.

There were few signs of change in the houses. The inner walls as well as the high outer ones looked like all mud walls during the months between the rainy seasons All had been conscientiously mud-plastered every year after the rains. Brass utensils for cooking and eating were drying in the sun. They were the minimum need for preparing food and serving the men. When the men finished eating, trays and bowls would be washed and used by the women and children. The string cots stood on their sides against a wall or were spread with homespun sheets on which grain was drying or babies were sleeping. There was not a plant or a blade of green. Instead, there were the usual stacks of fodder for the animals, and nearby a fodder cutter. No one had such an implement thirty years ago, but every owner of animals now aspires to own one.

I asked about other Farmer families. I knew that many of them were related to Ram Lal, but the women evinced no interest in the others. Their enclosure with its several subenclosures had enough women and children to provide all the variety, all the problems and gossip that women anywhere could want, without the need of going into neighboring houses. The older women being freer from chores sometimes went to see the nearest and most closely related families, but they had little to say about them. I reminded myself that not one of these women were related to the others, except by marriage, either in this house or in the houses next door. It is the men who

have family ties. Married women accept life with their
in-laws because they have no choice. Gradually, when
they have sons, their roots go deeper in the new soil,
and by the time the sons are grown, they regard their
husbands' homes and people as their own.

The following day I set out again for the khera,
fortified by the friendly reaction of Ram Lal's daughter.
My goal was a Farmer family on the far side of the main
road. I passed Ram Lal's house before the women had
gathered, and crossed the main road. Beyond it, I stopped to look through the wide open entrance of an enclosure which I recalled as being as large as Ram Lal's.
That day it looked larger than ever. Around the corner
was the very narrow lane I had hoped to find, with its
solid row of small dilapidated houses, all facing toward
the hillock. When I came to the entrance I remembered,
and went inside, I was greeted by men of all ages, still
at their morning chores. One of them led me to the nearest doorway which I had often entered. When we passed
through the cattle room and into the pleasant courtyard,
a chubby, middle-aged woman gave me the same warm welcome
as Ram Lal's daughter had. She was not a daughter of the
village, but a senior bahu (wife). She reminded me that
she was the shy young bahu, who had watched and listened
when I had come to visit her mother-in-law long ago. She
was old enough now to go down the lane to houses nearby,
but she preferred her own courtyard. We sat and talked
togehter on a charpai (string cot), while a younger bahu
continued grinding flour for the noonday meal. Later
from a storeroom she brought a collection of round baskets she had woven from reeds and decorated with bright
colored patterns, and reminded me that it was her mother-
in-law whose basket weaving I had admired.

But this was a large family, composed of an unknown
number of single families with separate courtyards as the
family that I had known before must have grown and been
divided and re-divided over the years. There could be
no privacy in such a situation, no opportunity for

conversation with one individual without an audience.
My search had not ended.

One afternoon about a fortnight later, a young man
walked into my courtyard, introducing himself as Bhalai
Singh. When I followed the accepted formula and asked
his father's name, his reply was startling. "I am eldest
son of Parbat, Farmer." Bhalai explained that he had
attended high school in Mainpuri. This was welcome news.
Apparently Bachan's plan for Parbat had been realised a
generation later, in Parbat's son. But the plan was not
working out as Parbat was not aware of the changes that
years would bring. There were many more boys finishing
high school now than there had been thirty years before,
and office jobs had not increased proportionately. Bhalai
told me that for the past two years he had been trying,
unsuccessfully, to get some kind of job in the district
headquarters in Mainpuri. He was "high school fail," and
although this might seem a poor qualification, in this
area no one is embarrassed when he must add the "fail."
The chances are that the class work of a "fail" student
has been as satisfactory as that of others who can add,
"first," "second," or "third" division to their names,
rather the fail student may not have been as adept at
memorizing passages from textbooks or had not been able
to pay a tutor during the final weeks before an examination. Few village boys had been able to attend high
school, and among them the majority were "fail."

Bhalai was now helping his father on their land, but
he felt that he should have a job with regular income.
His friends in town had not been able to help him, although their fathers in government offices had secured
posts for them. He needed some special contacts, and
hoped that I would recommend him to friends in offical
positions. I was doubtful but offered to try. As he was
leaving, I said that I should like to come to their house
some afternoon to meet his father when he came in from
the fields. Bhali apologized. In his concern over his
own problems he had forgotten to tell me that his father

and mother were expecting a visit from me.

Bhalai neglected to tell me that the old home as I knew it had been divided and that Parbat now lived in the far part of the house. When I went, I walked in the door I had used formerly, passed through the outer courtyard where the cows, buffaloes, and oxen would be tethered and fed in the evening, and on into the inner courtyard where I knew I would find the women. There I faced the coolest reception I had ever met in any village home, anywhere. I was obviously a complete stranger to the two women there, and strangers do not walk into a family courtyard without warning. The children, one screaming and the others too terrified to make a sound, ran to their mothers. Everywhere children in the village ran to me, rather than away, for they had assurance from parents that I was a friend. Here there was no one to speak for me. The women stopped their work abruptly to look me over. The younger one pulled the end of the dhoti far down over her face and peered out at me, while the older one stared without expression. I asked if either of them knew me. The older woman finally shook her head. Neither of them was old enough to have seen me in the early years, and their husbands must not have come to our grove. I explained that I was from the village, but this sounded so improbable that the older one looked suspicious. After another long pause, I asked about Parbat. "Parbat?"--they relaxed. If I sought Parbat, he lived in the far part of the house. The family had separated, and Parbat and his brother had moved out. At last the women showed active interest and were prepared to relate in detail the quarrels that had led to the building of the partition, the high wall which now separated the two branches of the family.

These women and children seemed healthier than those I had seen across the road. The women's arms looked strong enough to do the work of men and the children's bodies had smooth curves and their eyes were clear and bright. The women wore dhotis, soiled and slightly torn,

but of better material than those of their neighbors.
Numerous brass utensils were drying in the sun. Theirs
was a comparatively prosperous household, and the women
belonging to it were quite satisfied with themselves and
boasted that they had nothing to do with their neighbors,
related or otherwise. When I inquired about field work,
the older one said that she went out occasionally for
certain tasks when the men needed extra help, but not
the younger one. The younger one remained silent under
the heavy coverings, until she began to giggle. This
sent both of them into spasms of laughter. I could not
help laughing with them. Finally a schoolboy offered
to take me to Parbat's door.

Outside Parbat's door was a very wide, low platform
of earth which seemed inviting, and beside it an open
space shaded by trees. Two pair of bullocks were tethered in this space, and near them was a small hut for
implements and fodder. The house door stood open and I
went inside.

Parbat's wife, Shanti, was in their large outer
courtyard pulling peanuts from vines which she had just
gathered. The only word that describes her well is
"motherly." Later I came to know her as "mother of
Bhalai,: not by her own name nor as "wife of Parbat."
Her face was rather full and smooth with few lines. Her
eyes were kind and she laughed easily, as she did now at
the crowd of youngsters who had followed me in. She did
not drive the children away as some women do. They settled contentedly on the ground, while she had one of
them pull down a charpai and seat me on it. I relaxed:
there was no tension or restraint here. A young woman,
Bhalai's wife, ventured out from the inner courtyard and
sat behind the children to listen, with face carefully
covered.

Bhalai's mother told me that she vaguely remembered
seeing me from under her head covering when she was a
very young, very shy bahu. I had never had a glimpse of
her face, yet as we talked, it seemed as though we had

known each other for a long time. She asked the questions that village women usually ask, chiefly about my
three sons in America. She also had three, and two
daughters as well. They were all living together except
for the eldest daughter who was married. One of her
questions was, "How do your bahus get along when you are
not there to supervise them and keep them from quarreling?" I assured her that they were doing very well, and
that they live too far apart to work together or quarrel.
She did not seem shocked at this as most village mothers
are. Rather she was distressed that a family should have
to be so scattered. For each of her questions, I asked
one about her family, as is customary. Thus we made the
first steps toward an acquaintance which later developed
into a lasting friendship.

The bahu withdrew into the inner courtyard to prepare the evening meal and I was about to leave when
Parbat came in from the fields. He looked tired and
much older than his wife and was very thin and grizzled.
The barber is supposed to come and shave him once a fortnight, but had evidently skipped a shave or two. He wore
a small turban carelessly wound, and his white shirt and
dhoti were dirty. Yet in spite of his weariness, he appeared far from frail. He stood as most of the village
farmers stand, straight and at ease, with an indefinable
air of "I owe nothing to any man." His eyes were those
of a man who spends his days working in the glare of the
sun, but his grin was as reassuring as his wife's smile.

It was not until several visits later that I saw
Parbat again. He came into the courtyard with a finger
bleeding badly. He had tried to repair a charpai leg
using an old-fashioned fodder cutter with a broad, sharp
blade, instead of taking it to the Carpenter. When I
offered to dress the finger, he accepted without hesita-
tion, and came home with me. It was his first visit to
my house since the housewarming in 1958. When the
finger was bandaged he left; but to my surprise he
appeared again early the next morning for fresh treat-

16

3. Shanti, Parbat's wife

4. Parbat, Bhalai, Gopi, Pohtar and Bamar

ment. Men seldom bother to come more than once for first
aid unless the injury becomes increasingly painful. He
came three more times on his way to the fields, and each
time became more communicative. On his last visit he
lingered to reminisce, as others have done, about the fun
he had in our grove many years before.

After several more visits to Parbat's home and further conversations with him and his wife, I decided that
theirs should be one of the four families whose history I
would write. I had known Parbat from his boyhood and he
was regarded as a successful farmer. Aside from his ten-
dency to follow his father's example and move faster than
his neighbors, his family was like others in the khera.
They were better off than Ram Lal's family and less well
off than a few others. Like all Farmers, he and his
brother, Pohtai, were good stewards of their land, their
animals, and their home. The women obviously were good
housewives. One son, about twelve, was still attending
the village school as a number of boys from Farmer homes
now did. Bhalai had finished high school while Gopi,
Parbat's second son, had left school early and was helping his father on their land.

Personally I found the atmosphere of their home congenial. In some Farmer houses, a few questions were
enough to cause uneasiness. The women would urge me to
visit them, but when I did, they preferred asking the
questions. In Parbat's home there were no such barriers
to a free interchange.

The House Divided

I soon felt free to ask about the division of the
old home. What had led to it? I had heard a rather
vague and rather biased report from the women on the
other side of the barrier. Parbat tried to explain with
help from Shanti. The more involved the explanation became, the more confused I was, especially as to names
and personalities. Parbat finally suggested that I
should have the history of the family to help me under-

stand. When I left, he sent Bamer, his youngest son home
with me, to get a sheet of clean paper because in most
houses, the only paper available comes from old school
copy books. A few days later he arrived in my dining
room, which also serves as a common room, with his family
tree copied in Hindi on the paper, along with notes re-
garding each generation. In addition he gave me more
detailed information as we talked.

It started with his great-great grandfather, Rajan,
who had settled at the foot of the Khera. Rajan cultivated five acres of land which he held from the landlord
under marusi rights: he could use the land during his
life-time and could pass it on to his sons, but he could
not sell it. If in any succeeding generation there were
not sons, the land would revert to the landlord. Rajan
lost several children and only one of his sons lived to
manhood and inherited the five acres. Like his father,
this son, Sohan Lal, had two oxen which are considered
enough to work this much land.

Sohan's two sons, Bhim Sen and Ajit, lived jointly
with their families. With the cooperation of the landlord's agent and because unclaimed land was still available, they now held thirty-six acres under the same
rights as their father and grandfather. They still had
only two oxen, but they purchased one buffalo so that
they might have plenty of milk. From their increased
acreage they grew more food, and consequently could sell
the surplus in order to buy clothes. The house still had
the original mud walls, but the brothers made them higher
and thicker. Bhim Sen had one son, Bachan while Ajit had
two sons, one of whom died while small: the one who
lived was Punni.

Bachan and Punni considered themselves brothers, as
most men do who have grown up as sons in a joint family.
They lived together with their families in the old house
and cultivated the thirty-six acres together, although
according to the land records, each one owned eighteen.

After this, the family relationships became more
complicated. Punni was married three times. His first
wife had no sons but four daughters. Evidently all four
were married and sent to live with their in-laws. When
his first wife died, Punni took another woman into his
house, nominally as his second wife. She was a distant
relative who was about to be turned out by her own family
who had found that she was pregnant before going to live
with her in-laws.

Punni had granted her refuge, and set aside a room
for her with her own chulha separate from his household.
Here her son, Ulfat, was born, and here she remained,
living apart but accepted as a member of Punni's family.
Punni always spoke of Ulfat as his son and arranged his
marriage. Ulfat and his wife lived with his mother.

When Bachan, Parbat's father, died, Parbat was about
nine and his brother, Pohtai was not yet born. After
Pohtai's birth, Punni took Bachan's wife as his own. She
was counted as his third wife and no ceremony was necessary. They had one son, Chakku Ram. Punni accepted responsibility for Bachan's children as well as his own
and Ulfat, providing them with food and clothing and
supervising the field work of Parbat and Pohtai. Parbat's
marriage to Shanti had already been arranged by Bachan
but Punni arranged for the marriages of Bachan's two
daughters and for Pohtai.

It was chiefly Punni's complicated role in the family that led to trouble. He was foster-father of Ulfat,
father of Chakku Ram, and uncle and step-father of Parbat
and Pohtai. Then he was gone, these complex interrela-
tionships no longer allowed unity. For a short time after his death the various members of Parbat's generation
continued to live together and share in the work. However, no one was willing to follow orders given by another. There were discussions about legally dividing the
land; but before the final decision could be made, Parbat
made the devastating discovery that Ulfat and his mother
had arranged with the land recorder, at a price, to

transfer all the joint property, including his and
Pohtai's share, to Ulfat's name. Bitter accusations en-
sued followed by threats on both sides. They finally
took the matter to the district court which upheld Ulfat's
claim. However, no villager gives up land without a
struggle, even though he may exhaust all his savings--
stored gold and silver--on it. Land is a villager's
most valued inheritance; the family's security as well as
its livelihood. Parbat, with the help of the village
council, took the case to a higher court. There it was
decided that he and Pohtai had a right to their father's
share of the property--18 acres--while Ulfat and Chakku
Ram were granted Punni's 18 acres. During all this up-
heaval Parbat, Pohtai, and Chakku Ram with their wives
and children continued to live together, while Ulfat
and his wife were with his mother.

Chakku Ram was now drawn closer to Ulfat with whom
he was sharing half the land. Parbat did not foresee the
estrangement that was bound to result. As the eldest of
the men he accepted the responsibilities of head of the
family. He did for Chakku Ram all that Punni had done
for him. But Chakku Ram felt that he should be head of
the family as he was Punni's own son, and had looked up
to Punni all his life as head of the family. Parbat and
Pohtai were Bachan's sons and did not have the same claim
to the homestead that he had. Parbat, having no inkling
of this, was shocked and deeply hurt when, during a minor
disagreement later, Chakku Ram told him that he, Parbat,
and Pohtai would have to move out with their families and
set up their own chulha in the far portion of the house.
The reason he gave was that his own family was small,
while both Parbat's and Pohtai's families were increasing.
They already had five children between them, and might
have more. Chakku Ram should not be expected to provide
as much grain and other farm produce for the joint family
as they. With just his own wife and two children to
support, he could have more grain and a good deal more
cash.

So Parbat shifted to the far section of the house
with his wife and children and his mother, and with
Pohtai and his family. They erected a high wall between
their part and that occupied by Ulfat and Chakku Ram.
Erecting such a wall marks the division of a family as
irrevocable, for until that point there is the possibility of restoring fraternal relations.

Now there was no question of Parbat's and Shanti's
authority in their joint household. Their own children
and Pohtai and his wife and their children depended on
them for all major decisions. The relationship between
Parbat and Pohtai was more like that of father and son
than that of brothers. Pohtai had always followed Parbat's instructions in their work and in their home. He
could neither read nor write and his wife as more like a
girl than a woman, and her simple acceptance of whatever
came made life with her easy. Parbat and Shanti carried
the burden of providing care for all of them, in sickness
and in health. There was little time for them to concern
themselves with affairs outside of their home, either in
the village or in the nation. This was the "householder"
period for Parbat, in accordance with Hindu tradition.

One afternoon when the daughter-in-law was cleaning
a storeroom and Shanti and I were sitting together on a
charpai in the courtyard, I asked about her life in Parbat's family. Since I had first known her, she had seemed so poised that it was hard to think of her ever having
been disturbed. She assured me that there had been times
when she was not only disturbed but frightened. She recalled her own home where she had felt secure. Family
problems were in the hands of her parents and did not
touch her. Then came her marriage. Her brother's wedding had taken place a year before hers, and the only
share her family had taken was to invite certain relatives and friends to join the wedding party. Women
were not included. When her brother returned from the
wedding, he shook off the ceremonies with a brief report;
and his reference to his bride was indifferent. His

interest seemed to have been in his own importance for
three days, and in the two big feasts they had been
served by the bride's family. This had prepared Shanti
for the attitude her husband-to-be might have toward
her. All that she had overheard in her elders' discussions of her intended was that he was fourteen and had
been in school.

She had been taught by her mother, her aunts and
her sisters-in-law that every girl must be married and
that her husband must be her master, her lord, Because
of this, she was so in awe of Parbat that during the
wedding ritual she hardly dared lift her eyes to peep at
him through her heavy face covering. When she did, she
saw an ordinary boy like her brothers. But her future
actions toward him must approximate those as exemplified
by Sita, the ideal of Hindu women, toward the Lord Rama.
She must worship him; she must serve and obey him under
all circumstances. Regardless of what he might do of
good or evil, she must never question his actions.

When the last ceremony was completed, she was carried by her uncle to the special shrouded wedding cart
reserved for the bride. In it she rode alone, seeing
nothing, hearing nothing but the laughter of men in the
open carts until the curtains were lifted and she was
led into her new home. For her, entering Parbat's home
as a bride was a traumatic experience, as it had been
in the lives of other village brides I have known. Only
thirteen, she was expected to establish a whole new set
of relationships. During her brief post-wedding visit
in her mother-in-laws's courtyard, she was surrounded and
inspected by women of the family, with only glimpses of
Parbat when he came into the courtyard for his meals.
After three miserable days she was taken back home where
she was allowed almost two happy years of freedom with
her own family. Then, when she was brought here to stay,
it was to her mother-in-law that she came, not to Parbat.
She was known as Bachan's daughter-in-law, the family's
new bahu. Immediately she was set to work. It was

upsetting that her mother-in-law did things differently
from her own mother and expected her to adopt the new
ways without question. After what seemed a long period
of self-discipline, she, like most village bahus, learned
exactly what was expected of her. Tension relaxed. Then
the moment came which she had both dreaded and wished
for. Her mother-in-law informed her that she would be
the one to serve Parbat his evening meal. This is the
signal that the couple may meet alone for the first time.
That first night when they were along together in the
darkness of a storeroom marked the beginning of a new
relationship, that of husband and wife. Their meetings
were supposed to be clandestine, as are all husband and
wife trysts. Because they were brief, they were the
more valued. Life for both of them now followed a pat-
tern of work by day relieved by romance on rare nights.
Members of the older generation in the household hampered
communication between the two during the day. At the
same time, by making major decisions for them, the elders
spared them the arguments they might have had if they had
lived alone in a nuclear family.

The coming of their children drew them closer together. However, the children belonged to the whole family:
if a child of theirs fell ill, the elders decided whether
or not medical treatment was necessary, and if so, what
practitioner should be called. The death of their first
son, and later of the second, bound them even more closely together, although it was the elders who took charge
of the customary funerals. They continued to honor the
seniority of Punni and of Parbat's mother as long as
the two lived.

Then followed the difficult years when Shanti was
nominal head of the courtyard as Parbat's wife. Chakku
Ram's wife tended to be rebellious and sometimes refused
to follow her instructions; then there was constant interference from Ulfat's mother and his wife. The division
of the house forced upon them by Chakku Ram was intended
to hurt Parbat, but for Shanti it came as a relief.

Then, with the early fears and later conflicts left far
behind, she had attained the composure now characteristic
of her.

The word Shanti means Peace. Because it seemed so
appropriate I asked if I might call her that. She seemed
pleased. Only once had she whispered for my ears alone
the name that had been hers in childhood and was still
hers when she went home on a visit. In the khera, since
Bhalai's birth, she is referred to as "mother of Bhalai."
Parbat, like all village men, never addresses his wife
by name.

The land worked by Parbat and Pohtai was still
owned by the raja, whose ancestor had granted their great,
great grandfather land to use. Later a second absentee
landlord had taken over certain sections of the village
lands, but had not touched theirs. From the rent collected by his agent, the raja paid a portion to the government as taxes, while keeping a generous slice for himself.
Parbat and Pohtai held their land under marusi (hereditary) rights, like their forefathers. In 1951, four years
after Independence, the new government set out to give
farmers full ownership of the land they were cultivating.
The procedure was complicated by the fact that the government needed money with which to compensate the former
landlords. This money was to be paid by the new owners
in the form of a special tax equal to their tax for ten
years. Small scale farmers like Parbat did not have that
much cash on hand. However, after demands for payment
and subsequent threats of prosecution proved futile, government officials compromised and extended the period
allowed for payment. The outcome was that Parbat and
Pohtai gained full ownership of their fields and thereafter paid taxes directly to the government through local
officials. They no longer needed to fear the increased
demands of the landlord's agent should they succeed in increasing production. This gave them a new attitude toward
the land and towards themselves as landowners.

They bought two more oxen, giving them a total of
four to use for farming. They also had two buffaloes as
well as three cows, each with a calf. They rarely sold
any produce, with the occasional exception of potatoes
and grain surplus, for if they should oversell, they
would then be obliged to buy for family consumption before the next harvest. Their aim was to produce enough
surplus to cover taxes, clothes, and wages for any hired
helpers. They also tried to put by enough gold and silver to meet emergencies such as sudden illness, or for
irregular expenses such as a new ox, school books, or
a wedding.

By careful planning, hard work and thrift, Parbat
and Pohtai were able to support their joint family of
eleven members from the eighteen acres they held. One
reason why they succeeded with so little was that their
farming was a family affair. The two brothers, with
Parbat's two elder sons, when at home, all worked full-
time with their own hands and their own oxen. Farm equipment consisted of two plows, one of wood with only a small
metal tip made by a village carpenter, and one of steel.
They also had a shovel, two or three sickles for cutting
grain, a wooden scraper used in making irrigation channels and a large leather bag for lifting water from their
field well to the irrigation channels, and they had an
ox cart. Their land was not in one or two fields, but
in eight or nine plots scattered to the west and to the
south of the village, which meant carrying implements to
each different plot. The cycle of sowing, planting, cultivating, and irrigating, and later of harvesting the
main crops of grain and legumes occupied them all through
the autumn, winter and spring. In addition there were
the summer crops of musk melons, pumpkin, and other summer season vegetables. There was sugarcane to be planted, and eleven months later, to be cut and pressed for
the juice which they boiled down in huge pans to make
crude sugar. Peanuts had to be planted, as well as
potatoes, both sweet and white, for family consumption.

If they wanted rice, as most families do, they planted
it early in the monsoon and transplanted it as soon as
shoots appeared. Each sowing required using the steel
plow to break up the dry, hard ground, followed by ten
or twelve plowings with the village-made plow. For irrigating they used water from their own well or from the
pond. And once or twice during the winter season they
took their turn, by day or by night, making use of water
from the government tube well, which was electrically
powered. The women did their share in the courtyard and
Parbat felt free to call on his wife or his younger
daughter, while she was still at home, to help in the
fields. Pohtai's wife was considered too young an in-
law to venture as far as the fields except with Shanti.
One day as I walked into the outer courtyard, I met
Shanti and Pohtai's wife arriving, each with a large
load of peanut vines tied in a sheet and balanced on her
head. They pulled off the peanuts in the courtyard, and
used the fodder cutter to chop the leaves for the animals.
The women did their own gleaning at harvest time, rather
than leave this to women of serving castes, as Brahmins
do: they were able to gather an amazing amount of heads
of wheat or barley which the harvesters had left scattered
on the ground. There was always work waiting to be done
in the courtyard from before dawn until the men and children had been served their lunch. And again, after a
short break for their own meal and bath, the women
continued to work until long after dark.

One of their most time-consuming duties was feeding
their large family twice a day--once shortly before noon
and again in the evening. The daily bread served at each
meal consisted of chapatis, the flat, round cakes of whole
wheat flour ground freshly each day and made into dough
with water and a pinch of salt. At noon, the breads were
served with one of the several varieties of lentils from
the fields. The evening meal was the same, with perhaps
a different kind of grain with a different lentil or a
vegetable, also from one of their plots. Occasionally

there was rice which had to be husked and boiled. Festival days were marked by richer flat cakes, spiced and sweetened with crude sugar and fried in ghee, or in mustard oil, if there was no ghee. All of the utensils used for cooking or eating were of brass. When an article of brass wears too thin for use it can be returned to the brass seller who weighs it and deducts its value from the amount he charges for the new one. Iron is accepted for only two utensils--the convex griddle on which chapatis are toasted, and the basin used for deep frying. Fingers take the place of forks and spoons. Things like dish-towels or napkins are not needed.

For the whole family there was one hearth fire, the chulha. In cases where a new chulha appears in a different part of a house or in a separate courtyard, it marks the establishment of a new family. It is small and inconspicuous, made of a special kind of clay in the shape of a horseshoe, protected by a low wall of earth, surrounding a space just large enough for the chulha and one or two women who prepare the meals. Marking the heart of the household, it is given ceremonial care: each day at dawn or shortly before a bahu coats it with a fresh paste of clay. No one but the cook enters the now purified area.

The woman's chief responsibility was the care of all that the men brought in from the fields for family consumption. There was drying, husking, winnowing, grinding, and storing of grain. The women also made two tall jars of a special kind of clay, built up, layer by layer and dried in the sun, ready for storing grain after it also had been dried in the sun. Foods other than grain were kept in a storeroom in jars made and baked by the potter, of various sizes, all round bellied and covered with saucers of clay. Every possible means was used to keep rats from their food. Some jars, also carefully covered, contained legumes. Still others were filled with pickles or mangoes, limes, cucumbers or carrots stored in brine. Sliced, dried mangoes and

potatoes and greens were tied loosely in pieces of cloth
and suspended from the beams. When milking was done, the
milk was simmered, blended with curd and later churned.
The buttermilk was kept in a jar, ready for anyone in the
family to drink. The butter was collected for several
days until there was enough to be clarified at a high
temperature to make ghee, highly prized for frying special cakes. All the foodstuffs that might be needed before the next harvest were stored in the two storerooms,
each with just one door leading from the courtyard. As
in most village homes, the women learned the location of
all the containers and groped their way to the ones
desired.

Inside Parbat's house, every room was a storeroom.
No room was set aside for an individual or couple. No
room was designated for eating or sleeping. When the men
came in, they usually came separately, when hungry and
free from field work. They sat where they chose in the
courtyard and waited to be served. The women and chil-
ren ate after the men left, also sitting anywhere. The
women slept in the courtyard on charpais, a child or two
with each woman. In stormy or very cold weather, they
shifted to the shelter of one of the storerooms. The men
slept in the outer courtyard, among the trees, or in the
hut where implements were kept.

Shanti had learned something of Hindu lore while
still in her own home. She had also learned to read a
bit and keeps a copy of the Bhagavad Gita in her tin
chest. She brings it out and reads from it on certain
holidays. With her magnifying spectacles, she is quite
impressive. Like other village women, she is informed
on the religious significance of the grave of Khan Bahadur, a Muslim saint, at the top of the khera. There are
a number of legends surrounding the saint, all of which
end with the making of his grave by men grateful for his
services, especially his healing. Women and children
regularly go on Thursdays to Khan Bahadur with gifts.

On these occasions, a procession of village women

may be seen winding its way up the hillside. It is a straggling procession led by a ragged Muslim beating a drum. As one of the two stewards of the grave, he makes a meager living from the offerings of women seeking a blessing from the saint. At the top, the women spread a white cloth over the flat stone. In the center of the cloth and at the four corners, the women place copper coins. A number of the women bring miniature baskets filled with grain which they pour out on the cloth. Then everyone sits on the ground around the grave and sings familiar hymns and songs. That is the extent of the ceremony. After the women leave, the Muslim and his wife gather up the offerings and tie them in the cloth, thus receiving payment for their small services.

At other times of the year Shanti will worship Siyao Mata (the Lampblack Goddess) for blessings on her sons, or she will ask Devi, the goddess, for health for her family and long-life for her husband. All in all, she will participate in almost thirty major annual rituals.

Though considered a noncomformist in some respects, Parbat is strict in following the prescribed religious ceremonies. He is better informed than many as to the name and significant characteristics of the deity he worships at the time of each holiday, and what blessings this particular deity might be expected to grant. On the day appointed by the priests he performs his puja--ritual--beside his small worship center on the platform in front of the house. This contains a stone lingam, symbol of Shiva, and several other smooth stones. Like other village men I know, he makes no effort to enlighten his women folk on the religious aspects of the special holidays, but he expects them to make the elaborate festive dishes appropriate for each one.

The Younger Generation

There were two reasons why Parbat sent Bhalai, his older son, to high school. The first was Parbat's desire to give his son the opportunity that he himself had been denied. The other was more realistic. The eighteen acres of land that Parbat and Pohtai owned were enough for their family as it was at the moment, but soon it would be insufficient. His three sons would be married within the next few years and would presumably have sons of their own. Pohtai already had several children and might well have more. The needs of the next generation could not be met by harvests from only eighteen acres. At least one son must find work that would bring in cash to supplement what the fields could provide. Bhalai, as the eldest and most promising son, should be the one. The high school venture was costly. All boys going to school in Mainpuri had bicycles, so Bhalai must have one. There were textbooks to be bought, as well as clothes better than those needed in the fields. But the benefits would outweigh the cost. So both Parbat and Bhalai were disappointed when no government post was forthcoming. Finally after two years Bhalai decided to join the Army. He enlisted, was finally accepted, and was posted to Lucknow. Neither his family nor his neighbors knew anything about the Army which was part of the strange outside world. When they learned more about it from the Carpenter and the Shepherd, each with a brother in military service, they were sure that this was not at all what they had hoped for. With a clerkship in Mainpuri Bhalai could have lived at home and cycled to and from the office; the Army might send him anywhere. He must always take orders from others who, unlike his father, had no interest in him as a person. His parents were alarmed.

This was the first major crisis in the family since the dividing of the old homestead. To Parbat it was a blow. He was losing his eldest son. So to reassure the

women of the family and to relieve his own anxiety, Parbat undertook the journey to Lucknow. Many years before
he had gone to Allahabad for a court case; but since then
he had not traveled beyond our district or those adjoining it. He managed to locate Bhalai and returned satisfied. He son was well fed and well clothed, food and
clothing paid for by the government. Every day he had to
undergo strenuous drill, but that would benefit him. He
was receiving a monthly stipend. After hearing this news
the women were no longer hysterical, although they were
still distressed.

Two months later Bhalai, because he had completed
high school and had passed special tests given by the
Army, was assigned to a medical corps. This was a definite advancement. Because he could read and write well,
he was given the duty of keeping records of all medical
supplies. His training would be free and it would enable
him to get a good job when his military service ended.
The family was proud of him.

Bhalai's first leave gave the whole family the relief his father had' experienced. His mother prepared the
dishes she knew he liked best, told him how much they had
missed him, and wept while begging him to stay at home.
But when he explained that if he were to desert the Army,
there would be severe punishment for him and disgrace for
the family, she accepted the fact that she must face life
without him.

Bhalai's wife was torn. She was obviously proud of
him in his smart uniform, but at the same time she was
bereft. She had lost two babies and now she was expected
to give up her husband. All that had given meaning to
her life and work was gone. She might have made a scene,
but in the presence of others she did not raise her voice
in protest. She, too, had learned or was learning self-
discipline.

The sudden appearance of Bhalai as a full-fledged
soldier gave their neighbors pause. Over the years they
had become accustomed to belittling him. The older ones

had regarded Parbat as impractical and extravagant, sending Bhalai to high school when he could have been useful
on the land. Later they had smiled complacently over
each of Bhalai's failures to find work and had frequently
reminded Parbat that he had made a mistake. But now here
was a successful Bhalai, parading the insignia of the
Army Medical Corps, the importance of which he hastened
to explain to them. They felt obliged to treat him with
respect, whether willingly or grudgingly. The younger
Farmers either frankly admired him for his success or
envied him. Bhalai basked in his popularity. For any
visitor who came into their outer courtyard, he opened
his metal box and displayed the Army equipment that he
had been allowed to bring.

In 1962, a year after he had joined the Army, Bhalai
was transferred to the famous Red Fort in Delhi with a
generous leave at home en route. Again his parents were
upset until he explained that going to and from Delhi
would be easier than going to and from Lucknow. Also he
had heard that life in the Red Fort was more pleasant
than in the Lucknow barracks, and Delhi itself offered
many attractions, historical and modern. Soon after arriving in Delhi he was selected for service in the Anti-
Malaria Unit working on the eradication of malaria in
the Delhi area. Unit members occupied special quarters
in the Fort and were granted a number of privileges that
Bhalai had not had before. He wrote home that it was
hard to believe he was still in the Army.

By 1964 when he was well enough established to acquire one of the family quarters inside the Fort, Bhalai
came to take his wife to live there with him. This pro-
posal was startling: whoever heard of a young bahu leaving
the security of her in-laws' home to go off with her husband, alone, to a distant place where she would live a-
mong strangers? They had no precedent for such a risk;
but after extracting assurances from Bhalai, they agreed
to let her go, provided Bhalai's younger sister go with
her. His sister was married, which was an asset, and she

was not expected to go to her in-laws for another year.
So the three set out, sent on their way with tears and
warnings and provided with bundles of special food such
as those a wife takes when leaving her home for her
in-laws.

For almost a year they lived in the suite of rooms
provided for them within the Fort. Bhalai's son was
born there and Bhalai's mother came to visit. Every
afternoon for a full week, during Bhalai's hours off
duty, they all went sight-seeing. Until then, only one
woman of Karimpur had visited the capital and she had
been there for just one day. Bhalai's mother spent a
week and saw everything that any tourist could hope to
see, with her son as experienced guide. Since then no
matter how monotonous her life has been or how filled
with drudgery, she has had that week to think and talk
about.

Shortly after Shanti's visit Bhalai was transferred
from his service in the Anti-Malaria Unit to his former
post in the medical corps. He had barely made the transfer when orders came for all medical corps personnel to
report for duty on the India-Pakistan border where fighting had already begun. He brought his wife and sister
and the baby home by the next bus and left immediately
to join his corps.

Life in the Red Fort had transformed Bhalai's wife.
While there she had been head of her own small courtyard
as Bhalai's wife, no longer Parbat's daughter-in-law.
And in the section of the Fort where their quarters were
located, she was treated as an individual. Surprisingly,
when she was once more in Shanti's courtyard, she returned to her role of senior bahu without apparant effort.
The relationship between her and Shanti was that of traditional bahu and mother-in-law when in the presence of
other village women, although alone together they were
more at ease, especially when sharing their novel
experiences.

Meanwhile Bhalai had been in the combat area with others of the medical staff caring for the wounded, often under fire. However, the war ended shortly and he was granted two months' leave. He was soon back home but no longer so self-centered. His responsibility for his small family in the Red Fort had curtailed his visits with fellow soldiers to their favorite eating places, and with less money to spend on himself, his enthusiasm for costly diversions had wanted. Added to this, his experiences during the war, brief though they were, had sobered him. He came home with a changed attitude and with no apparent desire to boast of his exploits.

When Bhalai left home to join the Army, the family took for granted that Gopi would take his place as eldest son, but Gopi showed no interest in farming. Obviously he chose to remain the abused younger brother and ne- glected son. Both his father and mother complained that it was difficult to work and live with him, and when he followed his father's instructions in the fields, he did it grudgingly.

Gopi was four years younger than Bhalai which at once put him at a disadvantage. He was shorter and weaker than Bhalai and he disliked school intensely, preferring friends who had never been in a classroom. His father finally abandoned threats of punishment at the end of the fifth class. Gopi thought his elder brother foolish to load himself with school books until their father bought a bicycle and Bhalai went riding off to town each morning, when he discovered that now he was the one loaded, not with books but with field work. This he resented.

On Bhalai's first home leave, Gopi had watched and listened sullenly while Bhalai boasted of his successes. He said nothing until Bhalai had gone back to Lucknow. Then he announced that since he was eighteen, he too would join the Army. Parbat refused to let him go. One son in the Army was enough. Gopi did not run away

to enlist as he threatened to do, but he stubbornly refused to work in the family's fields. After a time he
found employment with the local land-recorder, measuring
the boundaries of disputed plots. But the job offered
no future.

Gopi returned home, not to work but to bring pressure on his parents to help him become a motor driver.
If he could not join the Army, he would be a driver.
However there were very few cars in our district, and
these belonged to government officials or successful
doctors or lawyers who employed poor relatives as drivers and who would certainly hesitate to hire a village
boy without experience. Although Gopi knew this, he
was convinced that he could get a job somewhere. In
desperation his father sent him to me and I offered
to consult friends in Delhi on his behalf during my
next visit.

When I returned, everyone I met was excited about
Gopi, who had suddenly emerged as a hero. He had saved
his family from a band of dacoits, robbers. It happened
during a violent storm, as is frequent before the monsoon
breaks, when the wind rushes over the countryside carrying what seems like a solid wall of dust with it, and
everyone runs for shelter. Branches are ripped from the
trees and even large trees are blown down. On such a
night, a gang of dacoits descended on Parbat's house.
Apparently they had been waiting for such an opportunity. They alone welcome these storms as cover. Parbat
had taken refuge in his implement hut, while Pohtai and
Gopi had shifted their charpais to a storeroom off of
the outer courtyard. The women and children had moved
into an adjoining storeroom.

After one of the dacoits found access to the house
over a back wall, he passed through both courtyards and
opened the heavy bolt on the inside of the one outer
door. The other dacoits, who waited there, came swarm-
ing in. The number of robbers varies with the narrator

from sixteen to forty. They had flashlights and guns,
which ordinary villagers rarely possess. Parbat heard
the shots and saw lights flashing. Guessing what was
happening, he ran down the narrow lane to get help, but
his neighbors were all tightly shut in their own storerooms and the roar of the wind drowned out his shouts.
Meanwhile the dacoits took possession of the house.
Shanti overheard the leader giving orders that no woman
was to be searched, so she and the others quickly hid
whatever jewelry they were wearing under their garments.
The two men, Pohtai and Gopi, were roughly treated,
pushed down on a charpai and their hands bound behind
their backs with strips of cloth. Two of the large homemade jars of grain in the storeroom were overturned and
the grain spilled out. These jars are considered a safe
repository for money. Chests in other storerooms were
broken open and everything of value was seized. Then
the dacoits discussed torturing the two men with a fire
of kerosene oil.

Meanwhile Gopi worked at the knots in the cloth
binding his wrists, until he was free. When the nearest
dacoits were occupied with their search, he crept out
into the courtyard, and in the darkness made a leap to
the narrow half of the earth stairway on his family's
side of the wall. He had climbed almost to the top when
a flashlight exposed his flight. With torches and staves,
a crowd of dacoits converged on him. Two of them grabbed
at his long loose trousers, but Gopi, sans trousers,
jumped over the wall and down into Chakku Ram's courtyard. Guessing that he would spread the alarm the whole
gang fled with whatever they had in their hands. Uncles
and neighbors came hurrying in with lanterns and staves.
Only the devastation and the terrified women and Pohtai,
still bound, remained to tell the tale. Parbat had given
up his attempt to find help and was stumbling back
through the darkness when the dacoits rushed past him

and away, fortunately turning their flashlights toward
the fields.

Not long after the incident, a self-confident Gopi
came to inform me that he was ready to go to Delhi at
any time. Having outwitted a band of dacoits, he was
prepared to face strangers in the outside world.

His opportunity came less than a month later. For
over fifteen years I had gone to Delhi periodically to
participate in what has been known as the Orientation
of Foreign Technicians--foreigners arriving in India
to become members of embassies or other organizations.
At the time when Gopi was to join me, good friends in
Aligarh, half way to Delhi, had been sending their car
and a driver to take me to their home for a day or two
before going on to Delhi by train. When the day came
for the next trip, Gopi was at my door long before the
car was due.

The journey to Aligarh was his first experience
riding in any conveyance other than an ox-cart. He was
all eyes, and tense with excitement as he sat beside
the driver. The ample shoulder bag which his mother
had made for him from scraps of old dhoti borders did
not contain clothing as I had thought: instead it was
filled with fried cakes and homemade sweets, enough
for his journey and his first few days in Delhi. This
was his only baggage.

During our weekend in the home of my friends in
Aligarh, Gopi was overwhelmed and uneasy. It was his
first experience in a city home with electric fixtures,
hot and cold running water, showers, flush toilets,
polished furniture, and separate rooms for eating,
sleeping and entertaining. To the amusement of our
hostess, he was never more than ten feet from me. While
my friends and I talked with guests who came in for tea,
he sat in the background watching and listening intent-
ly, although he could not understand a word of our

conversation which was in English. He could not eat our
food because of caste restrictions, but he sat near us
in the dining room during every meal watching our use of
knives, forks, and spoons. As for his own food, he kept
his bag in my room and made frequent trips to it during
the day. On the second morning, he accepted a cup of
tea and liked it. He had never drunk anything other
than water or milk before.

When I was preparing to travel on to Delhi by train,
he suggested that perhaps he should return home. To this
I would not agree. He would be more unsettled now than
before. He must go on. Never having been on a train, he
was worried by the crowds of people pushing their way
into and out of the compartments. When he heard I was
to travel in a compartment "for ladies" and knew that
he was to be separated from me in such a mob, he was
terrified. My friends found him a seat in the next
coach, but at each large station between Aligarh and
Delhi, he came to the window beside my seat just to
make sure that I was still there. At the big Delhi
station he stayed as close to my heels as the shoving,
shouting crowds allowed, while we followed Paulus, the
driver who had been sent to meet us by the friends whose
home was mine while I was in New Delhi.

Paulus immediately took Gopi under his wing as he
too had experienced the same fear and confusion long
ago. It was he who went with Gopi to get two new out-
fits of clothing for city living, as well as the utensils
and oil stove needed for preparing meals. And it was he
who arranged for a room next to his where Gopi could
sleep and cook. He also helped find a "driving school,"
of which there are many in Delhi, and saw Gopi safely
enrolled. When he learned that the actual teaching of
driving was limited to two hours each afternoon, he
helped Gopi get a morning job cleaning cars at an office
building. In two weeks Gopi knew the way to his school

and to the office building where he worked.

When I returned to Delhi, after an absence of two months, Gopi was at the station with Paulus to meet me. The station rush no longer confused him. On the drive to my New Delhi home, he used several sentences in English and announced, "Now I am a city boy." To establish himself indisputably as a "city boy" he indulged in disparaging comments on villagers, just as Bhalai had done before him. Villagers were narrow-minded, backward, with no interest in events outside the village, careless in their dress, content with houses of unbaked mud bricks that often gave way during the rains. None of this however, applied to his own family. Again and again he asked for news of them. And his eyes shone when I talked about his wife and the small son whom he had seen just once. He repeatedly expressed his desire to visit them all as soon as his training was completed, being careful to add, "But not to stay."

During the following weeks, Gopi learned from his driving teacher the fundamentals of driving. That was all. He learned more from the experienced drivers connected with the office where he cleaned cars, and still more from Paulus. The chief advantage derived from attending the school was that his test for a driver's license was simplified. The examining officer took for granted that the driver-students knew all that was necessary and passed them after a cursory test. When Gopi finally received his license from the manager of the school, he found to his delight that he was qualified to drive heavy, as well as light, vehicles. Now he could go home as a trained driver with a license bearing his picture to prove it. And he had found a job as a tractor driver.

When Gopi was ready for his job on the large government farm beyond Delhi, it took time and patient effort on the part of his supervisor to convince him

that he must live nearer to the farm. He was willing
to work, but he fought the idea of moving away from
Paulus, his Delhi friend. The farm was more than ten
miles from the part of the city where Paulus lived, and
there was no public transportation between the two areas.
Finally, after several weeks, he accepted the inevitable
and settled down with a distant relative in a room only
three miles from the farm.

Gopi proved to be a good mechanic as well as driver.
He was strong and ready to learn and undertake any task
assigned to him. His wages rose from barely enough to
cover his room and food to more then Bhalai was getting.
During his second year of service, he was selected to
go to other stations where an experienced driver was
needed. It gave him an opportunity to visit many parts
of India while the generous travel allowance added considerably to his income. He seldom came home, having
just one month's vaction each year. If he wanted to
make the trip between annual leaves, it had to be
when a special holiday covered more than one day.

Although the visits home were short, Gopi managed
to tell a good deal about his travels. Every young
neighbor who could, came to listen. On one visit he
flourished a watch, regarded in the village as the
first sign of success. He did not call attention to it
but consulted it frequently. On a later visit he
walked about the village with a camera slung over his
shoulder. This was an even greater sensation. Anyone
who owned a camera must have a great deal of money to
spend. Obviously, Gopi was enjoying his popularity.
He was now self-confident, established, and secure.

Following Bhalai's example, he made a trip home at
the end of two year's service to take his wife to Delhi
to cook for him and his cousin. He assured his parents
that his quarters were as good as Bhalai's had been in
the Red Ford. They were smaller, only two small rooms

plus a tiny kitchen and courtyard, but sufficient for three persons and were protected by a high brick wall. There were friendly neighbors on each side, and the older women would be glad to act as chaperones for his wife while he was away at work. She need not go out because he, like all the men he knew, did the shopping. After all, he was twenty-one and she was seventeen-- old enough to take care of themselves. By this time Parbat and Shanti were so accustomed to gossip that they allowed her to go without demanding that another woman of the family accompany her.

In Delhi, she was a success both as cook and as companion. Gopi knew just what sights Bhalai had taken the other women of the family to see, and he took his wife by motorcycle rickshaw to visit them all. On their first excursion, she saw little. She was so afraid that some man might have a glimpse of her face that she kept it well covered. Also she was still unaccustomed to sitting beside her husband in public, and was uncomfortable and self-conscious. She was just beginning to enjoy her emanciaption in Delhi when Gopi was obliged to take her back home. He explained to his village friends that he might be sent to some distant place and could not leave her alone. Actually, food prices in Delhi had become so exorbitant that his pay was not sufficient to provide for two. In his father's house, one more person to be fed made little difference. Also at home she could do more than cook two meals a day which was all that she found to do in Delhi. Her help in caring for raw products from the fields would more than compensate for the food she ate.

Less than a month after Gopi had brought his wife home, he was sent to the Punjab just before the conflict between India and Pakistan broke out. He was working in an area where there was no actual fighting; but after bombs had been dropped several times on neighboring fields, it seemed wise to abandon the project until later so he was transferred back to his regular job near Delhi. He was now listed as a "permanent" employee. Had he been in regular government service, this would have meant that no one could displace him; but he was employed by a private agency cooperating with the government, therefore it simply indicated that he was considered a good workman and that as long as his services proved satisfactory, he was secure. It also indicated that his supervisor approved of his work and that he would not be lightly dismissed.

Then, without warning, his supervisor was called to a post in Afghanistan. Because the conditions and language were entirely different there, he could not agree to Gopi's urgent request to be taken along. A new supervisor arrived. He found Gopi experienced and capable enough to be assigned added responsibilities on a farm being newly developed farther out. Gopi's house was located conveniently near the original farm, but far from the new one. Determined not to move again, he undertook the longer bicycle ride morning and evening. Many of his neighbors traveled as far or father, but they held office jobs which were less rigorous than driving a tractor.

Before this change in the location of his work, Gopi had discovered that other young Indians working on the farm were far better qualified academically than he. When fellow workers learned that he had dropped out at the end of the 5th class in a village school, they were scornful. Supervisors gave him credit for his skill and thoroughness and were aware that his practical qualifications outweighed theoretical preparation in college classrooms. At the same time, subordinates were able to outrank him in standing and pay because they had B.A. degrees. He decided that he must remove the stigma of being labeled a fifth grader. Without advice from anyone, he located a college in a different state where he could study "privately" at home. When he became "high school pass" in this way, he went on to college courses, hoping that some day he might receive a degree. His efforts were well repaid. When Gopi's employer's contract expired and the experimental farm was taken over by government officers, they accepted him as an employee, with the possibility of becoming "permanent" within two years. This could not have come about if he had not pursued further education.

*   *   *

Although the two brothers were much nearer each other now than while Gopi was in Karimpur and Bhalai in Delhi, they made little effort to meet. Only once Gopi had visited Bhalai at the Red Fort, and then it was to borrow money from him while he was receiving driver training in Delhi. Thereafter, on the rare occasions when they did meet, Bhalai reminded his brother of the loan, and Gopi assured him that as soon as he had a job he would repay it.

During the months of his training, when Gopi returned to his room, he hastily bathed and ate his meal then, if I chanced to be there we sat on the lawn while he told me about his adventures driving a car in the big city. He was excited about many things that people living there would not notice. One Sunday, when Bhalai was free, he came to call. My friends and I, with Gopi, were in the living room when Bhalai arrived. He brought with him not only the assurance of a man in a well-fitting uniform, but also the pride of a member of the esteemed Medical Corps. He knew enough English to converse easily with my friends, and he was as much at home in their living room as Gopi was on the lawn. He talked about the important sights in and around Delhi that he and his army friends had visited and which my friends did not know existed.

In Bhalai's presence, Gopi was deflated. Until this meeting he had regarded himself as a person of importance as a driver-to-be. Now, suddenly, he reverted to the younger brother with too little schooling and too little knowledge of the world--the city world. He knew just

enough English to realize that Bhalai was talking about
a Delhi he himself had never seen. While he had walked
the street to and from work, Bhalai rode in buses or
motorcycle rickshaws. While he sat on a dirty bench at
the driver's training school waiting his turn to drive,
Bhalai was living in comfortable quarters in the Red Fort
or going to cinemas and restaurants. Gopi was a raw
country boy and was acutely aware of it.

As I watched the two brothers, one so urbane, the
other so artless, I wondered if it were possible for a
young man to adapt himself to the life of a city without
losing all the spontaneity and freshness of the open
fields. Gopi's naivete, his quaint turns of speech, his
stride that could carry him for miles with ease, marked
him as coming fresh from the country. Could he retain
some of these traits when he had acquired sophistication
comparable to Bhalai's, which so obviously impressed
him? I have known older men in responsible positions in
New Delhi who have achieved this. With their years of
living in both environments and their balanced perspec-
tives, they have been able to sort out the values of
country and city, and retain the best of each.

Before leaving, Bhalai announced that the chief purpose of his visit was to invite us all to have tea with
him one afternoon soon. So one day Paulus, Gopi and I
drove through the great doors in the gateway, past sen-
tries and into the vast interior of the Red Fort. Gopi
had been here twice, but was as confused as we were. As
we drove slowly up one avenue and down another, we met a
number of officers each of whom inquired the name of the
officer we sought. The car and Paulus' uniform were mis-
leading. Our report, that we were trying to find a private, was a shock. However, when we added that this
private was in the anti-malaria unit, we were immediately directed to its quarters and there found Bhalai
waiting. He was surrounded by comrades eager to entertain his guests. Several disappeared to arrange for tea
while others took us on a tour of their quarters. The

two main rooms serving as offices were enormous, stone
walled and stone ceilinged. The sleeping rooms were also
large with ample space for each member of the unit. We
met two of Bhalai's officers, both doctors. Our tour
ended on a beautiful stone balcony looking out over the
Jumma River to the countryside beyond. This particular
section of the Fort, built by Shah Jahan, a Mogul Emperor,
must have been intended for selected members of his staff.
Bhalai and his friends talked with us while they served
tea and delicious cakes. Paulus, a South Indian who had
traveled a good deal, was immediately accepted by the
group. I enjoyed Bhalai's friends and enjoyed Bhalai
himself in this setting. Yet though at least half of the
conversation was in Hindi, Gopi did not speak, perhaps
fearing that his accent or vocabulary would betray him as
a country boy. He listened, watching and copying Paulus'
every move. No one seemed to notice that he was ill at
ease. As we drove out of the Red Fort I mistook the
brightness of his eyes as pride in his brother's distinc-
tion, but it proved to the gleam of jealousy.

On the drive home he announced that he was going to
learn English and speak it better than Bhalai, and that
he was going to earn more money than Bhalai. As a driver
he could easily do better than a private in the army. To
me it seemed a forlorn hope. Who would employ a young
man with inadequate training and no experience? However,
within a year I saw him in his khaki driver's uniform
self-confidently operating a large tractor. The pay was
far below his expectations, but there was promise of more
when he completed his apprenticeship. At least he had
enough to live on independently.

Not long after Gopi had been employed, the brothers
met again, this time with their father. Although Parbat
had accepted the decisions of both his sons to leave home
and enter occupations that he would not have chosen for
them, he still considered himself responsible for their
conduct. He made the trip to Delhi to talk with them,
to satisfy himself that each was doing his honest best.

Also he hoped that if he were with them in person he
could persuade them to contribute toward the expenses
of the family. He arranged to meet them at the Red
Fort. He left home with high hopes, but returned sad-
dened. Neither boy would part with any of his income.
Still worse, they had quarreled over the loan that
Bhalai had made to Gopi before Gopi found employment.
Bhalai insisted that Gopi, now earning regular wages,
should repay the loan. Gopi replied that he was earning
barely enough to cover the cost of food and lodging.
Why did Bhalai keep tormenting him over a little money?
He spent more on himself each month than he had loaned
his brother. Bhalai would have to wait. Bhalai's re-
tort angered him and soon the two were out-shouting each
other. Parbat finally parted them, but he left Delhi
feeling ill and shamed. Going to a big city and earning
cash had demoralized his sons.

Neither of the brothers seemed to understand the
depth of Parbat's sacrifice in granting them their freedom. He had denied himself the security which would
have been his with two stalwart sons beside him. He had
lost two pair of strong arms needed in cultivating the
family's fields, and yet he could not count on help from
his youngest son, Bamar, who was still in school. He
and Pohtai worked harder than ever before. Also, it was
necessary to hire one or two men to do the work that the
two boys could have done. When he had humiliated himself
to the extent of going to his sons to solicit the help he
was sure they could give and which he thought it their
duty to give, they had treated him disgracefully.

Over the years Parbat had met and weathered storm
after storm of adversity. Now, without warning, came a
blow that threatened to be fatal. Pohtai deserted him.
Parbat had counted on having Pohtai with him always as
his younger brother. Pohtai had willingly left all responsibility to Parbat and had accepted his decisions
without question. Obviously someone had prejudiced him,
and Parbat was convinced that it could only be their

half-brother, Chakku Ram. Since the day that Chakku Ram had denied Parbat and Pohtai the right to share the old home where they had all lived together, he had used every means possible to cripple Parbat. Parbat was sure that Chakku Ram had instigated the robbery, which would have impoverished him if it had been successful. Now, after a series of petty persecutions he had estranged Pohtai. When Pohtai insisted on having half of whatever the robbers had left, Parbat tried to divide all that remained of the clothing and jewelry, but Pohtai was not satisfied. To Parbat it was the kind of disagreement they could resolve amicably. To Pohtai it was serious enough to warrant a complete severing of fraternal ties. He insisted on a re-division of the house. He would take the outer courtyard and the storerooms connected with it, while Parbat would occupy the back courtyard and storerooms. This in itself was an affront to an elder brother, an affront which Pohtai could not have conceived without prompting from someone more shrewd. The front half was preferable from the point of view of thefts. It would be more difficult for thieves to climb a wall facing the public road than to climb a back wall where no one passes. However, with the increase in traffic on the district road, the front portion would be more exposed to clouds of dust and the roar of heavy vehicles. When the division had been completed, the only change Pohtai made in his section was to apply a thick plaster of mud over the door that had connected the outer and inner courtyards. It was in Parbat's en- closure that changes began to appear and have continued since.

Parbat had scarcely recovered from the division of their home and the setting up of a separate chulha, when Pohtai struck a second blow, more devastating than the first. He announced that they must divide their land. When Parbat heard this he was more firmly convinced that Chukka Ram was using Pohtai to destroy him. The division of the land was most unfortunate coming as it

did shortly before the official evaluation of each family's scattered plots for purposes of consolidation. The
evaluation would determine the acreage and quality of
the consolidated field or fields assigned in exchange
for the old plots. With their joint holdings, they would
have been assured of a field large enough to cultivate
profitably. With the property divided, both holdings
would be reduced to fields of less desirable soil and too
small for the efficiency which consolidation plans had
promised. Nevertheless, the division was carried out.
Pohtai's next demand was that each of them retain one of
the two oxen they were using for field work. When a farmer has depended on a pair of oxen, he feels like half a
farmer when left with one. For Parbat having only one
ox was a constant reminder of his humiliation. He sold
his ox and solved his problem temporarily by working on
shares with a farmer who had only one acre of land, but
who owned two oxen. Parbat would get only half the produce, but with the reduced size of his family he would
have food enough. They had always been frugal, now they
must be even more so.

A man of Parbat's standing runs the risk of becoming
a target for others who want to displace him or perhaps
replace him. Where there are two or more grown men in a
family their position is comparatively secure. But one
left alone like Parbat, now without brother or son beside
him, is vulnerable. And it is a man's own relatives who
are most apt to attack. Parbat was aware of this, knowing of similar cases in the village. Some of his Farmer
neighbors thought his misgivings unjustified. Others
agreed that if they were in his situation they would feel
as he did. Men in both groups regarded his place of
seniority in their community as being so stable that his
strained relations with his half-brother could not weaken
it. This was small comfort to Parbat.

With each fresh blow he and Shanti had become more
despondent. Theirs was a house of gloom, and when the

daughters-in-law were away it was worse. Parbat had
aged perceptibly during the past months. He and Shanti
had lost their two eldest sons, had been robbed of their
goods, and now had lost half of their house, land and
oxen. Shanti complained that she had too little to do.
Where there had been ten or more to look after and two
daughters-in-law to direct, now she had just three to
cook for--Parbat, herself, and Bamar. Parbat complained
that he had too much to do for a man of his age, but the
added work could not account entirely for his weary
stoop. In every conversation he returned to his grudge
against his half-brother, Chakku Ram, whom he held responsible for all of his troubles.

Following Pohtai's estrangement and its consequences, other misfortunes beset him. Their crops were
suffering from lack of rain. But though the maize might
survive if he could get water from the government tube
well immediately, it would yield a meager harvest. The
sorghum and millet had already withered and would provide nothing more than fodder. The peanut crop was safe
but they had planted less than in other years.

It was no longer a pleasure to sit with Shanti or
with the two together in their courtyard, and I postponed visiting them. When I did go, about ten days after
hearing Parbat's lament over the drought disaster, the atmosphere had completely changed. A card had come from
Bhalai saying that his leave was due, and that they
should expect him any day. Parbat had made a quick trip
to bring Bhalai's wife and two children from her parent's
home. Parbat had also sent a post card (villagers limit
themselves to post cards) to the father of Gopi's wife
asking that someone bring her: her parents would understand that Parbat would be too busy to fetch her. Even
while we were speaking of her, she came in, escorted by
an elder brother, and was as excited as the others over
Bhalai's coming. Her own husband was not free to join
them now, but she looked forward to helping with the
special dishes they would prepare for Bhalai. With the

presence of the two daughters-in-law and the children,
Shanti's smile returned, and gloom gave way to laughter.

The next morning Bamar, Parbat's youngest son, appeared at my door with the news that Bhalai had arrived.
I must come to see what he had brought and to hear about
the plans for changing their house. Their courtyard,
when I stepped into it a few minutes later, was the scene
of a full-scale homecoming. Bhalai was obviously delighted to be home again. Former visits, except for the
one following the war, had been sensational, always centered around his exploits. This time he wanted to display the gifts he had brought as a surprise. They were
spread out on two charpais for the family to enjoy and
visitors to admire. There were plain white shirts and
dhotis for his father and Bamar, white dhotis with red
or green borders for the women as well as flowered
blouses, and the brightest clothes of all for his children. Shanti sat relaxed on a charpai, looking and listening; and Bhalai's and Gopi's wives missed nothing
while they went on frying cakes that filled the courtyard
with the aroma of festival preparations. Parbat had
stayed home from the fields to share in the first happy
occasion his house had known for a long time. Bhalai's
choicest gift was a bicycle for his father. He could not
have thought of anything more needed or better appreciated. When word of a brand new bicycle spread, men stopped by, and as Parbat exhibited it just outside the door,
his eyes had the twinkle that had been absent for months.
He had missed the old cycle which Pohtai now owned, and
found it difficult to get to town or to neighboring villages without it. He still had his oxcart, but he had
not reached the point where he was willing to be seen
going to town on the district road with a team of ungain-
ly water buffaloes. From now on he could ride anywhere
on his own bicycle, as any self-respecting elder.

Shanti had been ailing for some time. Parbat had
written to Bhalai about it, and Bhalai had brought special medicine for her, suggested by one of his officers.

On that first day of his visit, she looked and felt
better. She was not sure whether it was the result of
the medicine or the pleasure of having her son at home.
Neighbor women, other than one family's hostile relatives, began coming in to admire and exclaim over the
gifts and to sniff the delectable odors coming from the
kitchen corner. When they finally left and the men had
gone home for their mid-day meal, Parbat came in tired
and hungry. The food was ready and the two bahus were
waiting for someone to appreciate it. They expected no
praise from Parbat, but were sure from his manner of
eating that he appreciated it.

Bhalai had brought plans for remodeling the house
and studied them as he walked through the storerooms
and courtyard, impatient to show them to his father.
He had stopped in Delhi on his way home to spend a day
with Gopi. Since Gopi's repayment of the irritating
loan and their heavier responsibilities, plus the sober-
ing effect of the war, their relationship had changed
for the better. Together they had made these rough
drawings which were now more important to him than food,
even rich festival food. As soon as Parbat had finished
eating, he was ready to look and to listen.

Measurements and blue prints are not considered
necessary in the planning of a village house, but the
sketch Bhalai showed us was almost professional. It
was also revolutionary, so much so that no one could
comprehend it except Bhalai. After the last flourish of
his pencil and the final gasp from his audience, he was
ready to eat, and ate with such relish that both cooks
were delighted. He often boasted of the good meals
served in the medical corps, but the women of the family
were positive that he preferred their cooking. After the
meal, they expected him to recline on a charpai for the
afternoon, as had been his habit during the first week
of former leaves. He announced, however, that he was
going to visit the mason whom he intended to hire, to
confer with him on materials needed for the first stages

of rebuilding. When he returned late in the afternoon he expressed pleasure over the bicycle and satisfaction over the building estimates agreed upon.

Although he had not spoken directly to his wife during the morning or while he ate, she knew that every word he had addressed to others was intended for her ears as well. When he spent time playing with their children, she was sure that he was thinking of her. She knew as Bhalai knew, that when others no longer claimed him, they would be together. Others did claim him before he could finish his evening meal. Several young Farmers shouted to him from outside the door, demanding that he join them. As always, they expected to be entertained by his tales of adventure. This time he could report the danger to which he had actually been exposed since last they met, and exaggeration was not necessary to make it breath-taking.

However, when morning came, the house again took first place. The mason arrived and with Bhalai went over every inch of the section to be attacked first, measuring and re-estimating the number of bricks and bags of cement needed. When the mason left, Bhalai went off on the bi-cycle, first to a brick kiln near Mainpuri and then into the town market to order cement. On the way home he lo-cated and hired two men, glad to earn meals and cash for a month or two.

Building, whether with sun-dried or kiln-baked bricks, moves slowly in Karimpur, but Bhalai's impatient prodding accelerated the pace. He was to be at home for two months and was bent on making as much progress as possible each day. The three women of the family emptied their well-filled storerooms, and on their trail came the two men Bhalai had hired, pulling down walls and scatter-ing rubble. The women struggled for privacy, first in one spot and then in another. Their freedom from village restrictions while in Delhi spared them embarrassment now and they were amused more than they were upset by the confusion that prevailed.

When Gopi arrived, unannounced, a few days after
work had begun there was more excitement in the courtyard. He was greeted as son, brother, husband, father
and workman. He had brought gifts less spectacular than
Bhalai's, but explained that he had been saving all of
his overtime pay to help with the house. He had been
riding in a rattling, uncomfortable bus all night and
gladly accepted the puris and warm milk his mother
pressed upon him. Then he quickly exchanged his city
clothes for the well-worn mechanic's outfit and plunged
in.

With another man added to the team, the tempo of
tearing down walls and roofs mounted. It was impossible
to move without walking through debris or tripping over
discarded beams. Finally came the eventful day when a
new courtyard emerged, with plenty of space, taken from
two former storerooms. Part of the old courtyard was
transformed into a large, airy storeroom, such as they
had never seen. They accepted this as the army medical
corps' idea of a proper storeroom.

This was as much as they could accomplish during
Bhalai's two months leave. The following year Bhalai
again came home on leave, but with less enthusiasm over
house plans. His own daughter had died and he missed
her painfully. She had been a lovable child, almost six
years old. This was the first year, since she had been
able to walk, that she was not at the door waiting to
welcome him. He had received his father's postcard telling of her illness when he was too far away to come home,
although he had the assurance that his parents would be
doing all that he would have done. They had even taken
her to a doctor in town who gave her an injection and
provided them with medicine that he said would surely
cure her. When it brought no relief, they called a hakim,
a traditional doctor, whom Bhalai knew and trusted. Nothing had availed and she died only a short time before his
return. They had lost a son a few years before, and although they still had their one small son this made it

no easier for them to give up Rani Devi. Gopi too came
home as soon as word came of her death. Although Rani
Devi was Bhalai's child, she was a daughter of the whole
family.

Soon Gopi again came home. He had pressed for an
early leave when he received a card from Parbat reporting
that he had a baby son, his first child. For years
Bhalai had outshone him at every point and he had been
bitterly jealous, until he himself had become a success.
This made him Bhalai's equal, except that he had no children. Bhalai's wife went on having babies while his had
none. Now, he, Gopi, was a father. During his first few
days at home, he was glad to work on the house for it
gave him an opportunity to watch his own son lying on a
charpai or in his grandmother's arms.

The wheat harvest was not yet over, so Gopi offered
to help, along with the three men his father had hired.
Parbat provided him with the sickle he himself had used
until two years previous when his asthma had obliged him
to give up manual labor. Gopi, armed with the sickle,
took his place beside the hired men, squatting, cutting
a handful of wheat stalks and hitching himself forward to
the next row. By the time they stopped to pass around
the red clay pipe, he was tired and sore; and as he looked back over the ground he had covered, it seemed absurd-
ly small, much less than the others had left behind. By
noon he was famished and exhausted, and was relieved when
his father suggested that he might help with the threshing. Again his friends were far ahead of him as they
drove their oxen around their threshing floors near his;
and when it came to winnowing he discovered that he had
lost the knack of tilting and jerking the basket of
threshed grain in such a way that the chaff went flying
in the breeze while the kernels dropped at his feet. He
felt more and more awkward and finally gave up.

That evening as he sat with his friends, he was
ready to laugh at himself, with them. He was still a
farmer, but a mechanized farmer. If they would come to

the government farm where he worked, he would show them how, in a few hours with his big machine, he could carry out all of the steps in harvesting that kept them busy for weeks. They were impressed. But then came the question--What ordinary farmer could buy such a machine? Even if all the Farmers in Karimpur pooled their money, they could not afford one. And if they could, such a machine would occupy all of the space in one of their plots, with no room to turn it around. Perhaps when plots were consolidated, the one or two landowners who would get large fields could use one.

From this the conversation turned to the topic uppermost in the thinking of all landowners, large or small--the Consolidation of Holdings. The young men in Gopi's circle were not directly involved, but their fathers were. They had been hearing about consolidation for several years and thought the plan a good one. They had been told that in place of small, scattered plots, each land-owning family would be given one or two consolidated plots, equal in quality and acreage to the original plots. This would lighten work and would be more efficient. They would no longer be obliged to carry their plows and other equipment, first to one plot and then to another as they were now doing. They could concentrate their energy, their seed, their fertilizer and their irrigation on the one field, or perhaps the two.

Later, when the consolidation team arrived, its members dominated the village, and life revolved around them. Superior officers remained at district headquarters in Mainpuri. The A.C.O., assistant consolidation officer, was chief among those sent here. He and his subordinates, down to the clerks who kept all records, demanded houses or portions of houses for themselves and in some cases, for their families. The village was shocked at such full-scale intrusion, but acquiesced as it always had when face to face with officialdom.

As the measuring and evaluating of plots progressed, tension between farmers and officers grew. Farmers

discovered that the consolidation was not entirely for
their welfare, but was for the benefit of the officers
as well. As a result, they accused the officers of showing partiality to those who granted them favors. The
officers in turn complained that they were harrassed by
importunate farmers. Worse than this--neighbor became
suspicious of neighbor as each man wondered what his
neighbor might be doing to win an officer's favor, in
order to get land of better quality or in a better
location.

By the time Bhalai and Gopi came home on their next
leave in 1968, part of the money they had saved for rebuilding was needed for the consolidation of their father's land. Parbat must have cash before the final
allotment of fields took place, if he were to be granted
a desirable piece of land. Parbat consulted Gopi on the
choice of land that he should request. This was an hour
of triumph for Gopi. Parbat had respected his judgment
above his own. After surveying each piece of land that
Parbat had designated, he advised against applying for
the field to which Parbat had given priority, that with
the highest quality of soil. Some Brahmin in a position
of power would surely lay claim to it, and even if Parbat
might be granted such a field, it would lead to serious
trouble between him and fellow Farmers. He considered it
wiser for Parbat to ask for two fields: one had soil
that was moderately good, better than they now had, and
conveniently near their house while the other was farther
away with soil most people would consider low grade but
which he knew he could improve. The obvious disadvan-
tages of this second field would offset the advantages
of the first field and divert at least some of the suspicion which might easily be directed at Parbat. Bhalai
agreed; and when Parbat had had time to discuss reasons
and to cogitate, he finally expressed approval.

For Bhalai and Gopi, that summer marked not only the
final steps in rebuilding, and new land problems, but
also their discovery of Bamar as an individual. He had

been a child when they left home, and on their annual
visits they continued to regard him as the "little brother," living in a boy's world. He had listened to their
discussions of construction plans the year before, but
when he offered to help under Bhalai's direction, he was
assigned the job of carrying away debris. However by
1968, they could no longer overlook him. He was as tall
as Gopi, coordinated in his movements, and more communicative. As he talked with them, they realized that their
home was as important to him as to them, even more so.
He was actually living there, while they came as visitors.
When Parbat had originally suggested that the time was
approaching when they must find him a bride, his brothers
had laughed. Now they acknowledged that they should have
considered this earlier. Neither of them knew enough of
Farmer communities in the district to offer suggestions,
but they could consult their neighbors. They were leaving soon, but others were familiar with families near and
far with promising daughters, and were glad to pass on
the names to Parbat. Bamar's assets, financial and
otherwise, warranted a handsome dowry.

* * *

When the two sons arrived the following summer, 1969,
Bhalai carried out his ambitious plans for the front entrance to the house, one as imposing as the best in
Karimpur. The cement panels above the doorway and on
both sides are covered with formal floral designs. On
one side a tall niche has been added; and above it, also
of cement, is a large mogul-style lamp, purely ornamental.
Parbat was pleased with the whole effect. A short time
ago, neither he nor any other Farmer would have dared
make such a bold gesture. Now he not only approved, but
made his own contribution. He removed two small pieces
of delicate sculpture from his worship center and placed
them on a high shelf beneath the lamp.
    While the artist-mason was perfecting the entrance,
Bhalai and his helpers were building a large outer room

5. Parbat in front of his new door

beside it, similar to the outer rooms of houses belonging to my Brahmin neighbors, separate from the family
courtyard and storerooms. Men who expect to entertain
friends or relatives have such a room. Then Bhalai and
Gopi could not resist one final flourish; they bought
two straight chairs with wooden seats and a small table
for the new room. Parbat and other Farmers eyed these
with disfavor. Who wants to sit on a hard chair when
the ground or a charpai is more comfortable? I have
noticed that there are always two charpais in the room,
while the chairs and table are pushed aside.

When Bhalai left home that summer to return to
service, he knew that he would not be with the family
again for two years. He was to be in Ladakh, a distant
outpost, mountainous, cold and lonely. In 1971, he
returned a seasoned soldier, glad to be home again,
away from the rigors of mountain life and the strain of
always being prepared for alarms. His next post would
be a reward for special service, in Lucknow, where his
wife and elder son and the baby born after he left for
the frontier could join him. As always, Shanti was delighted to have another son at home while Parbat never
tired of listening to stories of life in the mountains,
and Bhalai's friends constantly demanded more tales,
this time of adventures which they will never be able
to experience

*   *   *

And now the autumn of 1971 has come. Bhalai arrived from Lucknow to spend a few days and has left with
his wife and children and their belongings, as well as
supplies from their fields. They went loaded with many
more bundles than on their departure for the Red Fort
seven years ago. The house seems quiet without them,
too large and too quiet for those left behind. Gopi's
wife and small son are still here, and Gopi is expected
soon for the annual Festival of Lights, the last of the
four major holidays of the year. Shanti had feared that

he might again follow Bhalai's example and take his family back with him; but this will not happen before he is securely established in his government post and in larger living quarters, perhaps in a year. And by that time Bamar's wife will have come. She was here for her three-day visit following the wedding and met with warm approval. Not only were Shanti and Bhalai's and Gopi's wives here, but the two daughters of the family came for the occasion. They all agreed that the newest, youngest bahu was all that any in-laws could want. Her dowry added to her success. It included a generous amount of money and personal gifts for members of the family and provided them with more brass utensils than they could use, at least for the present.

Bamar has already moved into the men's world, working in his father's two fields with a regular hired man and no longer needing his mother's care. He has not expressed any desire to leave home, either for further study or for employment elsewhere. Shanti has little to do so she often occupies herself with her basketry or with weaving of mats. Friends from down the lane may come to visit in the early afternoon. She herself seldom leaves the house and then only to help Bamar with lighter tasks in the nearest field. She knows that her sons and their families will come home whenever a leave is due and on special holidays. She also knows that when their services are terminated, they will be here to stay, and she will be able to enjoy her happiest role, that of grandmother. There are times when she and Parbat talk of the past. They find it difficult to believe that they were once beset by disappointment and disaster. Their memories now center around the days most crowded with activity and cheerful confusion.

Parbat is a man who has earned his retirement. Both Bhalai and Gopi have noticed on each successive leave that he has grown weaker and his asthma has made field work increasingly difficult. It had never occurred to his sons that Parbat might not always be carrying the

load, but now it is their responsibility to do all they
possibly can during their home visits to relieve their
father from overwork and worry. Parbat grins when he
talks of how tradition has been reversed as he grows
old. For many years he was the the one to make decisions
and give orders. Now it is his sons who have decided
that he is to live in a house of brick, not of mud. It
is they who have instructed him to give up active farming and let out part of his land on shares. If there
is not enough money saved for food or clothing for the
family, they provide him with whatever is needed. He
can work or not as he pleases. He can sit and enjoy
his family when they are all together or he can sit on
his platform with neighbors who like himself, no longer
work regularly. And there is the Ramayana to read. He
has no desire to retreat to an ashram in a distant forest
as he is entitled to do, in this, the last stage of his
life journey. Why leave his own home when all that a
man of his age could hope for is right here. He has
lost possessions. Twice he has been forced to leave
what he has thought of as his home, and he has lost his
only brother. But he has not lost his sons. And what
is of greater value to any man than loyal sons?

PART II

THE FAMILY OF DEVI AND BALRAM, CARPENTERS

BALRAM'S FAMILY TREE

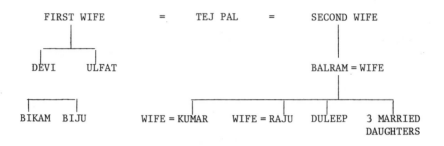

CHARACTERS

DEVI — chief among the Carpenters and
         head of the family from 1925 onward

DEVI'S WIFE

ULFAT — Devi's brother

BIKAM — Devi's older son

BIJU — Devi's younger son

BALRAM — Devi's successor as head of the family

BALRAM'S WIFE

KUMAR — Balram's oldest son

RAJU — Balram's second son

DULEEP — Balram's youngest son

BALRAM'S THREE DAUGHTERS

PRAKASH — Balram's counsellor and his strongest jajman

JIA — Prakash's wife

LAKSHMI, Prakash's daughter

The men who farm, whether Brahmin, Farmer or some
other caste, know that their strongest allies are in the
Carpenter community. A farmer's work is tilling the soil
and does not involve the repair of his implements! This
task he entrusts to a Carpenter. Why should he invest in
tools and take time from his field work for repairs, as
long as there is a Carpenter with the tools and the skill
to sharpen the metal tip of his plough or replace the
worn handle of a sickle with a new one? He is a farmer,
not an artisan. Each Carpenter regards himself as the
special employee of a number of farmers whose fathers had
depended on his father to maintain their implements. They
are his patrons, his jajmans. He may have five or six
jajmans or as many as twenty-five. A Carpenter never
offers to serve farmers other than his jajmans. And no
farmer would consider changing his patronage from his
particular Carpenter to another, even though the other
man might be capable of better work.

It was through our two young sons that we were introduced to, and later accepted by, the Carpenter community. The mango grove in which we set up our camp soon
became a lively playground as village boys still too
young to be apprenticed to fathers, and with parents not
over-suspicious of us, would appear at the edge of the
grove and gradually gather courage to come in. The red
wagon and the tricycle, unlike anything seen before,
along with swings and mango trees to climb were the at-
traction. We discovered that none of our young visitors
had owned a toy or any kind of play equipment, even
though some of them had fathers who were Carpenters.
But in return for the use of our sons' toys they taught
our sons games that could be played with sticks and stones
stones or with balls of clay and homemade hockey sticks.
In peanut season they taught them how to roast the fresh,
unshelled nuts in a fire of twigs, or to roast field corn
when it was harvested.

In the afternoon when games lagged, our sons and
their friends wandered into the village. In Humble Lane,

there was the old Potter to watch as he spun his heavy
wheel and shaped a lump of clay into jars or small saucers; and across the lane was the Grain-Parcher, at his
later afternoon task. While his homemade furnace roared,
he deftly ladled out blazing hot sand and poured it over
grain in a broken clay jar. There were always children
gathered around his small open hut, each hugging the
small basket of grain brought for "parching." The wheat
he roasted, the corn he popped, and the rice he puffed,
and returned each to the child who had brought it, keeping a portion for himself. There was laughter and fun
among those who waited and everyone sniffed the tempting
aroma of toasting grain.

Finally, on their way home, our sons invariably
stopped at the Carpenter's outdoor workshop under a large
tree and here we could always find them when we followed
later. Like them, we were captivated by the varied activities of the shop. I recall when there were eight men
at work, all apparently related. Two men were sawing the
length of a tree with a long, two-handled saw. Another
was planing a board and another was measuring with a
piece of string, several boards already planed. These
would be fitted together to make a door frame. Others
were repairing implements for the farmers who sat watching while visiting with them. One Carpenter had been
trained by his father to be an ironsmith. His forge and
anvil were just across the lane where he was busy sharp-
ening a plough tip with the help of his small son who
pumped the large bellows. One man was occupied with an
ox-cart wheel, a most exacting job. He had finished the
six spokes, made in pairs, each pair shaped like a slender V, designed to spread from hub to rim, like radii of
a circle and was now driving the first pair into one of
six holes cut in the hub. The only tools to be found in
the village were in the possession of the Carpenters, and
these were the bare minimum required for their services.
Each one owned a hammer, a hatchet, two saws--one short
and one long--also a chisel and a hand-manipulated lathe.

Their products were not as well finished as those made by city Carpenters, but were sturdy and useful.

By village standards, the Carpenters might have been considered "middle class." There was usually a stock of grain in their storerooms, though meager in comparison with that of their farming neighbors. If one of them succeeded in earning more grain than was urgently needed for food, he could sell it and buy clothing or invest the money in silver jewelry to be buried in the floor of packed earth or in a wall, ready for the next emergency. This was better than borrowing from a moneylender.

No one living in the village knew why the builders of Devi's house had chosen to locate it apart from the other Carpenter houses on an odd-shaped piece of ground between the village pond and the lane, with an open space just behind it for the workshop. When monsoon rains were heavy, the pond rose until water oozed into the courtyard and soaked the earth floor of the storerooms. Forebears of the other Carpenters had built their houses across the lane in a more protected location and close together. Devi, like his house, seemed aloof from the rest, but he was respected for being the most skillful among them and the most prosperous.

I had often visited the small Carpenter houses across the lane. Knowing that their husbands worked with Devi, I asked about his wife as I had never seen her and wondered why. In answer they simply shrugged. She had no place in their lives. Was she confined to her courtyard, because men might see her if she were to cross the lane to visit them, or had Devi forbidden her to leave? She never went, like the others, to the well. Instead one of the boys of her family filled the water jars and brought them home to her. Much as I wanted to know her as head of Devi's courtyard, I was unwilling to walk in without some friendly gesture from her or from him. Then, without warning, we met, not in her house but at the door of my tent. There she stood, just outside the bamboo screen serving as our door, a baby on her hip and two small bundles tied in cloth dangling from her free hand. Her face was covered and I had no inkling as to who she was. Other women who came were accompanied by relatives and were ready to explain their own ailments or those of their companions. A woman would introduce herself as "mother of Ramesh" or of Sundar, or one of the other boys we knew. This woman simply stood, mute, until one of the children playing nearby came up and explained that she was his aunt. But which aunt? Why, Devi's wife, of course. I was dumbfounded. I asked what I could do for her. She partially uncovered her face and announced bluntly that it was her intention to go into Mainpuri with us that noon. We were surprised that she had come this far from home and was prepared to go far-ther, without her husband. Village women do not walk out like this, especially one as secluded as she. Only des-peration could have driven her to it. The child, about a year old, was in a state of collapse. He had had vio-lent dysentery for several days. Her husband had told her earlier about our simple remedies and about the pa-tients we had taken to doctors in town. She had tried everything that the local hakim had advised and had called on the spirit exorcisor, but the child had grown steadily worse.

Taking a mother to town with her child is not simple. We could find a place for her to sleep, but what about food? She would not touch ours. In answer to our query she held up her bundles. One contained food enough for herself for three days and the other contained whatever covering she and the baby might need. It was warm weather so this was very little. She was wearing what was obviously her best full skirt and blouse and cotton shawl. I knew that if she were like other vil-lage women she would not own another such outfit to carry to town. Apparently she was going without a change of clothing. We sent someone to her house to make sure that she had Devi's permission. He came him-self to assure us that he had agreed to her going. They

would do anything that we or the doctor advised, in the
hope of saving their child.

Later, when she uncovered her face, I found her one
of the least prepossessing women I had seen in the village. Her features were large and uneven. Her front
teeth were gone. Her hair, straggling out from under
the edge of her shawl, was unwashed and stringy. There
seemed nothing to relieve her plainness. I would have
guessed her age to be fifty. But with so small a child
she must have been younger. If I had met her in her own
courtyard I would have thought her uninteresting, but a
woman with enough spirit to travel to a strange town
with strangers, alone, on short notice, must be far from
dull. We could not refuse her nor would she have
accepted refusal.

The next few days became an ordeal, both for her
and for me. The doctor gave strict orders that the baby
should have only water and the prescribed medicines,
given at regular intervals day and night. No milk. The
mother was prepared to give the baby the medicines but
to deny her child her own milk? Never. So we struggled,
both of us trying to save the baby's life by methods that
clashed. When a village baby cries, feeding him is the
first step in pacifying him. If that fails, jouncing
and making loud noises to distract him are resorted to.
What else is there for the women to do? The child was
too weak to cry, but his wailing was even more pitiful.

Keeping him in a room apart from his mother, as the
doctor advised, would have simplified the treatment, but
she flatly refused to do this. He had slept with her at
night ever since he was born, and during the day he had
always been in her arms or in the arms of an older child
in the family or on a charpai near her while she worked.
The only food he had ever had was her milk. She became
too frantic to listen to reason. After all, I was a
stranger, as was the doctor. On the morning of the
fourth day, when she threatened to carry the child home
on foot and I would have been relieved to have her do

so, he opened his eyes. The strain was over and, slowly, we both relaxed. From that point on there was no question of her cooperation. The child was not going to die.

She refused to go near our coal-burning range. Instead she set up a makeshift chulha in our small yard, and over the wood fire she toasted chapatis from whole-wheat flour, and cooked the pulses or vegetables brought from the bazaar. To our surprise she settled down in her routine without demur. By the time we returned to the village she was prepared to carry out all of the doctor's final instructions as to feeding and care, and the baby became healthier than she had been before the bout of dysentery. Our return would have been quite different had he died--which was what the doctor had feared on the first night. As it was, we were warmly welcomed by Devi and his relatives.

The Family of Balram, Devi's Half-brother

When we left Karimpur in 1930, Devi and his brother, Ulfat, were occupying the family home. And on our succeeding visits to the village we found them still living together and carrying on their carpentry in the familiar workship behind the house. Ulfat had no children. Devi, we thought, had four sons. There had always been four boys working with him as his apprentices. Later, one son died--the one we had managed to save as an infant. The other three had completed their apprenticeship and after Devi's and Ulfat's deaths they continued to serve the family's jajmans.

Not long after my return in 1961, I made the startling discovery that one of them, Balram, was not Devi's son, but his half-brother. Balram had spent most of his days in our grove with our two sons and Devi was among our most loyal friends, yet neither of them had ever intimated that their relationship was other than that of father-son. As I look back, I am not surpised that the taciturn Devi failed to mention it; and Balram was too engrossed in games to make any reference to his family.

Their neighbors had known of it from the time of Balram's
birth but by the time we came in 1925, it was too familiar a situation to seem worth discussing. Finally, it
was Prakash, who enlightened me.

This is the story as he told it: Tej Pal, Devi's
and Ulfat's father, was left a widower while the two boys
were still unmarried. A household needs at least one
woman to do the cooking and to look after the children
and Tej Pal had none, so he went in search of a substitute.
How he found the particular woman whom he then took into
his house no one recalls. All that is known is that she
had been married and had lived with her in-laws in another district, and that her husband had died. One thing
is sure--Tej Pal brought her into his house without benefit of priest or feast. Several years later Balram,
their only child and Devi's half-brother, was born. By
the time Tej Pal and the woman died, both Devi and Ulfat
were married and Devi, as eldest son, succeeded Tej Pal
as head of the family.

Asserting their rights as legitimate heirs, Devi
and Ulfat claimed all of Tej Pal's ten acres, ignoring
any claim that Balram might have; unfortunately Balram
was still too young to realize that he was left with
nothing except a home and the food which Devi provided.
Meanwhile, Devi accepted full responsibility for him and
found him a wife when he was thirteen. During her second year here, the wife died and Devi arranged a second
marriage for Balram. However, he continued to deny
Balram any share in their father's property. Land is
land, and no sentiment stands in the way of acquiring
all that one can. Then Devi's death led to serious conflict.

Balram and Devi's two sons, along with their families, lived together in what had been Devi's house. As
more children came, the courtyard was increasingly crowded and noisy, and the storerooms were inadequate. Balram
was the oldest of the men and the uncle of both Bikam
and Biju and either would ordinarily have assured him

6. Balram's wife and grandchildren

7. Balram's courtyard

recognition as head of the household. Likewise, his
wife was older than and by all rights superior to the
other two women. But neither he nor she could claim
authority because they were entirely dependent on their
step-nephews, who owned all of the land. Moreover,
theirs was the largest family in the household, which
made them unpopular.

In desperation, Balram went to Prakash, his closest
jajman and Prakash was sympathetic. When he was young,
he had had his own battles with rapacious relatives.
Also, he was convinced that Balram was entitled to a
share of his father's land; and he set about getting it
by the direct method. He borrowed three hundred rupees
from a shopkeeper in Mainpuri; and when the landlord's
agent came on his next rent-collecting tour, Prakash
offered him the money. The agent accepted it graciously,
and by skillful manipulation, had four acres of Devi's
land transferred to Balram's name in the records. No
one was inconvenienced. Prakash knew that Balram would
repay the three hundred rupees in labor. Balram welcomed any amount of labor if it assured him the permanent rights to the land. And the agent had a generous
gift in his pocket. As for the Raja who owned the land,
he would not question the transaction, even if he did
hear of it. And even though the land was under water
Balram was delighted: Overnight he had become a landowner. He was now in possession of four acres while
Devi's sons had only three acres each. He was familiar
with the field and was fairly sure that if the rains
were not too heavy, he could sow a small amount of grain
and peas on it as the water subsided. Whatever its
value, or lack of value, it was land and it was his.

Prakash advised Balram to keep quiet, at least until the nephews should uncover the transaction for themselves. It was possible for them to reverse it; but
with the lapse of time reversal would become increasingly difficult. Knowing Balram as he did, Prakash should
have been prepared for the inevitable. Almost immedi-

ately, Balram asserted himself as Devi's successor in the family. When his nephews challenged him he told them what had happened. At first they refused to believe him. But when they saw the records and found that he actually did have more of Devi's land than either of them had, they were stunned. When they recovered from the shock, they scoffed at him. What good was land under a pond? Only a fool would have accepted it. It was like no land at all. However, after they discussed it further with each other and with their relatives and neighbors, they were enraged. They had been outwitted, cheated by one whom they had fed and housed. They suspected Prakash's hand in the matter and turned on him, to no effect. He told them what they already knew: that if they chose, they could make legal claim to the land. But they also knew that a court case would be costly, more than the land was worth. Apparently, there followed accusations, vituperations, gesticulations, threats, and finally a court case. Soon everyone knew that Devi's orderly household had turned into a field of battle for survival and status.

Throughout the visits to the courthouse, Balram had had one distinct advantage. Advising him was Prakash, who had gone through this process successfully a number of times and knew that cold calculation was more effective in the courtroom than pleading or haranguing. Biju had no jajman to support him. His work of recorrugating grinding stones called for no close relationship with anyone. Bikam had jajmans but for some reason none of them felt obliged to help him. Prakash told me later that no bribe was necessary. The deputy who tried the case knew him and accepted his word as being more reliable than that of Balram's opponents. It had finally been settled in 1958 or 1959, with a verdict in Balram's favor. And it must have been 1950 or 1951 when he was originally granted possession of the land. Prakash is not sure but it would not have been later, as the Act abolishing large scale landlordism, including that of rajas, was passed in 1951; and it was the agent of the Raja who had manipulated the transfer.

Long before the case was settled, Balram had persisted in sowing and reaping crops on the contested field even though he had to be content with one partial harvest per year. Unlike other farmers, he benefited from scant rainfall--the less rain, the more land he could use and therefore the larger his harvest. Along with the grain, he had the stalks and leaves as fodder for his buffalo. Best of all, he could inform everyone that he was a landowner. By 1961 Balram had emerged as a firmly established landholder, with more than twenty dependable jajmans and a home which was called his.

In spite of his new status, Balram often seems more like the lanky boy who frequented our grove than like the father of six children. He is usually talking, when there is anyone to listen. His eyes are always bright with excitement or dark with displeasure or indignation. His voice is so high pitched that when he comes into the courtyard, agitated over some occurrence, no one else can be heard. When he handles his tools his movements are precise; but when he is excited, and he is often that, he is uncoordinated. He flaps his arms while his words come tumbling out. He doesn't stutter, but he sputters and spits.

He is completely unselfconscious. Like most of the men, he gives no thought to clothes. While at work he wears a tattered shirt or none at all. His dhoti is wrapped carelessly. His hair is cut short and his head is usually uncovered, although occasionally he wears, at an odd angle, the round white cap popular with villagers; or if he is to be out in the glaring sun he winds a small hand towel around his head in lieu of a turban. If he wears shoes they are over-worn and over-sized. He is usually unshaven.

There come times when Balram grows restless. If no jajman is waiting for work to be done, he throws down his tools and prepares for adventure. This may take

him to a fair, near or distant, or perhaps just to town.
At such a time he suddenly becomes conscious of his
appearance. When he has located the Barber and has dug
his best shirt and dhoti and shoes from a metal chest far
back in the storeroom, he steps out, a different person.
The garments are presentable but unironed. The village
Washerman has a rock on which to beat dirt out of clothing but he does not possess an iron. This is of no consequence to Balram. He has enough money in his pocket
for bus fare and perhaps for sweets. He has become a man
of the world. Unfortunately, he can do nothing to change
his puckish face. To city men he must appear the typical
country bumpkin. But within the village he is respected
as a good workman, sometimes irritating, often irascible,
and amusing, but sufficiently childlike to be free from
the suspicion that men ordinarily cast on relatives and
neighbors.

It is this childlike quality that tempts those who do
not know him well to think him stupid. This was my earlier impression, but I have learned, as others have, that
he is capable of being amazingly competent. My first intimation of this came one morning when I heard him shouting just outside my front window. His high pitched voice
indicated that excitement was brewing. I looked out and
there he stood in front of a crowd of farmers waving his
arms toward the lane in front of my house that leads away
from the village. He was elaborating on the dangers of a
deep hole in the lane, about half a furlong from where
they stood. They all knew that the pipe carrying water
from the government tube well to fields farther out passed
under the lane at that point. They also knew that the
pipe had broken under the weight of heavily loaded ox-
carts and that the leak had become serious. Water flowing from it had soaked the dirt surface of the lane so
thoroughly that the carts driving over it had dug a hole
too wide to be bypassed. It was a menace to oxen and
carts. The well operator ignored it. The farmers had
endured it without considering the possibility of doing

something to prevent it. "Why should we wait any longer for action by the well operator?" asked Balram. "He is merely a government employee, not a farmer. Something must be done at once before a cart loaded with grain capsizes in the mud or an ox breaks its leg." If they would work together and fill the hole, the well operator would recognize the emergency and feel obliged to have the pipe repaired.

A few hours later I was surprised to see the men of my family with their hired men, and other farmers with their hired men, and a few men who had just come along out of curiosity, all gathered at the spot and all busy. The farmers were digging earth from the side of the road and younger men were carrying it in baskets on their heads and dumping it into the hole. When it was filled they were satisfied. They had done a good job, and they shared the credit with Balram. They reported their voluntary services to the tube well operator, expecting him to respond by calling engineers from district headquarters. He did nothing, except to cut off all water from that one channel as the easiest solution of the problem. Not until ten days later did he go to headquarters with his report; and not until several days after that did the engineers come. Meanwhile crops in fields beyond the broken pipe were suffering from lack of irrigation.

Balram was crestfallen and expressed his indignation freely. The more he talked, the more skeptical were the farmers who had worked with him on the road. They agreed that he was not thinking of the welfare of the village, as he had shouted. He had made use of them, as influential farmers, to coerce the well operator into action that would benefit him. Two large plots which he was cultivating on shares were beyond the leak. Balram, considered a simple Carpenter, had been clever enough to get them to work like unskilled laborers, on his behalf.

Throughout the village men chuckled over his impetuous outbursts and his exploits. Tales of Balram have become popular in evening circles where farmers gather as neighbors to share the red clay pipe, along with local news and gossip. Two of the more recent tales have to do with his encounters with government officers. When a petty officer came to take away his buffalo because he had not paid a certain tax, Balram slapped him twice. Later, when asked why, he asked, "Why not?" The officer had insulted him, belittled him in the presence of his neighbors. The officer left abruptly and of course reported it. Shortly thereafter Balram borrowed money from a jajman and paid the tax plus a fifty rupee fine for assulting an officer. On another occasion, when called before the District Magistrate on some minor offense, he abused the magistrate in the courtroom. Suddenly aware of the consequences, he fled. The magistrate sent an orderly after him. Before the orderly emerged from the door Balram was quite a distance from the courthouse. He saw the orderly coming, and ran. He kept running until he reached home. The orderly gave up long before this; and apparently there were no repercussions.

Among the tales of Balram a favorite is of his rash encounter with cattle thieves. One night thieves came and stole his buffalo while he was sleeping nearby to watch over her. At the first sound of the buffalo's chain being shifted, Balram was up and after the thieves without taking time to call for help. Nor did he stop to consider his chances against an unknown number of adversaries. He plunged into the night, but the thieves had a head start. His eldest son, Kumar, awoke, heard Balram shouting the two words "thieves" and "buffalo" and so joined the chase. He overtook his father and in the darkness thinking he was one of the thieves, he grabbed Balram and threw him on the ground, breaking Balram's wrist. By the time Balram got his breath sufficiently to shout "Are you going to kill your father?" the thieves had gone. Kumar picked his father up and helped him home. Yet while Damar, the bonesetter, mended his wrist, he mourned the loss of his buffalo more than the pain.

The Household of Balram and Biju

By 1961, Biju and his wife and child occupied one corner of the house while Balram's family occupied more than two-thirds, Bikam having moved to a house near the bus stop. There were two separate chulhas, Biju's wife cooking on one and Balram's wife and bahu on the other. This considerably reduced the chances of friction among the women. Moreover, Biju was no longer a competitor of Balram as he specialized in the rechipping of mill-stones for village housewives, while Balram served a number of Devi's jajmans as carpenter. Biju has had little success farming. He depends on dung from his one buffalo to fertilize his three acre field, but what she contributes is sufficient to enrich only one acre. As a result, he is limited to fertilizing and cultivating only one acre for two crops a year. The other two acres must lie fallow during the winter and spring. Early in the rainy season, he cultivates them without fertilizer, in the hope that they will yield a harvest of rice when autumn comes. Chemical fertilizer would meet his need for all three acres but costs more than he can afford.

Biju is old for his years, stooped, gray-haired, with few teeth left. It is hard to imagine him fighting anyone, as he and his brother must have fought Balram. Either he has lost whatever verve he had, or it was Bikam who did most of the fighting. Biju is often ill and his wife is afflicted with leucoderma, with white patches spreading over her breasts and shoulders. Her few remaining teeth are broken and discolored. With bedraggled clothes and unkept hair, she seldom shares in conversation and seems apathetic, except when there is laughter: then she smiles and her eyes dance. The son is a sad child, hindered by his parent's poverty and lack of success.

Beyond establishing himself as Devi's rightful suc-cessor, Balram has done little to support his claim to kinship to his nephews. True, he has met his obligations to the jajmans whom Devi had served, by keeping their

implements in working order. But he has shown small interest in carpentry other than this routine. Anything
more difficult does not appeal to him. As for his stewardship of the family home so faithfully cared for by
Devi, he has left it entirely to the mercy of nature, and
nature is merciless, particularly during the rains. In the
beginning he had a far better enclosure than the Carpenters across the road. But he has done nothing to preserve
it. By 1959, the roof of the cattle room had collapsed.
And one more rainy season washed down three of the walls,
leaving the one at the back battered but still upright.

Both Balram and his eldest son are able-bodied, and
judging from observation, the two younger boys would find
it fun to help build. But nothing happened. By 1961,
only a small section of the rear wall of the cattleroom
was still standing. At this point Balram prevailed upon
two of his jajmans to send an application to the state
government on his behalf. They applied for 500 rupees
on the grounds that the heavy rains had destroyed the
house and this amount would be needed to rebuild. The
request was considered and the money granted. But during
its progress from the state capital to the village, it
shrank to 100 rupees. This was not sufficient, so Balram
refused it and forgot about repairing the house.

The courtyard of the women of the family was now
completely exposed. If the house were facing the lane as
most houses do, they would find it intolerable. However,
because of the angle at which it is built, only men coming
in from the fields in ox-carts can peer at them if they
choose to. Men who sit beside Balram in front of the
courtyard while he repairs their implements are careful
to face away from the house. It would not bother Balram's
wife if anyone should watch her. She is old, and her
head is always covered. Biju's wife can work in her corner of the courtyard where she is partially protected so
it is only when she must cross the yard to dump waste
into the drain or to pick up a utensil drying in the sun
that she is exposed. The only one for whom it is really

awkward is the wife of Balram's eldest son, Kumar. She
struggles for privacy by keeping deep inside the courtyard or slipping through the door to the storeroom. Or
she sits at the end of their verandah where a low wall
surrounds the cooking space. She is careful to keep not
only her head covered, but her face as well. I have
sometimes wondered why her husband has not made a move
to put up a screen of mud across the front of the courtyard. There is plenty of mud on the edge of the pond
beside their house, and there is material for thatch in
their own fields so it would cost nothing. But he has
always waited for orders from Balram in his carpentry,
and apparently has no intention of making a start in
anything without instructions.

Balram's wife is now undisputed mistress of the
household. In temperament she resembles her husband,
and with each year they have become more alike. It is
amazing that the serious-minded Devi managed to find
Balram a wife who carries responsibility as lightly as
he. Because of her age and her greying hair she moves
about the neighborhood with her face only partially
covered. She enjoys diversions as much as does Balram.
Once when a special fair was held at the temple near
Mainpuri, six miles from here, she wanted to go. They
do not own an oxcart nor did she have bus fare. So she
went and returned on foot, delighted with all that she
had seen and heard, and, except for tired feet, not much
the worse for wear.

She spends most of her time sitting in her own courtyard where she can watch all the comings and goings in
the lane. Or she comes to my courtyard, where there is
less to see but where she has more companionship. She
is old enough to be free of most restrictions, so when
one of the sons of Prakash's family comes into the courtyard his own wife and younger bahus cover their faces,
Balram's wife carries on in her high pitched voice with
whatever tale she is relating. Prakash is the only man
in the family older than she, and in his presence she is

8. Balram and his youngest son

9. The pond behind Balram's house

subdued, but not always silent. Jia and the bahus enjoy
her. She is not fussy, nor is she easily offended, and
seems able to create laughter at all times. Circulating
gossip--amusing gossip--is her chief contribution. Like
Balram, her face is seldom in repose and her eyes reflect
her mood. The dhoti she wears most of the time consists
of pieces of three old ones sewn together by the Tailor.
Originally they were of different colors with borders
that varied in design. But many beatings on the Washerman's rock or on the stone slab in her courtyard and many
days spread on ground or wall in the sun to dry have
blended them to the same gray hue. Laughingly, she shows
off her three-in-one dhoti as something unique. Once or
twice a year she indulges in complaining, continuous and
bitter, especially when one of her bahu's relatives comes
to take her home for a visit, leaving her to face more of
the household chores. Other women do the same things
regularly; but her taste of freedom as mother-in-law has
made routine work seem heavier than it was before. Occasionally, she quarrels with Balram. They curse each
other in shrill tones; and if she goes too far, he may
beat her. And once in a great while he gives her a beating simply because he thinks she needs correcting. Otherwise, they are congenial.

Both are satisfied with a life of minimums. They
do not ask for comfort or convenience. The things they
value and for which they work are physical necessities--
food and clothing, and partial shelter for themselves,
their children and their animals. Theirs is the way of
easy laughter and easy tears.

Balram and his wife have paid little attention to
their children. They may have punished one of them when
exasperated, but not for the purpose of discipline. As
for intentional training they have never heard of it.
As in other village families I know, the older children
learn from companions still older, chiefly through play;
and they in turn apply their lessons to younger brothers
and sisters. Their "big brother" treatment is harsh and

sporadic, but effective. It is an informal, communal type of upbringing which seems to produce results fitting for a village environment. In the early stages of adjustment around the age of five-six, a few may rebel against the strict supervision of school master or parent, but they are abruptly and promptly set straight.

Balram's children have all been well liked among their peers in the village. The daughters left home while still young and tend to be forgotten. However, they seem to have succeeded in adapting themselves to the ways of life of their in-laws. When an in-law comes to take one of the girls back to her husband's home, he often spends a day or two here rather than rushing away. Among villagers this is considered an indication of favorable relations between the families of the husband and of the wife. A very brief visit indicates the opposite.

Two of their children, the second son and the youngest daughter, resemble their parents in feature, but lack the sudden changes of expression characteristics of both Balram and his wife. The eldest daughter has been married for several years. She comes home only rarely, bringing one or two children for her parents to enjoy. She has lived with her in-laws so long that their home is now hers.

The second daughter comes more frequently. She is the most attractive of the three, poised, charming, and friendly. Like her sisters, she is married to a man of Carpenter caste whose home is quite a distance from Karimpur. She speaks of life with her husband's family as pleasant. The work is heavy but her mother-in-law and her husband are both considerate. She timed one visit to coincide with the marriage of Lakshmi, Prakash's younger daughter, and brought her new baby, five months old, and one other child with her, leaving her two older ones with her in-laws. Like most village daughters, she enjoys the freedom of her father's house and the added gaiety of a wedding made that visit very special.

Balram's third and youngest daughter lacks the charm of her sisters. She is a friend of Lakshmi and the same age, about fourteen. Lakshmi told me that her friend's wedding had taken place some months before my return. Then when I had been back about four months, I learned that she had just come home from her in-laws, but I did not see her. A week later, Balram's wife burst into our courtyard asking that someone come with her to see what was wrong with this youngest daughter's new baby son. The call came as a surprise because Jia, who is considered an expert in supervising midwives at births in our neighborhood, had not been invited to this one. The baby was three days old. Prakash's eldest daughter, home on a visit, and I went over. In a dark corner of the long storeroom, we found the young mother and her baby son who refused to take any nourishment. The mother lay on a sagging cot, in great pain. She said that she could not nurse him. Balram's wife took the baby in her arms to demonstrate the difficulty she had in trying to feed him. She dipped a small rag into a clay saucer of milk and put it into his mouth. He sucked a few times, and evidently getting very little, gave up. She put down the rag and said "There is nothing more that I can do. It is hopeless". He looked like a perfectly normal infant, and I was troubled. Prakash's daughter offered a number of suggestions. I had none. It was beyond my understanding. No one was called again, not even Jia. Two days later they told us that the baby had died. They were sorry, but what could they do, more than they had done? The young mother improved rapidly and within a week was at our house visiting Lakshmi; and soon she joined Lakshmi and me on our evening walk through the fields.

I wondered about several things. Why did Balram bring his daughter home from her in-laws without the usual preliminaries, especially as he usually makes a great stir on any such occasion? Why had he brought her such a short time before her confinement? Why had they not made a more serious effort to save the child? And

why had they not asked Jia to come over when they have
always felt free to call on her for less important mat-
ters? It was Jia who gave me the answers. After the
wedding, just nine months before, the bride had gone to
her husband's home along with the wedding party. This
is customary. But this initial visit is supposed to be
brief, not more than three or four days. It gives the
mother-in-law and sisters-in-law an opportunity to look
the bride over and allows time for the girl and her in-
laws to take the first steps in getting acquainted. She
is carefully chaperoned and should only glimpse her husband when he comes into the courtyard for meals. While
he is present, she sits in a corner and keeps her face
discreetly covered. They are not supposed to speak to,
or touch, one another and act as though they are not of-
ficially married. After this visit, the bride returns
home for some time--maybe six weeks, maybe a year or more
depending mainly on her age and on the need of the in-
laws for her help. In this instance, Balram, who was
supposed to go for his daughter, neglected his duty.
He may have been exhausted after the wedding, or he may
have had enough excitement to satisfy him for a while.
However, neighbors say that if he were unable to go, he
should have sent his eldest son. The girl was left in
her husband's home for at least a fortnight, during
which time she became pregnant. In village eyes this
was a disgrace, for which Balram, as her father, was to
blame. The bridegroom's family also held Balram responsible, and all that he could do to make amends was to
bring his daughter home for her confinement. Had the
child lived, neither the baby nor his mother would have
been popular. In every society, there are unwanted
babies, and this was one of them.

If Balram was at all penitent, he showed no sign of
it. When the girl's brother-in-law came to fetch her
and she departed, he shook off the whole affair. Since
then, this same daughter has had three more sons in rapid
succession. When she comes home for a visit, Balram

proudly brings the newest one over for us to admire.
All is well, as far as he is concerned.

Balram's sons, like others of the village, have remained here. Kumar, the eldest, has almost completed
his apprenticeship under Balram and helps in the sharecropping as well. He has had enough schooling to be
literate, but has no desire to expand his formal education. The second son is several years younger than Kumar.
After he had failed twice in lower classes in the local
school, Balram decided that he should become a Carpenter
apprentice. According to other farmers in the community,
the boy is the hardest worker of the three and he makes
better progress in farming than in carpentry although his
mother objects to Balram's insistence that he have both
kinds of training, saying it is too much for a teenage
boy. One evening when I stopped to watch Balram and
Kumar working with their forge and anvil I was conscious
of tension. Balram's wife and second son were on the
verandah at the back of their courtyard. Suddenly the
mother stepped forward into the courtyard screaming imprecations which she kept up until Balram dropped his
work and rushed at her and the boy. There was a tussle
and for a few minutes it was impossible to see who was
fighting whom. Then Kumar dropped his hammer and dashed
back into the courtyard, attacking his father. When the
air cleared onlookers discovered that the battle was between Balram and his wife over the son. Balram had ordered him to join Kumar and himself at the forge because
blacksmithy was a necessary part of his apprenticeship.
His mother had seized the boy's arm and refused to let
him go. He was caught between his parents, struggling
to be free from his mother, while trying to escape his
father's blows. The quarrel was a violent one; but having expressed their hostilities so vigorously, both
parents were soon tired of the argument and dropped it.
According to neighbors who watched the scene, there has
been no aftermath.

The third son, two years younger than the second, is still in school, and promises to be the brightest member of the family. As yet no pressure had been brought on him to work except for routine chores. Like his eldest brother he is relaxed and friendly.

The *Jajmani* System

It was Balram who first taught me the significance of the *jajmani* system, by his treatment of me as a non-*jajman*. In the process of settling into the house on my return in 1961, I found that a shelf was needed for the makeshift kitchen. Because Balram was Prakash's Carpenter, and because Prakash regarded me as part of his family, it seemed logical to call on Balram. He planed the board that I had purchased, and stood it up against the kitchen wall, saying that he would come the next day to put in the necessary brackets. Each time the shelf was mentioned he looked pained. How could anyone doubt his intention to come the very next day? Weeks passed. I do not know how many times he was in the courtyard on some exciting errand, but the shelf was never completed. Finally I employed another Carpenter. This did not disturb Balram, as it would have if I were a bona fide *jajman*. Rather he seemed relieved for now no one could bother him with reminders of the unfinished job.

The lesson was repeated later. My good friends from Calcutta, who had designed the house, came to visit me to see what shape their blueprints had taken. While here they decided that I should have a special table for the dining room--long and narrow with a solid top. A few weeks later it arrived in a large packing case, brought from the Mainpuri railway station by oxcart. We lacked the tools with which to open it but Balram was curious enough to be eager to do it. He came over on the morning after the crate arrived and worked feverishly until the table appeared. As soon as the table was removed to the courtyard he was dancing with impatience. He had done this for me. Now would I please give him money for an angocha, a loosely woven cotton scarf which serves many purposes. He insisted that he must go into town for it at once. The bridegroom's party would be arriving at our house (for Lakshmi's wedding) that very evening and how would he look without an angocha? So I gave him the money, far more than he had earned, after exacting a promise that the empty case and packing materials would be removed from the lane into the cattle yard before the wedding guests arrived. But is was a fortnight before the removal finally took place because with the angocha safely in his possession, his interest in the case had declined. Lacking the authority of a jajman, there was little I could do to apply pressure.

The Carpenters appear to be more favored than other kamins (employees) and receive their pay in a more dignified way than the rest. Ganesh is one of Balram's jajmans. At the time of each harvest, spring and fall, Balram goes to Ganesh's house to collect payment, rather than to his field as do other kamins. Ganesh gives him 60 kilos of grain--30 kilos per plough. Ganesh decides which kind of grain he will give but has it threshed and winnowed before giving it. In addition, if Balram works on anything other than the repair of regular farm implements, Ganesh pays him in cash, with the amount paid determined by Balram before he undertakes it. He knows what should be charged and he knows that Ganesh knows, so there is little scope for bargaining. Such additional work from a number of jajmans provides Balram with the cash needed for clothing and extras. As a Carpenter he has another advantage over other kamins. At each of the four big festivals, he and his sons call at the homes of his more prosperous jajmans where they are served whatever rich foods the household has to offer. They are urged to eat all they can hold, and they are able to consume enormous quantities. Humbler employees, such as laborers, Oil Pressers, and Sweepers, are not seated and served, but are given food to take home, and then only a token amount. The tie between Prakash as

jajman and Balram as kamin is stronger than most, though
not unique. In return for his care of Prakash's implements and his readiness to meet any additional demands,
Balram receives a variety of services from Prakash. Not
only did Prakash secure the contested land for Balram,
but he has helped and continues to help solve the problems Balram creates for himself and others. Whatever the
situation he is not taken by surprise, having long passed
the point of being surprised by anything Balram might do.
Prakash provides the stability, the experience, the fore-
sightedness that Balram lacks. When I hear Balram's
voice approaching, on a higher note than usual, I con-
clude that he is in trouble and has come to Prakash for
advice.

In the beginning, I took for granted that Balram
depended on Prakash more than his other jajmans because
of their proximity as neighbors. But another jajman,
Sohan, a Brahmin, lives even nearer. His house is between Prakash's and Balram's and yet his relationship
with Balram is far from cordial. They communicate only
briefly when Sohan or his son takes an implement to
Balram for repair or when Sohan calls Balram to his door
to work on a broken oxcart.

One year in the spring, just before Holi, Balram
and Sohan had a dispute so heated that it nearly came to
blows. For several weeks the boys of our neighborhood
had been collecting wood, chiefly branches and twigs of
thornwood, for the community bonfire. It was ready to
be lit on the morning of Holi. In passing by, Sohan detected a large piece of wood near the base of the pile
that looked suspiciously like one he had been saving.
He went home, inspected his store of wood and found just
such a piece missing. He came out to the lane between
his house and Balram's and shouted at Balram's youngest
son, accusing him of stealing it. Balram came running
when he heard Sohan's accusations and retorted that
Sohan's own son must have taken it. What other boy
would dare to touch Sohan's wood pile? Each man tried

to outshout the other in blaming the other's son. Suddenly Sohan stormed over to the pile and yanked out his precious piece of wood while neighbor boys looked on in dismay. This aggravated the quarrel, and the two fathers resumed their accusations with greater venom until onlookers began to leave and friends persuaded them to retire to their separate homes. All the next day, they exchanged curses until their vocabularies were gradually exhausted. There was no noticeable aftermath; Sohan continued to call on Balram for service and Balram treated him as a jajman. But the tension was, and still is, there.

At one time however, relations between Prakash and Balram were so strained that I wondered if Balram would refuse to consider Prakash as his jajman any longer. The trouble started when men came to provide the village with poles and wires in a few of the lanes, to be ready for long-anticipated street lights. To clear space for the wires the men were obliged to remove branches from trees along the way. The understanding was that the owner of a tree would be reimbursed for the branches sacrificed. When the men reached the big tree behind Balram's house, the Carpenters began arguing violently over the ownership of the tree; and the hotter the argument, the higher rose the estimated value of the wood in the branches involved. Balram claimed that he owned the tree because it was directly behind his house. Tesu and a neighboring widow claimed that it was theirs as it was directly opposite their enclosure. The battle became an all-village affair and was finally referred to the panchayat, the council. When the council could come to no agreement, it passed the burden of making the decision on to Prakash. He was not a member of the panchayat, and refused. Eventually, however, he was persuaded to examine the matter. This he did, and came up with the verdict that the tree belonged to Tesu and the widow. Balram stormed. He could not believe that his own jajman would cheat him of what was lawfully his. His shouting might have moved a weaker

man, but the more agitated Balram became, the firmer was
Prakash. Balram made several calls on Prakash, shouting
his imprecations. After his fifth or sixth visit, he
left vowing never to darken our door again.

Meanwhile, the affair had become ridiculous. So few
branches were cut that their value was not worth the
quarrel, especially after the proceeds had been divided
between the widow and Tesu. Still further, the wires
that caused the trouble have never been used. But for
almost a fortnight Balram stayed away from our house.
Then suddenly he was back, as though nothing had happened. By that time he had worked off all resentment and
was ready to consult Prakash on a minor problem, as he
might have done before the trouble started. Prakash, who
had ignored the turmoil over the tree, treated Balram as
he always had. It would take much more than a passing
quarrel to dissolve a relationship as strongly established as theirs.

Then disaster struck not only Balram, but the whole
village. In 1963, when everyone was anticipating a rich
autumn harvest, the whole village was plunged into de-
spair. For years to come, men and women will tell the
younger generation about the "Rains of '63." The deluge
came late in the season when corn, millet, and sorghum
were ripening. Lanes and fields were flooded. Houses
collapsed. Even Prakash's sturdy house was threatened.
It was at this time that the last remnant of the wall of
Balram's cattleroom reverted to a pile of mud. More a-
larming was the rapid rise of the water in the pond. It
overflowed and joined the stream that had formed in the
lane in front of my house, coming almost to the packed
surface of my verandah, over four feet above ground
level. During the first few days, everyone was stunned
and all movement stopped. Then people tried wading
through water almost hip deep to reach the fields and
grazing grounds. We were marooned, as were Balram's
family and others along our lane. If the water could
have been drained from the fields, crops might have been

saved. But the one channel which, in years of moderate
rainfall, carries surplus water from fields on our side
of the village to the river between us and Mainpuri was
blocked. Engineers came out to investigate and reported
that it was too late to salvage crops that year. The
harvest would bring most people only fodder for their
animals. But Balram's misfortune was greater: he had
lost his half of the harvest of the fields beside the
overflowing channel, which he had been sharecropping,
and his own field would remain waterlogged indefinitely.
It would be at least a year before he could count on
even a small harvest.

I could not reach any of the Carpenter houses, but
Balram often came to mine. There was no field work to
be done and there were no demands for implement repairs.
Moreover he was worried about the safety of his family
as they were obliged to spend their days and nights in
the one dark storeroom where the floor was so saturated
with water from the pond that it might sink beneath them.
Finally I suggested that I would assist him in rebuilding. His reaction was mercuric. The amount was limited
but he seemed to think it a fortune. He rushed out,
waded down the lane and quickly disappeared into his
family's storeroom. In less than an hour he was back,
with the plan he and Kumar had worked out. They would
make use of a building site across the lane, safely removed from the treacherous pond. A Carpenter relative
had once lived there, but now only mounds of earth remained where walls had stood. Bricks were ordered and
a mason hired to do the work, aided by Kumar and the
two younger boys.

The result was a surprise. I had supposed that
they would build the room for their animals at the front
of the lot, as is customary. Instead, they began at the
back. It was not long before the room was ready, larger
and sunnier than their old storeroom. Then came another
surprise. I took for granted that the family would va-
cate the hazardous old enclosure at once. But after the

rush to get a safer house built, they chose to remain in the old, soaked room--all but Balram, who immediately moved into the new one taking the animals with him. Apparently the fear that the ground of the old house might give way was forgotten as the level of the pond water became lower. When I asked Balram why his family did not join him, he shrugged, as he always does when dismissing a trivial subject. His only reply was that he must sleep there to guard the cattle from thieves. He was comfortable and satisfied. They now had two houses (actually two storerooms) and he had a choice of a place in which to eat and sleep.

Two years later the room I had anticipated at the front of the new enclosure partially materialized. Several weeks before there was any evidence of a room, Balram had purchased a doorframe of mango wood with a delicately carved border, inlaid with brass. Few doorframes in the village could compare with it and it stood in the far corner of the new back room where he proudly showed it to visitors. But it was a mystery: Why should Balram spend money on such an expensive doorframe when he could make an ordinary one himself? Then came word of the approaching marriage of his second son, and the presence of the doorframe was explained. When the boy had been considered old enough to be eligible as a bridegroom, several Carpenter fathers of adolescent girls had sent emissaries with proposals of marriage. With Kumar's help and advice from Prakash, Balram selected the girl who would bring the most money, brass utensils, and gifts into his household. Her beauty, or lack of it, and her disposition were disregarded.

Three times, on behalf of this three daughters, Balram had borne the burden of entertaining a bridegroom's party and the expense of a wedding. Now it was his turn to reap the benefits. However, the father of the bridegroom must observe certain prescribed formalities before the departure of the wedding party and after its return from the bride's home. In addition, he would be expected to entertain large numbers of relatives and to invite certain men to the village to a feast. Preparations soon began, and as an added flourish, about a fortnight before the wedding, a room without a roof was constructed at the front of the new enclosure, to serve as entrance. The walls were of baked brick and the front wall was built around the beautiful doorframe. Then the bricks were covered with a layer of cement by a special mason, skilled in shaping pillars and elaborate designs in relief. The effect was striking although there was no door for the frame and there was nothing beyond it except a partially leveled courtyard. Since taking that ambitious step, Balram has done nothing more, either to the new house or to the old. The elegant doorframe with its ornate setting was only a facade, intended to impress wedding guests. However, for Balram it may well have been a symbol of his aspirations.

Balram's Good Fortune

It was the final decision made by a deputy of the district court in 1959, that led eventually to the change in Balram from dreamer to realist. After years of arguing the case of Balram versus Devi's two sons, Balram had won. The long disputed four acre field had become legally his, and when he went to plough around the edges of the pond that covered it, he was walking to his own piece of land. He was getting a small amount of grain from it, enough to give him satisfaction; and year by year, it became more important to him. His interest in farming was stimulated. If only he had more land, real land, he would have more grain and be less dependent on what his farmer *jajmans* might choose to pay him. He decided that carpentry was not enough. Even though he could not acquire more land there was another possibility. He could become a cultivator in other men's fields, on shares. He discussed the plan with two of his *jajmans* who had more land than they could cultivate and they agreed, on condition that he provide the oxen as well as half of the

seed and fertilizer. He had the oxen and they had very
little work to do on his own field, hardly enough to be
worth their fodder. Now they would be working full time.
The seed store set up by the government in our village
had begun to function and he was able to borrow both
seed and fertilizer. And Kumar, the eldest son, could
work the fields with him.

Together they went into sharecropping in earnest.
Later, they added a third member to their team, Balram's
second son, Raju. By 1967, they were sharing crops with
three jajmans: a six bigha plot (5 bighas = 1 acre) of
Prakash's, four bighas of Madan's and three bighas of
Laja's. Their carpentry continued to occupy their mornings and evenings and during busy seasons claimed their
noon rest time. Service to their jajmans still came
first, although farming was equally profitable.

They were drawing near to security, the goal of
every villager I know. Yet they felt that to be really
secure they needed more fully productive land of their
own. At best, their one plot was uncertain. The jajmans whose fields they cultivated were satisfied with
their harvests, but no landowner would risk sharecropping
for more than two, or perhaps three, years with one cultivator, lest the latter claim the land. They would have
to change from field to field, and would have difficulty
saving enough to buy more land.

Balram had no inkling of impending prosperity. But
one day district engineers arrived with plans for a drain-
age system that would prevent further flooding of the
village fields. With a corps of workmen they installed
a brick-lined drain that started on the east side of
Karimpur, bypassed the village of Anjani, and continued
across country to Isaf Nadi. the nearest river. The drain
would assure protection from floods to farmers with fields
along the east side of the village, two of which Balran
and his son were working on shares.

However, the new drain did nothing for the land to
the west of the village beyond the khera, where Balram's

four acre field was. But then the engineers reappeared.
This time they created less excitement, with simpler
equipment and fewer laborers. They went about digging
a wide, open ditch that looked like a gulley, which,
they said, started at some distance in a neighboring
district and which would move on from our village to
Isaf Nadi, like the first drain. It looked too ordinary
to be effective and farmers working in the vicinity paid
it little attention. Apparently no one knew when or how
it began functioning. It was Balram who made the startling discovery. One morning he went out to see if a bit
more of his submerged field was dry enough to be plowed.
When he came near it he rubbed his eyes and looked again.
He recognized the plots around him and knew that he was
on the right spot. But where was the pond? All along
both sides of the drain, water was seeping down and land
was appearing, where before only water had been visible.
Here before him were acres of damp, rich earth, and four
of those acres were his! When the truth finally dawned
on him, he rushed back to our house and around the village spreading the good news. Some refused to credit
his report and went out to see for themselves. There it
was, a whole area, still partially submerged, but with
long stretches of soil exposed, richer than that in other
fields of the village. Balram's spirits soared higher
than when the plot had become legally his. Now he, like
landowners he had envied, could have two full harvests
each year, in addition to whatever he got from sharecropping. Not for one moment did he consider deserting
his jajmans or his traditional trade. He was still a
Carpenter. But, asked Balram, was ever there a Carpenter
as fortunate as he?

*   *   *

Balram's two older sons have reached the age and
standing when they can be considered able Carpenters.
If Balram were to follow Devi's example, they would be
working along with the men from across the lane, in the

open-air shop behind his house. But instead Balram suddenly and inexplicitly set up his own shop at the front of his own courtyard. Prakash is familiar with his motives, but even he cannot analyze this, although he surmises that it was an outcome of the quarrels between Balram and Devi's sons, or it may simply be a display of his own self-sufficiency. In any case, Balram is obviously satisfied with the present location. While he sits on the ground working or supervising, he can watch what goes on in the exposed courtyard, except for the bahus who discretely remain at the far end. And he can shout at his wife without effort, knowing that she will hesitate to scream back in the presence of his jajmans.

Balram's sons still acknowledge him as head of the family. Thus far Kumar has made no effort to carry responsibility in their carpentry, and has expressed little interest in farming, despite his original enthusiasm over sharecropping. He has been overshadowed by his voluble father for so long that no one expects him to have ideas or ambitions of his own. Several times he has mentioned the empty space in the new house, and the possibility of constructing a room on one side of the courtyard. It may be that the mounting quarrels between his mother and his wife will drive him into action, at least to the point of building a room and installing his own family in it. I have known a number of sons who have resorted to this. He seldom visits the younger men of our family, and he is rarely seen in a group gathered for singing or fun. In the shop he repairs the implements handed to him by his father, but does no more than he is obliged to do. And the same is true of his field work.

Raju, the second son, was called stupid by his school masters and fellow pupils. To him school seemed useless, a waste of time. In contrast, his initiation into farming delighted him, and he has been a first class farmer ever since. His eyes are bright and his expression alert as he talked with us in his father's field beside the drain. Experienced farmers respect his ability and stamina and are glad to engage him to cultivate their land on shares whenever he is available. He likes working in Balram's shop, is as able as Kumar, and works more steadily. He is both genuine Carpenter and farmer, an unusual combination in village tradition.

The youngest son, Duleep, is Balram's pride. When he was praised as a clever student Balram began making plans for his future in some government office. Neither carpentry nor farming would be his lot. He passed the examinations of the eighth class, which is as high as the village school goes, and which was all that he needed for the post his father intended him to have. With plenty of cash available and with his rising prestige, Balram had entree with officers of the rural development department in Mainpuri. He had come a long way from the days when he was repeatedly in trouble with representatives of the government. They found a job simple enough for a middle-school graduate and Duleep was hired. He has a bicycle and comes sailing into the village each evening, dressed like a townsman and he has acquired a slight swagger, typical of young men who have jobs in town. He impresses other boys of his age, but not his own brothers. They ignore him until he changes to his ordinary village clothes and becomes the least among them. Duleep reports that he is doing very well and is liked by his superiors, boasting being another trait of young men who want to make sure that their value is understood and appreciated.

Now, in 1970, Balram has reached the peak of his ambitions. He should be enjoying the fruits of his past labors, as other men of his age are glad to do. But his restless spirit rebels against retirement. He misses the striving and the fighting that have stimulated him during his climb. Life has become empty. He indulges in complaints, some real, some imaginary. His sons do not always obey him as they should. His wife quarrels noisily with Kumar's wife when not quarreling with him. He is not allowed to see the faces of his sons' wives, more attractive he is sure, than his wife's. They fly

to a dark corner when he comes to the verandah to be
served a meal; or they whisper together and giggle, probably over some silly joke about him. He is assailed by
physical ailments, chiefly in his legs and feet. At
times these become so painful that he cannot leave his
charpai in his room at the back of the new house. When
his morale is at lowest ebb, he sends his wife to call
me, as one person who has known him from his healthy,
carefree boyhood and understands his maladies. He tells
me that the men who praise him as successful carpenter
and fortunate landowner know little of the burdens he
must now carry. When he is well enough to walk to our
courtyard, he regales us with tales of his good fortune
and his success. If he could not boast, he would no
longer be Balram. He still looks forward to fairs, in
our district or one that borders ours. He dresses in his
best garments, clean but wrinkled, a white cap at a jaunty
angle, and shoes, and off he goes, recapturing some of his
earlier zest. Between fairs or trips to town, he wears
torn, soiled shirts, or none at all, and loose white pants.
His wife still takes pride in showing us her dhoti made
from scraps of old ones, frayed and soiled. Their new
house, which I expected them to enjoy, is just as it was
when they first built it, except for the embellished front
doorframe and the room far at the back, now a stable which
cattle share with their master. Meanwhile the old house
becomes more dilapidated each year; walls are crumbling
and the courtyard is fully exposed. The large, rusty iron
basin, minus a bottom, still lies at one side among broken
clay jars. Old garments are strewn about, on the ground
or on a worn charpai leaning against the wall. Such details do not concern Balram. His carpentry assures him
of a definite role in the life of the village. This is
essential, just as sons are essential. Best of all, he
is sole owner of the coveted piece of land which has be-
stowed the prosperity and security so important to him.

PART III

THE FAMILY OF DINESH, OIL PRESSER

DINESH'S FAMILY TREE

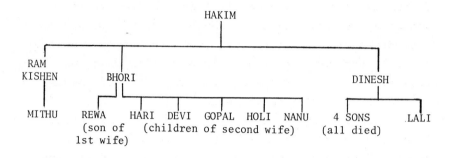

CHARACTERS

The old _telin_ - mother of the three Oil Presser brothers

The _hakim_ - father of the three brothers

Ram Kishen - eldest brother

Mithu - Ram Kishen's only son

Bhori - the second brother

Hari - Bhori's eldest son, the son of his junior wife

Rewa - Bhori's second son, the son of his senior wife

Dinesh - the youngest brother

The wives of the three brothers, daughters-in-law of
the old _telin_

The second old _telin_, living next door

The _mahajan_ - Shopkeeper whose mill in Karimpur curtailed
Bhori's oil trade

The Goldsmith - manager of a second mill in Karimpur

We had never heard of Oil Pressers before coming to live in Karimpur. When farmers or housewives spoke of them as holding an essential place in the village community, we were puzzled. Who were they? In our Hindi dictionary we found that the word was derived from tel, oil, and when translated into English meant Oil Presser. In cities where we had lived, people bought whatever cooking oil they needed from shopkeepers. In the village it came directly from the seeds of mustard plants sown by the farmers between rows of wheat and barley. When the plants had been threshed and winnowed and the seeds had been dried, they were brought to the Oil Pressers, the telis. They extracted oil from the seeds to be used in every household in the village for frying vegetables and legumes. Clarified butter, ghee, was reserved for puris and other special cakes for festivals. As far as we could discover, there had always been Oil Pressers because there had always been a demand for oil. Their income depended on the sale of the residue left in the bottom of the press after the oil had been removed and given to the farmer. Known as "oil cake," this residue was purchased by owners of animals as a valuable addition to ordinary fodder.

The Oil Pressers were classified as Sudras, lowest of the four large varna divisions. Sudras are the menials who serve farmers and their families either directly as servants or laborers, or indirectly through special services like those of the Potter, the Barber, and the Oil Pressers. Their homemade grain jars, never full, were often empty before the next harvest. Their clothing was barely sufficient, with perhaps one change kept for special occasions. Yet they had their own homes, their children, their place in the community and did not regard themselves as poor.

The Oil Presser Family

During our early years in the village, there was just one large family of Oil Pressers occupying an enclosure

facing the village pond and the mango grove in which
we camped. We had passed their house often, but had
not gone inside. Finally we made a visit: just as we
reached the doorway, a man came hurrying out with a jar
on his shoulder that looked like the familiar water jars.
This one, however, was oozing oil. In that moment,
"teli" took on meaning for us. He recognized us easily
for like the rest of his family he had watched us from
his doorway, so he set down his jar and led the way
directly into the courtyard. There was no entryway and
stable room like those we had found in other houses.
The courtyard was smaller than we had expected for so
large a family, but was filled with women and children,
along with two or three men, all sitting on the ground.
Others quickly emerged from dark doorways. Everyone
seemed saturated with oil. Someone dragged two oily
charpais from a wall against which they were leaning.
The men and older boys gathered around the one on which
they seated Bill, and the women and girls and small children sat close to the one assigned to me. The women and
girls wore the customary long blouses with long sleeves
and full skirts, although any color that the garments
may have had originally was gone. The men wore shirts
and dhotis, once white, now gray. Older children were
in an assortment of ragged shirts, some too large, others
too tight and short. Because the weather was mild,
younger children wore nothing at all. Everyone was
friendly and frankly curious. On that first visit
neither Bill nor I was able to ask the questions we had
come prepared to ask. We were too overwhelmed by theirs,
and by their steady chatter and ready laughter.

A week later, as we passed their door, they invited
us to see their three oil presses, the source of their
livelihood. Each one was inside a small dusky room, the
only light provided by the low, narrow doorway. When we
entered the first room, groping our way, all that we could
see was a blindfolded ox. Then, as our eyes adjusted to
the dimness, we discovered that it was plodding in a

circle, around what we were told was the mortar for the
oil seed. This had been cut from the trunk of a large
tree and imbedded in the earth floor with the top about
three feet above floor level. It had been gouged out
into the semblance of a mortar and lined with metal.
The tall pestle, pressing oil from the seed, was made
from a much smaller tree, smoothly rounded at the base,
and reaching almost to the ceiling. To give it added
pressure a heavy beam revolved around the mortar as the
pestle turned. It was this beam that the ox was pulling.
But how could the beam turning outside the mortar affect
the pestle inside? One of the men pointed to a sapling
tied by a piece of rope to the upper tip of the beam.
To add more weight, a rock rested on the beam and beside
it sat the wife of one of the men. We discovered on
subsequent visits that one or two children might join
the woman to add still more pressure. Someone was responsible for checking the oil, dripping into a clay jar
at the base of the mortar and when it was filled, the
jar was replaced. They knew just how many hours an ox
could work at one stretch and how much oil could be produced in one day. The whole contraption was incredibly
cumbersome and unwieldy. When we asked the man supervising the work that day if this press was like the one
used by his forefathers, he assured us that nothing had
been changed except for the pieces of rope that held
the parts together, and the ox. Yet, primitive as it
appeared, it kept pace with the village demand for oil.

One particular man aroused our curiosity. He was
a member of the family, but we rarely saw him in the
courtyard, nor did he bear the marks of oil-pressing.
We met him more often in the lane or in a higher caste
home. Upon inquiry, we were told that although he was
an Oil Presser by caste, he was a respected hakim, a
practitioner self-taught in the use of herbs, roots,
and leaves for the treatment of disease or infections.
Like the villagers we were impressed by the large volume
he always carried with him but which we never saw him

open. This was all we knew about him at that time. I
had to wait thirty years to hear his story.

The Family of Dinesh

Before I had settled in our house after my return
in 1961 and before I had time to call on friends other
than those near my home, I suddenly became involved with
the Oil Pressers. An old, stooped woman hobbled into my
courtyard, shivering with cold and coughing violently.
Her face was deeply wrinkled, and she was without a
single tooth. She wanted something to relieve her
coughing that made it impossible for her to sleep or eat.
When I had given her tablets for her cough and asked her
to come again, she left. Just outside the courtyard
door, she screamed. When I reached her, she was sitting
on the ground, crying and holding her leg. I was horri-
fied. Jia, at the time my next door neighbor, had also
heard the scream and had come running over from her
courtyard. When she saw the woman and discovered what
had happened, she covered her face with the end of her
dhoti and shook with laughter. The woman continued to
groan. When composed enough to speak, Jia said, "The
dog knows who is low caste and bites them. She thinks
they don't belong here. She never touches brahmins or
fair-skinned persons." This bothered me more than it
did the telin. When Jia saw my shocked reaction, she
added, "No one has trouble with her bites afterwards."
Then, for the woman's benefit, she raised her voice to
threaten harsh punishment for the dog when she was found.
Thus having handled the situation, she returned to work.
I bathed the tooth marks with antiseptic, bandaged the
leg, and walked with the telin until she was a safe
distance from our house. There was no sign of the dog.

Two days later I visited her. The Oil Pressers
were living in two enclosures instead of the one which
we had visited thirty years before. Everyone along the
lane knew about the dog bite, and several children led
me through a passage just wide enough to allow for

tethering of bullocks and buffaloes to the second of the
two enclosures. The passageway ended in an open oblong
space, evidently serving as outer court for three branches
of the family. The doors to the three homes stood open,
as all do throughout the day. Here in this outer court,
I found the old woman squatting in a patch of sunshine
as it was the cold season, when anyone not busy working
looks for a sunny spot. She welcomed me with groans,
uncovering her leg and displaying a now filthy bandage.
While I prepared to apply a clean one and more antiseptic, four women appeared in the doorways. Two emerged
from the door farthest to our left; a woman slightly
older came from the middle one, and the youngest of all
came out of the third door on the right nearest to the
spot where we were sitting on a charpai. I had not met
any of them. They were obviously bahus who had come here
recently as brides. If the bahus had any sympathy for
the old woman, it was overshadowed by their curiosity.
They stood and stared while I bound up the leg. Finally
the eldest one asked. "Are you the Mem Sahiba?" When I
acknowledged that I was, all four came nearer. When I
took a new white dhoti with a red border from my shoulder
bag and gave it to the old woman, they came even closer
to feel it and to comment on it. The old lady snatched
it from them and laughed with delight as she spread it
out to make sure that it was the proper length. When
all five had expressed their approval, the bahus reminded
their mother-in-law that she should thank me. This she
did, with injury forgotten and eyes bright with pleasure.
When I asked politely if these were her bahus, she suddenly looked sour. "They are supposed to be mine," she
said, "but not one takes any thought for me, and not one
will prepare my food." At this, all four drew their
dhoti ends over their faces and giggled like school
girls. The oldest of them finally recovered sufficiently
to speak. "She fights with us," was all she said.

On my next visit the old woman was wearing her new
dhoti and was in a more mellow frame of mind. When I sat

down beside her and the bahus came from their doorways,
she announced that she had something of importance that
she wanted me to hear. The four bahus immediately sat on
the ground beside our charpai and several neighbor women
joined them, ready to pass their time with gossip or any
other entertainment, even the secrets of an old woman.
When she had glared them into silence, she began her tale.

Until she was twelve, she had lived in this very
house. This was her home village. At twelve, she had
been married to a boy of another village and had gone to
his home to live. During her early years, she was allowed
to come home twice or thrice a year for a fortnight's
visit. Her brother always brought her here, and her husband or one of his brothers came to take her back to his
home. When her third child was to be born, she expressed
a desire to be with her mother and to be cared for by the
dhanukin (Midwife) of her family. A girl's mother is more
concerned about her care and her comfort than a mother-in-
law is expected to be. Her brother brought her here. The
child was a boy, another son to help in the oil-pressing
as soon as he was old enough. Her husband came several
weeks later to take her and the baby back to his people.
While he was waiting for her mother to prepare the fried
cakes and sweets that must go with a woman for her in-laws,
someone in the village discovered that he was not only an
Oil Presser, but also a hakim--a self-taught practitioner.
A Brahmin family asked him to come to see the father who
was ill. They had tried several hakims and spirit charm-
ers with no results. He visited the patient and agreed to
treat him with his own mixtures. The family was impressed
by his manner and by the large volume he carried, which he
said contained all knowledge of cures. Within a few days
the Brahmin improved. Word of the hakim's skill spread
and before he left he had helped several others. By the
time he came on his next visit, the Brahmins were convinced
that they should keep him here and urged him to settle in
one of the Oil Presser houses. Prospects were better in
Karimpur than in his home village where there were already

too many Oil Pressers so he agreed to remain and his wife's brothers offered him a small courtyard and store-room. His profession lent prestige to their family. Thus, it came about that he and his wife went counter to custom and brought their family to live here with the wife's people instead of with the husband's.

After the hakim's death, when his sons might have been expected to return to the parental village, they chose to remain in Karimpur. Their mother was happy to live where she had been as a girl. No one in the family knows what happened to the impressive volume. They think that an uncle sold it to another hakim or perhaps to a shopkeeper, just for the value of the paper. They were not concerned about it. We had sometimes wondered if the hakim actually read it, or if he could read at all. However, Dinesh, his son, has told me with pride of his father's ability to read. He had attended school just one day during which his master had beaten him for something trivial. He felt that the beating was unjustified, and he never returned to school. However, one of his father's jajmans took an interest in him and helped him to learn at home. By the time he was grown, he could read difficult books like the one which everyone had admired. Dinesh himself does not read, nor do his brothers; and none of them has aspired to follow the father's profession.

For generations the Oil Pressers had accepted their position and their role in the community without question. They were never prosperous, nor did they expect to be. Like their forefathers they were content with a small but regular income. Then disaster came. After 1961, indus-tries began to move into Mainpuri, six miles away, and oil mills were among the first to arrive. They were in-tended to press peanut oil since the district was consid-ered a peanut area. As the demand for peanut oil in-creased both within India and abroad, still more mills appeared. But pressing peanut oil is a seasonal occupa-tion limited to a short period after the peanuts are harvested. So to keep the presses working between

seasons, the mills began pressing mustard oil. Soon
farmers began taking their seed to town and discovered
that the mills could offer better rates than the local
Oil Pressers. One by one, the farmers took their seed
to the mill while the Oil Pressers suffered. They had
depended on their farmer jajmans for their livelihood,
but now they found themselves without work and without
income; in addition, there was no possibility of restoring their traditional rights as hereditary servants.
For some time they were too bewildered to grasp the situation, but when their trade had dwindled to the point
where there was not enough food for themselves or their
oxen, they gave up. Where three oil presses had been
kept busy, now only one is functioning.

Finding New Occupations

Ram Kishen, eldest of the three sons of the telin
soon after the mills appeared found an opening in a new
occupation. With the help of a farmer jajman, he was
given employment in the Karimpur Seed Store which was
affiliated with the cooperative loan society also located
in Karimpur. The loaning of improved wheat and barley
seed is the chief function of the seed store although
other cereals and some pulses, including gram and peas,
are handled. There are two busy seasons; one, at the
time of sowing the two main crops in the autumn, and the
other at harvest time in the spring when gram is collected. Ram Kishen's job was to weight the grain for each
farmer at the time of borrowing and again at the time of
repayment. The seed store manager paid him and his co-
worker a small stipend, and each farmer gave them one
kilo of grain for every eighty kilos weighed. The two
men set aside the grain they received and divided it
between them at the end of the day. It provided their
families with chapatis during the months when they were
employed and several weeks following.

The work was heavy, and neither man was robust. The
bags of grain weighed from ninety-four to ninety-six

kilos each. However, the working period in the fall was
just one month, and in the spring only three months. During the intervals between these periods of regular employment, Ram Kishen found work on plots belonging to farmers
whose grain he handled in the seed store. When his only
son was strong enough for field labor, he sent him out to
search for a job on his own. Finding a job was difficult
in the beginning because farmers looked on an applicant
in his early teens as an uncertain investment. Gradually,
however, he became known as being reliable and was steadily in demand as a day laborer.

Not until he was sixteen did his father make arrangements for his marriage, and held the _tika_ _charan_ ceremony,
the first step towards a marriage. At this time the father of the prospective bride visited the father of the
groom as a humble petitioner, bearing appropriate gifts.
At the ceremony he imprinted a _tika_ (red mark) on the
forehead of the bridegroom as the first visible sign that
a wedding would take place. Later came the _lagan_, the
second and final pre-wedding ceremony which seals the
marriage contract. In this ceremony the first installment
of the dowry is made and the marriage date is set. A
few weeks after that Kishen and his son and a few car-
loads of relatives set out for the bride's home for the
wedding ceremonies and feasts. When they returned, they
brought the bride with them for her post-wedding visit,
along with the dowry. Shortly thereafter, her brother
came to take her back. The brass utensils from the dowry
were stored in a wooden chest and Kishen's household
settled back into the old familiar routine with little
to remind them of the wedding. Because she was very
young and because in a small family like Kishen's the
need of another pair of hands to help in the courtyard
was not urgent, a year passed before the bride came to
stay. This was her _gauna_, or ceremony of the consumation
of marriage, for which her parents sent additional gifts.
There were several clay jars, the size used for water,
each decorated with conventional designs in bright,

contrasting colors. Some jars contained articles of clothing for her mother-in-law, father-in-law, or husband. Still others were filled with fried cakes and sweets. There was a small basket of bamboo covered with paper and gaily painted. In it was an odd assortment of glass bangles, trinkets and ornaments which serve as village costume jewelry. She also brought several additional brass utensils to be added to the family's supply.

Ram Kishen's wife was not in need of a daughter-in-law for her small household, but she welcomed the girl when she came. She wanted a <u>bahu</u> in the house not so much to help with the work as to bear sons. She looked forward to a grandson although they had little to offer him beyond the bare necessities.

Finally Ram Kishen and his son managed to save enough money to buy a pair of bullocks which made working on shares with landowners possible. It was left to the son to do the sharecropping. When Ram Kishen was not on duty in the seed store, he preferred the freedom of casual labor. He could work when someone called him and he needed the pay or he could sit at home on his <u>charpai</u> knowing that his son would provide them with food. They lived well at harvest time when he was bringing home grain from the seed store and his son was doing the same with his half of the crop from two fields. Ram Kishen's wife made her contribution as well. As the eldest of the <u>bahus</u> her seniority and age made it permissible for her to go to certain fields to glean with her mother-in-law. Day after day she brought home her large basket filled with heads of wheat or barley.

Several years ago Ram Kishen and his two brothers applied for and received a small plot of land which had been made available by the government for poor families. The land was alkaline, regarded as unproductive for any crop but rice, and not wanted by farmers who owned better plots. When the <u>pradhan</u> (headman) first told them about the offer, they were skeptical. How could they, Oil Pressers, expect to own land? Nevertheless, each

brother gave the <u>pradhan</u> one hundred rupees and received
official papers confirming their ownership of three
<u>bighas</u> each. Nothing equal to this had come to them
before. They had lost their trade, but they were now
landowners. They knew the poor quality of the soil,
its undesirable location beyond reach of irrigation,
and realized that they could hope for only one minimal
crop a year. But one harvest of one kind of grain is
better than none. Even more important, they had land,
a form of security which every villager covets.

*   *   *

Bhori, second of the brothers, proved most enter-
prising of the three. He created a new occupation for
himself, related to the old, but far more remunerative.
He could not compete with the oil mills, but he could
profit from their services. Instead of pressing oil,
he began distributing it. He found farmers who had no
way of carrying their mustard seed to Mainpuri; so he
worked out a system by which both he and the farmers
would benefit. If a farmer needed five kilos of oil,
he called Bhori and gave him fifteen kilos of mustard
seed. Bhori took the seed by bicycle to an oil mill in
town. The mill pressed the seed, charged Bhori one and
one quarter rupees for the service, gave him back a total of approximately fifteen kilos which included about
five kilos of oil for the farmer and ten kilos of oilcake for himself. He brought the oil home on the back
of his bicycle in a canister made in Mainpuri and de-
livered it to the farmer. Then he sold the oilcake.
The price of oilcake varied, but he could count on six
or seven rupees for the ten kilos. This gave him a
profit of about five rupees, considered handsome by villagers. If he carried seed for more than one farmer,
his earnings that day were still greater. If a villager
had no mustard seed, Bhori bought oil for him from a
mill in Mainpuri, paying four rupees for each kilo and
receiving four and a half or five rupees a kilo. Bhori

could not read, but he could keep accounts and knew exactly how his business was faring.

Bhori had been the favorite son and it was he who knew where their father kept his small hoard of gold and silver jewelry. After the father's death, Bhori refused to share what he had found with his brothers. Though hidden treasure like that of the hakim's is intended for security; more often it is the cause of trouble and insecurity. There were bitter quarrels, but finally Ram Kishen, the eldest brother, the Dinesh, the youngest, accepted the situation and have managed to survive on their meager incomes.

Bhori's father probably had comparatively little to hide, but whatever the amount, it provided Bhori with the capital he needed and the bicycle which made his new venture possible, with enough remaining to replace the mud walls around his courtyard and double storeroom with walls of baked brick.

Bhori needed to earn more than either of his brothers because his was the largest family of the three. He also had the burden of supporting two wives, a predicament he did not get into deliberately. His first wife was an ailing woman who had no children and gave no hope of having any. Bhori sent her home to her people as useless and took unto himself another wife. The new one was a buxom young woman who fed him well and who quickly bore him a son. Before her second child was born, the first wife returned to stay. Bhori was trapped. He had married the first with all of the customary ritual and was bound to give her a home. This he did, and she reciprocated by bearing him a son. The first wife had no children after the one son. The second wife continued to have babies, three more boys and a girl, including one son who died while an infant. The contrast between the son of the first wife and the children of the second wife is striking. Her son is always serious, tall for his age and very thin. According to the boys of my family, he was a good student at the village school.

The children of the second wife are plump, lively, and sturdy like the mother.

The two women quarreled, but no more than any other two confined to a small courtyard and obliged to work together. The older woman retained her position as senior wife and left all household duties to the younger one. The senior wife was not strong and spent most of her time making petticoats for herself by hand. Her stitches were as fine and as even as those of a machine, and the narrow tucks looked professional. She trimmed each petticoat with elaborate embroidery, a skill rare among village women whose hands are too rough from heavy work to handle embroidery silk. The petticoats were never worn, but were carefully stored in a chest. Eventually she grew weaker, and Bhori consulted a doctor, who diagnosed asthma, which partially explained her constant ailing and complaining.

Except for the senior wife, the family seemed to be thriving and healthy. Then tragedy struck; the second wife died. It was during the heaviest of the rains of 1963. Bhori had managed to wade through the flooding to ask me for medicine. When he described the swollen and ruptured glands on both sides of his wife's throat, I knew that she must be taken to a doctor. Communications were reduced to almost nil, and I heard nothing more about her. It was almost three weeks before I could reach their house again. In the passageway, Bhori's senior wife met me, bursting with the news that the one who had considered herself healthy had died while she, the weak one, had survived. Bhori explained that he had taken his wife to the doctor in town. The doctor gave her an injection and some medicine to take home, but the trip by ox-cart had been hard on her. After they returned home, she grew rapidly worse and died a few days later. He accepted her loss as he had other losses, with a sad smile and sigh of resignation.

Now the senior wife found herself in a position of greater importance, which she enjoyed; however, with this importance came harder work, which she resented. If she had just herself, her son and her husband to cook for, she could manage; but the burden of the hungry sons and daughters of that other one was more than she could cope with, although, she looked better and seemed more vigorous than she had for years.

Bhori's daughter tried to help, but she resented her stepmother's constant nagging. Whenever possible she slipped into Ram Kishen's or Dinesh's courtyard with a younger brother or sister. She knew that her stepmother would not follow because she refused to enter either house. She herself was welcomed by her aunts as a daughter of the family and given lighter tasks or none at all. Her stepmother was sure to scold her when she returned home, but scolding was easier than working hour after hour under her sharp eyes and tongue. It was not long before her stepmother gave her up as useless and worried Bhori to find a pair of stronger and more willing hands to take over the heavier chores. Bhori solved the problem by arranging for the marriage of his junior wife's eldest son, the simplest way of procuring domestic help.

From among the families I know well, Bhori holds the record for the speedy acquisition of a bahu while remaining within the bounds of tradition. The girl's father must have made overtures earlier, and arguments between the two families must have been curtailed, to make it possible to hold the first ceremony in a very short time. Then, less than a week later, Dinesh came to our house to invite Prakash and me to the lagan ceremony that night.

Bhori's courtyard was ablaze with light from three lanterns borrowed for the occasion. Men from Brahmins down to the Washerman came surging in and sat crowded close together around the traditional design on the ground. The women of the family and their relatives had retired to the roof where, screened by darkness, they could watch all that went on and sing songs honoring the groom and defaming the bride's family.

Bhori along with his son and the family priest was

seated on one side of the ritual area, while the bride's
father with his priest and barber was seated opposite.
The brass tray presented by the bride's father and containing all of the prescribed articles was between them.
Beside the bride's father was a large open basket filled
with grain. At the beginning and at the end of the ceremony someone shot off a gun outside the door as an added
flourish.

The lagan ceremony is comparatively brief, its purpose being to make the marriage contract final in the
presence of priests and witnesses. When the bridegroom-
to-be rose and picked up the tray to carry it to the
storeroom, the bride's father took a roll of bills from
his pocket and laid it in the center. Instantly, Bhori
transferred the roll to his pocket to be counted later.
He knew the exact amount it was supposed to contain. As
the guests were leaving, basket after basket filled with
puffed sugar candies was brought from the storeroom by
Bhori's brothers, and each man was given a generous handful. Wheat or barley had been brought by several guests
in miniature grain baskets for Bhori's Barber, who acted
as the go-between, and a few coins were given to the
family priest.

Just a week after the lagan, Bhori and his son and
their party set out for the wedding at the bride's home.
Three days later they were back with the bride for her
brief post-wedding visit. Very shortly afterwards Bhori
went to summon her, and obediently she came. Ordinarily
she would have been allowed to remain with her own people for a longer period, but she was needed. For her
the change from daugher to daughter-in-law must have
been traumatic. Any girl finds it difficult to be
wrenched from her home and set down among strangers, but
she was given no opportunity to make the adjustment.
For two days she was a bride, dressed in finery and
decked with jewelry; then suddenly she found herself a
drudge, working for her husband's family. She was barely thirteen and her husband, a schoolboy, slightly older.

The stepmother-in-law was now able to sit back and talk while someone else worked. Only once during the first year did I see the girl's face. Her stepmother-in-law ordered her to lift the end of her dhoti to uncover it; then instantly she continued with her scouring of brass utensils. Among women in the village it is proverbial that a mother-in-law may be a thorn in the heel, but the greatest of all trials is a stepmother-in-law.

The little bahu, frightened and overtaxed, discovered how true this is. There seemed no relief from her misery until here in this hateful courtyard she found a friend. Her husband's sister, just her age, was still at home unmarried and free of care but with no companions other than her aunts. Now she returned to her own courtyard, warily beginning to help as she had once helped her own mother. Her stepmother was as severe with her as with her new daughter-in-law, which served to draw them closer. They discovered that when two are sharing the work it moves faster and is easier than when one must do it alone. It might be loosening the husks from rice, pounding it bit by bit in the stone cup with two clubs instead of one, or beating the kernels from heads of millet with two sticks instead of one, or removing small lumps of dirt or unwanted scraps from a pile of wheat with two pair of hands. Even the upper mill stone whirled more swiftly and easily over the lower one when two hands were gripping the peg that turned it. They were not supposed to speak while at work, but they were sometimes able to whisper. When they were giving the children their food, they could talk and laugh with them and with each other. Again at night, when the last chores were finished and the children and their task-master had fallen asleep, they talked quietly until they, too, slept.

The astute Bhori planned the future of his two elder sons while they were still young. They were not to be oil sellers. His eldest son, Hari, whose marriage was first to be arranged, was strong and capable of farm labor. Bhori invested in a pair of oxen to give him a

start in sharecropping. Then later when granted the
piece of alkaline land, he assigned the cultivating of
this plot to Hari. He himself had never been interested
in farming, and now he was too occupied with selling oil
to spend time on his land. Hari did well at sharecropping. Shri, third son of Prakash, who has land of his
own, offered to share one of his fields with Hari. Shri
was one of the most progressive and exacting of the farmers. After watching Hari at work, he chose to share a
large potato field with him. When Bhori heard of this,
he was assured that he had been wise in making a farmer
of his son.

His second son, Rewa, was thin and frail like his
mother. He liked school and studied through the sixth
grade. His free time was spent watching their neighbors,
the darzis (tailors) and Bhori considered the possibility of having him trained as a tailor. He apprenticed
Rewa to one of the neighbors. When Rewa had learned all
that he could about the making of shirts and pajamas for
village men and blouses and petticoats for the women, he
was sent to a Tailor who catered to men in the town.
He taught Rewa how to make the kind of shirts, trousers,
and even coats that townsmen wear; under him, Rewa stepped into the "professional" class. When he returned
home, his father set him up in a shop of his own in a
mud-walled room constructed beside the workshop of
Dwarka, the Carpenter. Next, Bhori invested in a trea-
dle sewing machine. Only one of the village Tailors
owned such a machine. The others turned theirs by hand
while sitting on the ground. Because of his more sophisticated training, Rewa was regarded with greater respect
than an ordinary village Tailor. He did not compete
with his Tailor neighbors who had taught him this art.
The garments he made were carefully measured and fitted,
appropriate for trips to town, whereas the other village
Tailors simply cut and stitched clothes with little concern for fit or style.

Bhori's senior wife maintained her position as head

120

10. Dinesh and his wife and daughter

11. Bhori's son, now a tailor

of the courtyard although her asthma made it impossible
for her to take any active share in the work. The two
girls were under her surveillance as long as she could
sit or lie on a charpai. The combination of her illness
and disposition made her increasingly troublesome. Her
death in 1967 was a relief to her, to Bhori, to his family and to the families of his brothers. But so tena-
cious is custom that when she died the women dropped their
work to carry out every detail of mourning. When I
visited the day after her death, they were gathered in
Bhori's courtyard talking cheerfully. When one of them
saw me approaching, she spoke to the others and all of
them began rocking and wailing. Bhori came to the door
and shouted at them, whereupon they stopped without taking an extra breath. Every eye was dry. I had felt
sorry for her, but I had not been obliged to live with
her.

The wailing proved to be only the beginning. Bhori,
who had reason to relax and forget, felt obliged to follow all traditional observances, especially the feast on
the thirteenth day. He had been unable to do anything
to honor his younger wife because the roads were impass-
able at the time of her death and relatives were unable
to reach the village. This thirteenth day observance
was for her as well as for the wife who had just died.
He and Dinesh and a neighbor cycled to Mainpuri, and
each of the three came back with a load of wheat. It
cost Bhori one hundred rupees, a prodigal expenditure
for an Oil Presser, but it had to be wheat for puris.
No inferior grain would do. As soon as the grain arrived, the women worked together cleaning the large pile
bit by bit. When it was free of stones, chaff, and
dirt, each branch of the family undertook to grind one-
third. In Ram Kishen's courtyard were his wife and
young bahu; in Bhori's, his daughter and bahu; and in
Dinesh's, his wife and mother. One niece of Bhori's
also came to help. The men worked together, patching
and smoothing the mud walls, making the passageway

presentable, and arranging for the comfort of the visitors and their oxen. Relatives were coming from their father's village and others from the families of their wives. All of the guests would be men. The old mother enjoyed her importance as head of the house where a feas would soon be held, and she became more dictatorial than ever.

Observing them working in harmony, one might gather that they were a united, congenial family. Yet for at least a fortnight preceding Bhori's wife's death, the only communication between them had been glares or gali (a variety of graphic abuse). Not only were the women at war, but the brothers as well. The old woman was most vocal of all, keeping tempers hot. When I went to call during the days of high tension, it was necessary to go into one courtyard at a time and to refrain from mentioning members of the other two households. There was none of the gathering of wives as in times of peace. Oil Pressers can be humble and long-suffering, or completely uninhibited, quick with fun and laughter, or with anger. If one of them suspects deliberate provocation on the part of a relative there is a clash. Resent- ment may linger, or it may subside abruptly when an important joint project like a funeral feast diverts them.

On the day of the feast, all of the wheat had been ground; and before dawn the older women began frying the hundreds of puris required, while the younger ones cook- ed the pulse and the potatoes to be served with them. The men collected quantitites of milk from which the wo- men made curds. They employed no help from outsiders as a more affluent family would have done. It was tiring, but the food was plentiful. When it was over and the guests had departed, everyone in the three households rested for several days and continued to feast on what had not been served. Bhori, as master of ceremonies, had met every known obligation and was relieved and satisfied.

A few months later, he arranged for his daughter's

marriage and conducted the wedding. This demanded additional feasts for a larger number of guests. Once more
the family was his chief support, and all labored and
survived together. The cost was staggering and this he
had to bear alone. At the time of his son's wedding,
he had hastened to call the bride here, to serve him and
his family. Yet when the bride was his daughter, he explained to her in-laws that she must remain at home for
a longer period than was customary because his wife had
died and his son's wife was pregnant. In the absence of
the disagreeable stepmother, the two young women carried
out the household chores without complaint. Laughter
revived. When the bahu's baby was born, they were both
delighted. They did not think of him as a responsibility, an infant to be cared for, rather they played with
him as they might a doll. As he grew old enough to respond Bhori's younger children joined in the entertainment. They thought it fun to pinch him lightly or to
give him a small brass bowl or other bright object and
then immediately snatch it from him. When he burst into
tears, his mother or aunt was ready to cuddle and kiss
him until he laughed again. They were constantly feeding or jouncing him, and he thrived on it. Theirs was
a contented family. Bhori, too, enjoyed his freedom
from his ailing wife and he had two cheerful young
women doing their best to serve him well.

His oil trade was established, but suddenly again
he was threatened by competition, this time from within
the village. His new competitor was a mahajan, a Shopkeeper by caste, who lived beside the district road with
his two younger brothers and their families. Their aunt
had opened a shop on the roadside. It had been small,
catering to men passing by on the way to or from Mainpuri. Her nephews' shop was larger and better equipped.
Shopkeepers are known to be keen businessmen, so when
the eldest nephew built an extension to house a mill,
no one was surprised. Several years earlier there had
been a flour mill across the road, using coal as fuel.

It had failed, and no one had attempted a mill since. Perhaps the Shopkeeper would succeed.

He did succeed, but not until he had spent two years in tireless effort to secure permission to use electric power coming from Mainpuri. He was told again and again that there was barely enough for the government tube wells located along the district road, but he knew that the power plant in Mainpuri was being enlarged and was positive that when it was completed he would have as much power as he needed. He filled out forms and haunted offices until he got what he wanted. When the wires were finally connected, his building was ready and equipped with the very simple machinery called for. He included a light placed over the entrance to the mill to announce to the village and passersby that a mill was functioning. Quickly, the millstone began turning. He would be dealing with farmers and knew that they would insist on flour ground between stones like those used in their homes. His customers proved to be the larger, more prosperous land owners of Karimpur and men from other villages without mills as most families in the village continued to grind their grain at home where bahus charged nothing for their labor. Not long after the flour mill began bringing him cash, he invested in an oil press far different from the oil presses once seen in the Oil Presser houses. When Bhori heard this news, his reactions surprised the men around him. He rarely talked and was never fluent, even at the time of weddings or funeral feasts. Other blows he had accpeted philosophically.

"But," he asked, "how could any man be resigned to this?" The gods had given him success only to make his fall greater. He, an Oil Presser, had always depended on oil for his livelihood. Now a Shopkeeper who had never dealt in oil would far surpass him, all because he had the capital which Bhori was denied.

After this first outburst, he refused to discuss the new mill and avoided looking at the building when he passed. As he had done several years before when faced disaster, he adjusted his oil business to the new situation. He discovered that many of his patrons found it more convenient to hand their mustard seed to him at their own door and to receive their oil from him there, rather than make the necessary trips to the mill. Also, there was still a demand for oil from families without mustard seed. A Shopkeeper with a busy mill could not be bothered with storing oil and selling it by the kilo. So he started buying oil from the city mill on trips when he had no orders to fill and kept it in large tins in the outer, lighter section of his double storeroom which became his "shop." He could not hope for profits like those he had once made; yet he was earning more than he had expected to when the Shopkeeper's press began functioning. His two grown sons were bringing home grain or cash, which helped to balance any decline in his own income. He was better off in every way than he had been as a presser of oil.

*   *   *

It was Dinesh, youngest of Hakim's sons, who suffered most deeply when men no longer came to him with their bags of mustard seeds. He clung to his press long after his brothers and cousins had concluded that oil pressing on a small scale was doomed. Even when his ox died he seemed confident that someone would help him buy a new one. He knew no skill other than his oil pressing and had depended entirely on this to support his small family.

One reason for Dinesh's reluctance to seek out employment stemmed from his pronounced limp. The villagers did not treat his handicap as a bad omen as they would have done had he been born lame. Until he was twelve or thirteen, he had been a normal, active boy. Then he became involved in a plot against Prakash: a certain family in the village had long been a rival of Prakash's in the struggle for local power and desired to weaken his claim to prestige in the village. The surest way to do this was to damage Prakash's reputation, so a member of the rival family reported to a subordinate police officer that gold jewelry had been stolen from his house. At that same time, he bribed Dinesh to confess that he had been persuaded by Prakash to steal the jewelry for him. On the basis of the report, one night the police came to Prakash's house and demanded to be admitted.

Prakash was ill at the time and Jia, his young wife, had to deal with them. Fortunately someone had warned her of their approach and purpose and she had quickly put on her neck and arms and ankles the few pieces of her jewelry not buried in the floor. Then she covered herself well with her long skirt and heavy mantle. When the police pounded on the door, she met them, head and face covered. She was indignant, but had to admit them. Dinesh, terrified at what he had done, stood at the door and watched.

Neighbors gathered as they always do where there is excitement. When they discovered what was happening, someone in the crowd managed to get the ear of the police long enough to explain the position of Prakash's family in the village. He insisted that Prakash did not need anyone's jewelry, nor would he ever be guilty of stealing. After a cursory search, the police finally accepted the word of several villagers and withdrew. But they were incensed at having been misinformed. Someone must be made to suffer for it, someone other than the influential man who had made the report. As they came out of the house, a man at the front of the crowd pointed to Dinesh who still stood at the door trembling with fright and looking guilty. When they grabbed and threatened him, he confessed to his share in the conspiracy. So they fell on the boy and beat him until he was unconscious. When the police left, neighbors carried Dinesh home. His father, the hakim, was dead. There were no facilities for first aid in the village, and no one offered to take him to the civil surgeon at district headquarters as that would involve a report against the police. He finally recovered sufficiently to work, but the limp remains.

Eventually he became a casual laborer, living from day to day on whatever job might be offered. When I asked why he had not applied for work in one of the city oil mills, he explained that men who went from here to any mill in town were hired as coolies, carrying heavy bags of peanuts or grain from shops of wholesale dealers or from trucks into the mill. Very few were strong enough to do it. Added to the hours of heavy work, there was the six mile walk to town in the morning and back home in the evening. Riding on a bus was possible, but the thirty-two paise fare each way reduced the day's pay. He had inquired about such a job, but it was beyond his strength. He knew that he must find some other way to earn. But how? Never before had he been obliged to make a decision, even a minor one. As long as he was the youngest son of a joint family, his work and his life were directed by his elders; first, by uncles and then by older brothers. When oil pressing no longer united them, each brother set up his own household apart from the others. Dinesh was lost until the pradhan provided him with temporary employment.

At that time, the pradhan was planning a number of projects and could use a man without skill, like Dinesh, to work under a mason. Our house was the first job as the pradhan and his father, Prakash, had volunteered to superintend the construction. The pradhan used part of our house as his office, and Dinesh came frequently to talk about building jobs on which he was employed. He seemed alert and was consistently cheerful. When I asked pradhan about him, he said that Dinesh was one of the best day laborers he had found even though until a short time ago he had spent his days pressing oil.

The pradhan's building program continued until the cooperative society offices and living quarters for the secretary were completed and three school buildings had been constructed. Then, again, Dinesh was out of work. He waited patiently for some new job to come his way. Before long it came in the form of road building. The

Public Works Department was reconstructing the road con-
necting the district headquarters in Mainpuri with the
sub-headquarters in Karauli. Karimpur is about midway
between the two towns. The practice is to engage laborers from the locality where the construction is going on.
When word came that it was our turn to provide workmen,
Dinesh and others joined the gang. For several weeks
they were occupied breaking up stones and bricks. But
this too ended when activity moved on to the next village.

The only opening left for a man without skill like
Dinesh seemed to be work on the land. At the times of
sowing and reaping there was a demand for all men of the
village, regardless of skill or experience. In between
times, landowners might employ men for regular or casual
labor, giving preference to those who had worked for them
for years or whose fathers had served their fathers. Men
like Dinesh had to wait their turn. When out of work for
several days, he walked down the lanes, stopping at the
doors of possible employers. Occasionally he sat on the
lane-side stoop of a Tailor neighbor where he hoped a
passing farmer night be reminded that his services were
available for the next morning.

Shri, Prakash's son, hired him occasionally, but he
complained that Dinesh did not always report for duty in
his fields when he had said that he would come. Shri is
an energetic, well-fed young man and a hard driver. He
rated Dinesh's behavior as irresponsible and spoke of
him as shiftless. I was tempted to agree until I questioned Dinesh when alone with him and his wife in their
courtyard. Yes, he had deliberately avoided going to
Shri's fields because he was not equal to Shri's demands.
He had not refused Shri's call to report the next day for
fear of antagonizing him. Instead he resorted to passive
resistance and stayed at home. This spared him an awkward encounter with a strongwilled man, but it forfeited
his chances of future employment in Shri's fields. Frankly, he did not like being bossed by someone younger than
himself. He had always worked with his brothers or alone

at his own speed, and he hoped to do so again.

After a long stretch of unemployment he decided on
an entirely new career, far removed from oil pressing or
farm labor. He became a vegetable and fruit vendor. In
the beginning he walked to Mainpuri to the wholesale
market for his wares. Soon he found it more convenient
and more profitable to go in the opposite direction, to
Karauli, a market town. It was equally distant, but was
smaller and he found it easier to bargain with wholesale
dealers there. The walk was difficult, for he had a
minor limp, and returning by bus with his large basket
filled was a daily battle of shoving and being shoved by
the crowd. Gradually he learned to assert his rights on
the bus, in the market, and at the doors of village homes.

My first intimation of this venture came when he appeared at our courtyard door, looking out from under the
large shallow basket on his head. He was smiling broadly
as he set down the basket and displayed his wares. These
consisted of a supply of small, hard green guavas, two
slices of pumpkin, a small pile of okra, and a few bananas. He explained that he had set out with much more
but had stopped at several houses and made sales on the
way. His basket was almost empty, but the bag containing
the grain he had received in payment was nearly full.
The children looked longingly at the guavas and I bought
half a pound. Jia bought the okra, a treat at this season of tasteless vegetables. Caste rules were not involved: no one in Jia's family would consider accepting a
drink of water or cooked food from an Oil Presser, but
raw fruit and vegetables are in another category. I paid
him in cash; Jia paid him with grain. He laid the okra
in the small flat basket suspended from one end of a
stick serving as balance scales. A piece of string held
in his hand supported the stick. Jia poured her grain
into the opposite basket until she and Dinesh agreed that
the stick was horizontal. Farm families prefer to pay in
grain, and Narayan prefers it as well for a cash purchase
is apt to lead to debate. At the end of his rounds a few

vegetables might be left in his basket, rejected by housewives. These he took home to his wife who, as a treat, added them to their evening meal of pulse and chapatis. The grain he had received she set aside in the storeroom ready for her to grind and make into chapatis for two or three days. This was the extent of the help she could give him, bound as she was to her courtyard or the space in front of her door shared by the three families.

His mother, however, was free to go anywhere in the village and seemed to enjoy a day selling while Dinesh went to Karauli for more fruit and vegetables. She conducted her sales in her own fashion treating housewives as she might her bahus. She refused to let them handle each piece of fruit or vegetable to examine it, lest it be damaged before her next sale. If she suspected that a woman was giving her an ounce less of grain than the weight of her vegetable, she raised her voice while she applied her special brand of abuse. No one resented her for she was an eccentric, a village character not to be taken seriously. At each harvest time she worked with the gleaners and brought home her basket of grain as well filled as that of her senior bahu who often accompanied her. At a certain season of the year she ventured far from the village to gather nari, a green leafy vegetable found on the edge of a particular pond. On her way home, she would exchange nari for grain in others' houses, just as Dinesh was doing with vegetables in another part of the village. She would reserve a bit, however, as a treat for her family.

While Dinesh peddled vegetables, he dreamed of the one business he wanted more than this--peddling oil. From the time Bhori began bicycling to an oil mill in Mainpuri, Dinesh had longed to go with him. But Bhori had the only bicycle in the family and although Dinesh knew how to ride, he was never allowed to touch it. Then in 1966, the unbelievable happened. He found himself in possession of a bicycle, not through his ability

to earn and save, but because of his helplessness. A
group of visitors from Delhi, knowing of his physical
handicap and of his hopes, decided to give him a bicycle.
He was overwhelmed: never had he owned anything beyond
the bare necessities, and certainly nothing as costly as
a bicycle. Now he could join Bhori in the oil business.

The next morning he located two old canisters in a
small shop and with one dangling from the handlebar of
his bicycle and the other rattling on his rear carrier,
he set off for Mainpuri. When he returned in the afternoon with the containers filled, there was no sign of the
triumph we had expected. Although he had no difficulty
selling the oil that same day, it was not long before
he abandoned his trips altogether.

Dinesh was naive. He had always looked upon himself
as subordinate to Bhori and took for granted that they
could share the oil trade as they had shared the oil
pressing, with Bhori as the master. Apparently Bhori regarded his younger brother as a burden or as a possible
competitor to be discouraged. He had fought his own
battles with the oil mills and must have known that
Dinesh could not succeed alone. Dinesh tried, but inside the city oil mill he was jostled and shouted at by
other buyers and by coolies bent low under heavy loads.
The flying belts and the roar and the vibrations of big
presses frightened him. No one bothered to direct him
to the sales section. Once there, he had to wait his
turn to deal with the short-tempered, harassed order
clerk. Then came the ordeal of carrying the two heavy
canisters to his bicycle on the outside. He was a
stranger and no one offered to help him. There was
also the problem of the toll. Everyone who brought a
product from the town to be sold outside had to purchase
a permit. Bhori's had cost him twelve rupees. Dinesh
did not have the twelve rupees demanded and consequently
was barred from the highway while Bhori continued his
oil trade unperturbed.

Dinesh returned to his vegetable buying and selling,

not with an air of defeat, but with evident relief.
At one time he longed for a bicycle as the first step
in establishing himself in the oil trade. Now he was
discovering what an asset it could be in his vegetable
business. On his first homecoming with the big loaded
basket on his bicycle, he was tired, but relaxed, entirely different from the disturbed man who had come in
weighted down with oil from the mill. He had obviously
enjoyed pushing his bicycle up and down in the open air,
wholesale market. There was shouting and confusion and
there were flies and dust, but it was all comfortably
familiar. The men who sat or stood beside their piles
of fresh produce were ready to bargain with him in a
way that he could understand.

The demand for his produce increased as housewives
found that they did not have to wait for someone in the
family to bring a bundle of vegetables home from town
but could buy them from Dinesh at their door. In spite
of all this, there was little or no indication that
profits had increased. He added no brass utensils to
their meager supply. His wife had a few more vegetables
to add to their meals, but the tall, urn-shaped grain
jar that she had constructed of clay remained nearly
empty while those in neighboring houses were comfortably
filled. Their clothing was adequate for warm weather,
but they had nothing to add when winter came. Their
one quilt resembled a heap of scraps and to keep warm
at night during the cold weather they spread rice straw
on the floor of a storeroom. Dinesh even abandoned his
habit of sleeping just inside or outside of their outer
door, and everyone shared the straw bed and the remnants
of the quilt.

One afternoon I went to call on his mother. Dinesh
was at home that day and invited me into his courtyard,
primarily to show me his oil press. It was still there
in a small, dark room at one side of the courtyard.
When I stepped into the room, it was easy to recapture

the scene of thirty years earlier when a child or wife
perched on the beam that turned the pestle, and the
underfed, blindfolded ox patiently trod the path en-
circling the room as he pulled the beam. The path
was still there, worn deep. In those early days I had
pitied the ox. Now I pitied the man who had lost his
ox but who still clung to the press. Dinesh sighed
as he patted the mortar and spoke of its service.

Back in the courtyard, he smiled and announced,
"You bought my wife for me." I was puzzled. He then explained, "I worked on your house as a laborer and earned enough money to pay for a wife." Then he went on,
"My first wife died without giving me any sons. She
lost her only child. I needed someone to cook for me,
and I wanted sons. Friends of mine offered to let me
have this woman if I paid." There were no formalities,
not even a feast. She simply came and has been living
with him. He took me proudly to the cooking corner of
the courtyard: behind the partition his wife was toasting flat cakes at her chulha. Her head was covered with
the end of her dhoti, and, embarrassed by her husband's
praise of her, she had partly covered her face and hung
her head. Then she lifted the dhoti slightly and gave
me a shy smile. She was the youngest of the bahus I
had seen on the first day. She was attractive and
healthy and judging from her husband's frank approval,
she must have been a good cook and able to bear sons.
Dinesh resumed his explanation. "We had three sons.
One died right after his birth. The other two died
when they were older. Now we hope to have another
and shall try hard to keep him well."

When Dinesh's wife was pregnant again in 1966, she
planned to go to her parents' home for her confinement.
She and Dinesh both felt that it was the only way to protect their child. This was to be her first trip to her
home since coming here to stay; however, long before she
was ready to leave, one of the brothers came to call for

her because, he said, there was illness in their family
and she was needed. This is a patent excuse offered by
parents when they want to see their daughter, especially
when they think that she has been away from them over-
long. In-laws find it difficult, if not impossible,
to refuse such a request, even though they doubt its
validity. Dinesh was reluctant to let her go, but he
could not deny her people a visit from her. He waited
patiently for two whole months, but life in the courtyard was bleak. His mother gave me no peace as she
grumbled constantly of the work she was expected to do.
His brothers laughed at him when he seemed anxious upon
hearing no news. Neither he nor his wife could read or
write, and bus fare to her village seemed prohibitive.
Finally after the third month of separation, he left
and went to fetch her. She was glad to return with
Dinesh to his home and hers. Dinesh's spirits revived
and again there was laughter in the courtyard.

She had nothing to do in preparation for the baby's
coming. Even if she could afford to buy a new garment,
she would not dare have it in the house beforehand for
no evil spirit must have an inkling of their longing
for this baby. If they wanted it enough to ready a
welcome, a spirit might want it too. The less attention
received, the safer it would be with them. So when the
baby was born, there were no soft wrappings or clothes
in readiness and no exclamations of joy. To the relief
of both parents and grandmother and the other two families, this baby was a girl. Now there was less need
to fear. What spirit would want to carry off a girl?

The baby arrived in July of 1967, when the rains
were late in coming and the heat was stifling. No
clothes were needed for a child of any age. Although
they were delighted with her, Dinesh and his wife tried
to restrain themselves. Apparently this was necessary
inside their enclosure, but not outside. One afternoon
as I moved about the village, I was aware of Dinesh
trailing me. Finally I turned to wait for him. When

he reached me, his eyes were shining with pleasure.
He had a baby daughter, perfect in every way. His wife
was waiting to show her to me. When I asked why he had
been so hesitant in breaking such important news, he
replied that he had not dared to mention it when others
were close around us. The men would think him foolishly
sentimental. They treated birth as a woman's affair,
handled by the midwife and women of the household. A
man should ignore it. The baby really was perfect and
for several weeks I followed the example of the family
and refrained from praising her beauty. Then as they
relaxed and expressed their delight in her, so did I.
They no longer felt bound by the fate that ordained
the loss of every child.

We sometimes hear of parents regretting the birth
of a daughter, especially if they already have three or
four. A daughter creates problems when the time comes
for her marriage. Among the parents I know in Karimpur,
however, a girl baby is loved and petted as much as a
boy. Anxiety over her wedding and dowry is postponed
until she is older. In Dinesh's courtyard this was
certainly true. They were constantly finding new charms
to boast of or exhibit. Their daughter showed every
intention of surviving and growing. The household was
now complete.

Gradually experience was developing in Dinesh a
self-assurance which he had earlier lacked. With his
wife's encouragement, he entered a new venture. He
made a contract with his young Brahmin neighbor to guard
the latter's guava grove for one season, with the chance
of earning more than ever before, or losing everything.

In the past, Karimpur farmers have not thought of
fruit as a product to be marketed. Anything from their
fields not needed for their families was sold but an
orchard was in a different category. Even the most
miserly were not tempted to make money from orchards
they had inherited. They raised their mangoes and
guavas, not as a source of financial profit, but as a

means of gaining religious merit (punya). They knew
that men in the hills made large profits from the sale
of apples, peaches, and plums, while to the south others
sold their oranges, grapes, bananas, and papayas. Less
than a hundred miles away there were men who owned mango
or guava orchards who only sold the fruit, but Karimpur
farmers expected no return, not even a share of the
fruit. Anyone in the village was allowed to eat the
fruit as it ripened and fell, but the trees must not be
damaged. Actually little or no fruit was allowed to
ripen. A dust storm with its high wind was welcomed as
a signal for a scramble for the green fruit blown down.
When no wind came, boys served as substitutes with sticks
and stones to hasten the fruit's fall. Green mangoes
suited their taste and that of their parents. Why wait
for them to ripen? As I studied the foods of the village, I came to appreciate the usefulness of green
mangoes in a monotonous diet.

The tradition of planting mango trees for punya
still holds, but it does not necessarily apply to guavas.
In 1967, Dinesh's prosperous Brahmin neighbor chose to
make a profit from his fruit. He made a contract with
Dinesh and the village priest. Each paid him twenty-
five rupees and accepted responsibility for the orchard
from the time the first fruit appeared until it had been
sold. The Brahmin was sure of his fifty rupees. Dinesh
and the priest accepted all risks and had only the promise of profits. They knew that if they could ward off
parrots and boys during the day, bats and fruit thieves
at night, and if hail and wind were not too destructive,
they could count on a good crop. The sales were in
their hands. Their success depended largely on their
vigilance in guarding the fruit. The priest constructed
a cozy hut of straw for himself, with a torn gunny bag
serving as a door. He settled comfortably in it and
left the duties of night watchman to Dinesh. Dinesh
could not protest, nor did he think of protesting. He
was poor and of very low caste, while the priest was a

Brahmin. His hut was smaller and open on one side. That
particular winter was bitterly cold, but with the help of
his wife and mother, he was doing well and looked forward
to the proceeds from a promising crop. Shortly before
fruit picking was to begin, however, he once more fell
victim to the bad luck that always seemed to follow him.
He and his wife fell ill from a serious and painful mal-
ady. The priest managed the sales and kept the cash except for the small amount Dinesh's mother forcefully
demanded as her son's share. This helped to repay them
for the contract and to meet the charges of the hakim who
came regularly for several weeks to treat both Dinesh and
the bahu. For some time after that Dinesh was unable to
salvage his vegetable trade; however, when the next autumn
came, he was ready to repeat the risk of sharing the contract with the priest. That happnened to be a poor year
for all kinds of fruit, and by the end of the season they
were both grateful for the small profit they realized.
Dinesh alone took the contract for the next winter, as
the priest was too occupied with the construction of tube
wells to be interested in fruit. By taking turns he and
his wife and his mother were able to protect and market
most of the crop. All three--Dinesh, his mother and his
wife--found their temporary claim to the orchard almost
as gratifying as actual ownership and they treated each
tree with as much care as they would if it were their
own. The guavas that Dinesh and his mother brought to
sell were superior to any I had seen in the village,
chiefly because they had been allowed to ripen. As fast
as the three of them were able to pick the fruit, he
took bicycle loads to Karauli. The whole transaction
was on a small scale, but for him it was tremendous. No
one knows whether Dinesh stowed any of it away or if so,
how much. This is information that even a man as naive
as Dinesh does not divulge. In his household there was
no indication of a better income. Only one change was
apparent. He felt freer to spend an extra day or two
at home between trips to the market.

But even greater than their satisfaction in guarding the orchard was their pride in the legal ownership of the three-fifths of an acre plot granted them by the government. When the grant was made, the two older brothers gladly accepted it as an addition to their supply of food and to their security. For Dinesh it was much more. Like his bicycle, it came as a miracle. He had not expected it nor had he earned it for he had simply borrowed the money to pay the pradhan for his services. He knew, as his brothers did, that the plot was alkaline. Only rice would grow on it, and they must depend on the monsoon for water. But at least they could hope for one decent harvest a year, and there would be rice straw for bedding, a comfort in cold weather.

Before the next monsoon, all three adults of the family worked in the field preparing it for planting. Each year since, the land has been given first place in their activities at the time of sowing, transplanting, and harvesting. They have become veteran rice growers, so much so that in the year when they lost most of the crop due to heavy flooding, they accepted it as other farmers always have done and began talking of the next season's harvest. For others, this meant waiting six months. For the Oil Pressers there would be nothing for a year.

*   *   *

The three brothers have little in common now that toil in the press is no longer shared. Yet on one point they have come to an agreement. They see no reason to better their social status by a change in their caste name. They have been advised to follow the example of other Oil Pressers in our region and adopt the title of rathor, a caste associated with the kshatriya varna, the second highest of the traditional status groups. This they refuse to do. However, without Bhori's permission, his second son, Rewa, has suddenly emerged as rathor. To make this fact known, he has added "Singh" to his name. To the best knowledge of our Brahmins no Oil Presser has ever been a "Singh." Some surmise that Rewa changed his name because he thinks himself better than his father. His father still handles oil while he, Rewa, sits at a sewing machine. He is a tailor. Yet what about his Tailor neighbors? They have not considered rising above their humble status. Others surmise that Rewa's contact with city men during his apprenticeship gave him such an ambitious idea. In any case, he cannot have become a genuine rathor. If he were, he would refuse to accept food from his Oil Presser sister and would not have an Oil Presser wife. They chuckle over the fact that the wife now has a baby. Will the child be Oil Presser or rathor?

Bhori and his brothers scorn the idea of being anything other than Oil Pressers. Once, in a rare moment when they forgot the recent troubled years, they went back to their origin to explain why they consider their name an honorable one. Long, long ago, far beyond the memory of men now living, farmers of North India looked for men who knew how to press oil. They needed someone who could take their mustard seed and turn it into the oil their wives wanted for cooking their daily meals. They preferred ghee from their own cows, but there was no longer enough of it. The men they found who were qualified to do the pressing became known as Oil Pressers. Oil Pressers they have been, down to the generation of the three brothers, and Oil Pressers the brothers will remain even though the farmers who had relied on them have denied them their place in village economy and the right to perform their traditional function.

Never again will they become dependent on jajmans. Jajmans, like other men, are fallible, thinking only of themselves. Each brother must find security in himself and his own immediate family. Regardless of the work they do, all three prefer to be known by the name of their forefathers. They do not object to Rewa's change of caste. It is not significant. To them he is still an Oil Presser, son and grandson of an Oil Presser.

PART IV

THE FAMILY OF PANDITJI, BRAHMIN

PANDITJI'S FAMILY TREE

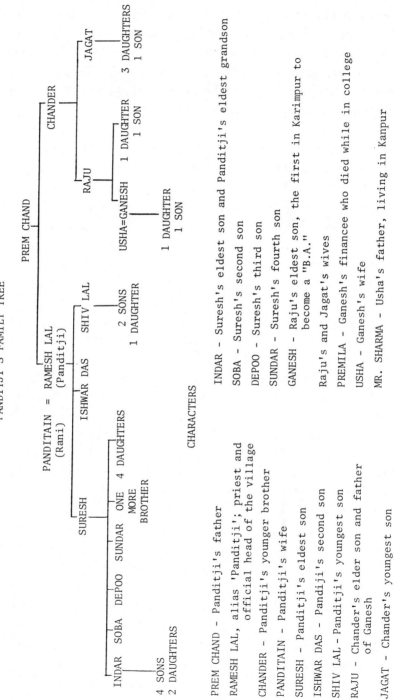

CHARACTERS

PREM CHAND – Panditji's father

RAMESH LAL, alias 'Panditji'; priest and official head of the village

CHANDER – Panditji's younger brother

PANDITAIN – Panditji's wife

SURESH – Panditji's eldest son

ISHWAR DAS – Panditji's second son

SHIV LAL – Panditji's youngest son

RAJU – Chander's elder son and father of Ganesh

JAGAT – Chander's youngest son

INDAR – Suresh's eldest son and Panditji's eldest grandson

SOBA – Suresh's second son

DEPOO – Suresh's third son

SUNDAR – Suresh's fourth son

GANESH – Raju's eldest son, the first in Karimpur to become a "B.A."

Raju's and Jagat's wives

PREMILA – Ganesh's fiancee who died while in college

USHA – Ganesh's wife

MR. SHARMA – Usha's father, living in Kanpur

The Brahmins, whose rank is the highest in the caste scale, dominate life in Karimpur. They attribute their high rank in this life, not to ancestry or achievements, but to their exemplary conduct in a previous incarnation. To have reached this status, to be born a Brahmin, a man need not have been generous or altruistic in his earlier existence or even strictly honorable in conducting his public or private affairs. It is enough that he followed the traditional code of conduct prescribed for Hindus. In contrast, a sweeper is reminded from infancy that he has been born lowest of the low because of his failure to observe the code in an earlier incarnation.

The more enlightened Hindu philosophers and Sanskrit scholars in universities interpret exemplary conduct as including altruism and honesty. For them the doctrine of transmigration, along with the accompanying reward and punishment for deeds of past lives, constitutes a man's karma; however, the scholar's interpretation has not yet reached the down-to-earth villagers. For them there are two forces controlling their lives here and now. The first is karma, as they understand rebirth and its consequences of reward or punishment. The second is kismet, or fate. Although kismet is of Arabic origin, it is a commonly used word. The better read Brahmins also use the Hindi, bhagya. Men of the village consider themselves in no way responsible for their bhagya. It comes uninvited and undeserved from a god or gods. Karma, on the other hand, is their responsibility.

Although there is less homage paid to Karimpur Brahmins now than in the past, they are still treated with deference. A young Brahmin woman who comes home from her in-laws frequently to visit often joins me when I go visiting. When we enter a non-Brahmin courtyard and are seated on a charpai, women of the family, particularly the older women, stoop down to touch her feet with fingertips and then touch their own foreheads. She acknowledges the gesture indifferently or ignores it. After all, she is a Brahmin.

Every Brahmin in the village belongs to a Brahmin clan. There are hundreds of these throughout India. In Karimpur, there are four clans. Pandeys constitute by far the largest clan with two divisions. There are the Pandeys of the East, living in the eastern section of the village, and Pandeys of the West, occupying the western section. There is rivalry between the two, and even more spirited rivalry in the factions within each branch. In addition, there are three other lineages representing other Brahmin clans: Dubes, Chaubes, and Dixits. All wives have come, not only from other villages, but from clans different from those of their husbands. According to village tradition, a girl's father is supposed to arrange for his daughter to be married into a clan a shade higher than her own. Jia, Prakash's wife, laughs when she tells about the mistake made by her father, a simple, uninformed farmer. He made arrangements for her to marry Prakash, who belongs to a clan slightly lower than hers. The blunder has not affected their relationship and she always refers to Prakash as "panditji," implying her respect.

The prominence of Brahmins in Karimpur is partially explained by their long-standing relationship with the village. Their scribes agree that it was they who established Karimpur as a flourishing town. Details vary, but the story most often repeated is that in the time of the Moghuls, or earlier, this was a large trading center, larger than Mainpuri is now. Brahmins and Warriors, known locally as thakurs, lived here, with members of lower castes to serve them and merchants to promote the trade on which the town thrived. There was rivalry between the two ruling parties, and this erupted without warning, with the slaughtering of Brahmins by the Warriors more experienced in the use of the arms of that period. Two Brahmin youths escaped because they had gone with their mother to visit her home village, a safe distance away. When news of the massacre reached them their mother vowed to avenge her husband's murder. She

employed men skilled in methods of warfare to train her
sons. When they were equal to the most clever of Warriors, she sent them to serve the governor of the area
in which Karimpur was located. When they offered to act
as the governor's attendants, he welcomed them as assets
to his prestige and power. They soon won his admiration
to the point where they could confide in him, telling
him of the fate of their people and disclosing their
purpose in coming. He ordered his army to support them.
They descended on the town, annihilated the thakurs, and
with the governor's blessing, settled there. A rule
made in the beginning still holds. It bars all thakurs
from living here or owning any property within the village limits. There has been an occasional thakur
schoolmaster, renting part of a house, but none of
them stayed longer than a year.

An added factor in the power of the Brahmins is
their land ownership. When Bill and I first went to
Karimpur they owned three-quarters of the village land
and they continue to own over half of the land today.
Brahmins employ a large number of people from other
castes on their land, a practice which strengthens
their influence on the economic life of the village.
The Farmers, the second largest landholders, control
approximately one-fifth of the land but work it themselves, employing very few non-Farmer laborers and
sharecroppers. Because of this they do not command the
power base that the Brahmins do and therefore are not
able to challenge the Brahmin's economic superiority.

In North India, any Brahmin may assume the title
of Pandit, and may act as a priest. But most of the
Brahmins in Karimpur are farmers and only a few have
ever aspired to priesthood. When we came in 1925, there
were two men acknowledged as priests. A few years later,
one of the two died, leaving no one to take his place.
This left Ramesh Lal as sole priest for the village. He
continued to carry his priestly responsibilities until
his final illness and death almost forty years later.

To the families of the village, he had the qualities of
an ideal priest and was revered above any other Brahmin.

The Family of Ramesh Lal

When we came to Karimpur in 1925, the District Magistrate had given us the benefit of his many years of
experience in selecting a village for our study and had
suggested that when we were ready to move we have a final
conference with him. So when our tents and camp equipment had been loaded on an ox cart and sent ahead, we
stopped at his office. As we were leaving, he handed
Bill a letter of introduction to the mukhiya, official
head of the village, remarking that whether or not this
man could help us, it was most important to have his support. As mukhiya he was serving as liaison officer between Karimpur and government officials at the district
headquarters; it was in this capacity that the magistrate
had found him exceptionally conscientious. His name was
Ramesh Lal, a Brahmin and a man worth knowing.

Before we were settled in our camp and before Bill
could call on him to present the letter, Ramesh Lal called on us. We found him very much a Brahmin, carrying
himself with a dignity that was natural. He assured us
that we were welcome to his village and that if we needed
help of any sort he would provide it. In spite of his
formal manner, we were both certain that he was sincere.
Ram Lal served not only as mukhiya, but as village priest
and his conduct in both offices was completely unconventional. As mukhiya he had no office to which men might
come for consultation, and as prist he had no temple over
which to preside. In his presence, there was no trace
of the formality that village men encountered in district
offices. Nor did he encourage the deference that some
priests of his standing demanded.

Every villager knew that he could count on finding
Ramesh Lal on his wide, high platform of packed earth in
the late afternoon when the chores were finished. The
platform fitted into a triangular space between two lanes

that branched off at that point, one leading to what I
call Humble Lane and the other to a Brahmin section of
the village. It was shoulder high and large enough to
accommodate a crowd of men as well as stacks of grain
brought in from Ramesh's fields. The high wall of his
granary stretched across the back of the platform. There
was nothing in the surroundings that might make the poor-
est villager feel ill at ease. Even the familiar chore
of chopping grain stalks for fodder continued on the
platform throughout every conversation, and the hired
man wielding the heavy chopper was free to listen or
make comments. There were always two or three charpais
scattered about, ready for visitors.

From his charpai Ramesh carried out his two functions. Men were free to come to him, whatever their
difficulty. Humble visitors or petitioners sat around
him on the packed earth of the platform. More important
men were seated on charpais. Each knew on which level
he belonged. They also knew that if they sought his help
as mukhiya, they must arrive before the sun was low, the
hour when he turned to his function of priest. Once he
opened his Ramayana, the epic of Rama, and began reading
it aloud, he refused to discuss personal or village affairs. His readings were primarily for his own gratifi-
cation, but if others wished to listen they were welcome.
Therefore, on some nights a large group was present; on
others Ramesh Lal was alone.

The post of mukhiya brought with it considerable
prestige and many responsibilities, but no pay. It had
been created by the government as a convenient link between local officials and villagers. The appointment
was made by the District Magistrate. In some ways, the
mukhiya's position was similar to that of the present
pradhan, president of the village council, except that
he had no elected panchayat, or council, through which
to work. His was a traditional panchayat, made up of
five elders of the village, (the word panch meaning
five). No one thought it necessary to elect them

formally. They were simply accepted as the wisest five
of the village, respected and acknowledged as leaders.
When their advice on some dispute was acted upon, it was
because they had convinced the opponents that this would
obviate the expense involved in a court case. No one was
bound to abide by their judgments, and their decisions
had no weight in the district court. Some cases which
they considered too serious for them to arbitrate were
sent directly to the district court. When the lawyers
and court took over, the council was relieved of its responsibility; but not the mukhiya. Ramesh Lal frequently
made trips to the district court with village men for
each case demanded not one trip, but several. Men would
go on the date set, and after waiting for some time they
were not surprised if told that the case had been postponed, perhaps for a few days or weeks. Villagers who
became involved in a court case looked to Ramesh Lal for
advice as they were suspicious of townsmen, and of lawyers in particular. They had difficulty in understanding
what they were told and were often not understood when
trying to give evidence. Because there was no bus service and Ramesh Lal did not possess a bicycle, either he
walked the six miles to court or took his light bullock
cart.

It was this self-imposed court duty, along with the
hearings conducted on Ramesh Lal's platform, that cement-
ed the friendship between him and Bill. If we happened
to pass by while some problem or quarrel was being discussed, he would call Bill to join him in trying to give
unbiased advice. He formed the habit of coming to our
office tent to consult Bill on the justice of his action
in some serious court case. He realized that the Sahib
was in a position to be objective and that he would not
betray a confidence. The latter meant a great deal to the
mukhiya. Villagers simply cannot resist the temptation
to pass on any bit of local news or gossip, be it harm-
less or serious. In his particular position, Ramesh Lal
had a store of information regarded as confidential.

Even though he was not always successful in the cases he carried to court, and even though he sometimes made mistakes, his integrity was never questioned. The money offered him by influential friends who wanted to add to their wealth or property by means of false evidence could have made him rich, but during our five years in the village we never heard of his accepting or paying a bribe. Rather he sometimes loaned money to men who needed it badly when involved in a court case. His interest rate was low and he never used the ruthless methods of moneylenders to force men to repay. Consequently, his influence grew while his finances suffered.

His activities as mukhiya were limited to legal concerns. Neither he nor the magistrate who appointed him associated his office with the development of the village as a community. Occasionally, when an officer of the welfare or of the agriculture department came on tour, he would ask the mukhiya's cooperation in gathering the villagers to hear his advice or to observe his demonstration. They came and listened or watched dutifully hoping that they might learn something that would help them meet their immediate problems. Afterwards, they sat in their evening circles, discussing the poor sanitation, the rutted lanes, the pests, the inferior implements or their exposure to epidemics as presented by the particular officer on that day. The conclusion usually reached was--"Perhaps he is right. His ideas are good for people like him with time and money to carry them out. But for us, all of our hours and energy must go into feeding and clothing our families." Ramesh Lal would encourage them to attempt suggested practices that were within their reach and which might result in better crops or improved living conditions. More often, being close to the burdens and difficulties of each one, he could only agree that for the villagers there is unremitting daily labor while for townsmen there is easy work at desks.

His position as pandit, priest, was hereditary.
His father before him had served as priest and had made
arrangements for Ramesh to be taught Sanskrit while he
was still a small boy and he continued his studies for
many years. As word of his training spread, he was called on first for simple family ceremonies and later for
more formal occasions. There were more than forty Brahmin families in the village, all of whom could be called
pandit, but, when anyone mentioned "Panditji," he meant
Pandit Ramesh Lal. Panditji was not like the sadhus who
periodically came to the village wearing saffron robes
and carrying begging bowls for donations of grain. Some
of them were and still are genuine religious mendicants;
others are fraudulent. They do not offer to teach or to
help anyone on their visits, but they do carry away a
generous supply of grain.

Panditji was also different from his cousin who was
a baba. Karimpur has produced several babas. Villagers
who work hard to support their families smile wryly when
one of them is mentioned. They are regarded as men who
give relatives the privilege of supporting them and their
families while they themselves are free to live in some
temple to which they attach themselves. Like the sadhus,
some babas are genuine and others are not. Ramesh's
cousin made a striking figure with his flowing white
hair, his long beard, and the bright mark of Shiva on his
forehead. He always appeared in a white dhoti and draped
white shawl, cotton in summer, wool in winter. His beads
were conspicuous, dangling from his hand and he carried
his volume of the Ramayana for all the world to see. In
contrast Panditji was dressed like other village men,
only his demeanor setting him off.

When a family has cause for rejoicing, as at the
birth of a son or grandson or some other good fortune,
they hold a katha, if they can afford it. They invite
their friends to a feast prepared by women of the family,
and at the same time they call on a priest to add his
blessing with his reading of a religious work. Ramesh

Lal had developed a reputation as a reader: often we met him on foot in one of the lanes leading from our village on his way to some other village where a katha was being held. At each such katha he read or recited portions of one of the sacred books, preferably the Ramayan. Then there were times when a different kind of priestly service was called for. A family might hold a song fest called a kirtan to mark some special occasion. Ramesh was also a popular kirtan leader.

In addition to these special occasions, there were and still are festive holidays celebrated at intervals throughout the year. The whole village shares in these, high caste and low, rich and poor. As each one arrives, it is savored to the full. The year ends with Holi, the most colorful and gay of festivals. Then after a series of lesser ones comes Raksha Bandan during the rainy season when girls are called home from their in-laws and tie bracelets of colored cotton or silk on their brother's wrists. The brothers then pledge themselves to give lifelong protection to their sisters. Again, after minor holidays, the excitement and drama of Dashera sweeps the village. Dashera celebrates the conflict between the hero-god Rama, and the demon, Ravana and ends with a battle in which Ravana is destroyed. Finally, twenty days later, there is Diwali, the Festival of Lights, when the flames of hundreds of tiny clay saucer lamps shine from wall tops and niches along village lanes. Every holiday brings its special festivities and delectable foods. Men, women, and children are all prepared to enjoy them. Ramesh Lal was one of the few members of the village concerned with the religious significance of each festival: while revelry occupied his relatives and neighbors, he spent his time meditating and reading.

I did not learn until after his death that he had also been guru, a spiritual guide, to a number of individuals. Bari Amma, a eighty-year old relative of Prakash's family, was one of them. As she told me about him in his role, she spoke with reverence. One

ordinarily thinks of a guru as a devout and learned Hindu
who lives in a forest, surrounded by disciples. Panditji
did his instructing here in the village. He in turn had
a guru, a Sanyasi Baba living in a forest near Sitapur.
He came to Mainpuri from his forest retreat, his ashram,
once a year and addressed thousands. Everyone who could
went to receive the blessings of his presence and perhaps
to listen while he spoke.

Ramesh Lal was never able to visit the ashram of his
guru, but he undertook other pilgrimages. He went as often as possible to the Ganges River for the special blessing granted to those who bathe in its waters. There are
two places on the banks of the Ganges near enough for our
people to easily visit. They go when the moon is full,
particularly at the time of some religious festival or on
some special family occasion. When Panditji went, it was
usually with a group. As in trips to the district court,
those with less experience depended on him as guide.

During the years when he and his brother were prosperous, he felt free to go with other Brahmins on longer
pilgrimages. He entrusted village affairs to the council
of elders, and left his family in the care of his brother.
He undertook one pura tirth, a complete pilgrimage, taking
Panditain with him. Three other couples joined them.
They went back into the Himalayas, to Badrinath and to
Kedarnath. There is motor service to these holy places
now, but at that time everyone went on foot, climbing the
foothills and then up the mountains to the snow covered
peaks, carrying the minimum of clothing and just sufficient utensils to cook their food. They felt rewarded
for the vicissitudes of the journey when they walked into
the temple at Badrinath, knowing that they would receive
the rich blessing granted to the faithful ones who had
persevered to the end. Kedarnath again revived their
spirits with its promise of a blessed future.

They were disappointed to discover that the visit to
Gangetari, source of the Ganges, would be beyond their
strength. Instead, they turned back reluctantly and made

their way down the rocky mountain paths, finding comfort
in the sight of two tributaries of the Ganges along the
way. Finally in Rishikesh, at the foot of the Himalayas,
they came upon the Ganga itself, a mighty river emerging
from the mountains and roaring down to the plains. From
there they traveled more easily by bus to Hardwar, the
Gateway to Heaven, several miles down the river. In
Rishikesh there were ashrams with their rishis to visit,
and in Hardwar there were temples beyond number, each
with its priests. For men like Panditji and his friends,
this was truly the gateway to heaven.

When they arrived in Allahabad, they went directly
to the city which appears new each year on a wide stretch
of sand near the sangam, the point where the Ganges and
Jamuna and mythical Saraswati rivers meet. Panditji
found the priest they sought by locating the banner flying above his hut. The priest expected them and was
prepared to be their host throughout their stay, guiding
them in all their worship. He had set aside two thatched
huts of bamboo for them, one for the three women and one
for the men. By this time it was January and bitter cold.
but every morning at dawn they made their way with thousands of others to bathe in the river, struggling to
reach the sangam or as near to it as possible. Ten days
later they moved on to Benares. Here they bathed in the
Ganges once more and worshipped in a number of large
temples. Then followed a visit to the famous temple of
Kali in Calcutta. After only two days there, they traveled by a small steamer to Ganga Sagar where Panditji
pictured the goddess as she must appear at the time of
her annual emergence from the waters of the Bay. Finally they reached Rameshwaram, the southern-most point of
their pilgrimage, where they worshipped Rama, king and
god. It is believed that from this spot Rama crossed
the channel to Lanka, now Ceylon, and destroyed the
demon-king, Ravana.

For Panditji, the whole pilgraimage had been a
blessed opportunity to worship gods and goddesses who had

now become realities, dwelling in temples built for them by devout worshipers who had gone before him. Each step he shared with the men who joined him on his platform in the evening.

*   *   *

On our visits to Karimpur during the years after we had left, we followed the changes in Ramesh Lal's fortune and activities. At some point in the 1940's he asked the District Magistrate to confer the office of mukhiya on his brother, Chander, as he could no longer cope with the duties it entailed. Then Chander died. A man unrelated to Panditji was appointed as mukhiya until India gained independence and the first elections, when the Panchayat became an elected body with a pradhan (head man) elected as its president. During this same time period, there were reverses in Ramesh's fortunes and he was left with no store of gold in his secret place. All of these changes seem to have relieved rather than disturbed him. During the day he could be found in his young mango orchard where he could read without interruption and, at the same time, keep birds from eating the fruit. In the evening he sat as he always had on the same charpai on his triangular platform. There he continued his reading unless called on for personal advice or asked to tell more about his pilgrimage. His back was as straight as it had been when he was young and proud. His poise was unaltered, and he was greeted by villagers with respect even deeper than before.

When I finally returned in 1961, Ramesh was the first to call. As he walked from the door to a charpai, I noticed that he was limping. He seemed to have lost some of his vigor, but certainly none of his dignity. He had come, not only to welcome me, but to tell me of the adventure that had disabled him. The story as he told it was mystifying and is still a mystery to me.

During the preceding January he had gone on a pilgrimage to Hardwar. January is the month of a special

Mela (religious celebration) and people come from very
long distances by train, by bus or on foot and remain for
days or weeks for daily worship and bathing in the Ganges.
A group of men from Karimpur and nearby villages hired a
whole bus for the trip to and from Hardwar. They arrived
in Hardwar in the thick of the Mela and at once became a
part of the driving, overwhelming, cheerful crowds. They
bathed along with thousands of others while other thousands waited their turn. They visited several temples
in which they worshiped and presented their offerings.
By evening they were exhausted. They bought fried unleav-
ened cakes from one of the many stalls, and all but Ramesh Lal ate theirs and lay down in one of the rest houses
built for the use of pilgrims and slept.

Instead of eating and sleeping, Ramesh Lal sat repeating "Ram, Ram." A sadhu passed by, and Panditji gave
him cakes. Then Panditji fell asleep. Some time during
the night, the mendicant returned, advising Panditji to
visit other temples which he had missed during the day.
The city was quiet, and it seemed an appropriate time for
worship. He followed obediently. They walked through
several dimly lighted temples and then moved out of the
city into darkness. On all sides of Hardwar there is
dense forest: Panditji followed the mendicant into this
forest. As it grew denser, he was badly scratched by
thorns and he tripped over vines and rocks. Then, suddenly, his guide disappeared, leaving him alone. He was
distraught. He had heard enough tales of the wild beasts
of the forest to know its dangers.

As it grew light, he hurried toward what he thought
was Hardwar. He knew that his friends would be searching
for him, but he had lost all sense of direction. He had
twisted his knee during the night and it was painful, as
were his scratches and bruises; however, he stumbled on.
When he was growing desperate, he suddenly came on a
small temple with a priest sitting in the doorway. The
priest told him that he was to remain there. He was too
tired and in too much pain to argue, and stayed. He

spent three days at the temple without food or care.
Here at least he was near another human being.

Then the mendicant reappeared as mysteriously as he
had vanished. He addressed Panditji, "Now is your opportunity to leave the world entirely and give yourself to
worship and meditation. If you still feel bound to your
family and friends, you should return to them; but I advise you to let them go." Panditji explained that he
could not desert his people at this time when they must
be greatly distressed on his account. He could leave
them later when they were prepared for his renunciation.
The mendicant said, "Very well. If this is your choice,
follow me." Again Panditji followed in a daze of hunger
and pain. Finally they arrived in Hardwar where his
guide led him to the railway station and remarked, "Now,
go to your home." "But I have no money for fare," pro-
tested Panditji. "There are three rupees and some coins
tied in the end of your dhoti," said the mendicant.
Panditji found the money, the exact amount stated. He
had no recollection of how much he had had when he entered the forest. Said the sadhu, "This will be enough to
get you to Aligarh. From there you can take care of
yourself." Again he vanished into the crowd. Panditji
boarded the first train.

When the ticket collector came to his compartment,
Panditji explained his plight. The ticket collector
counted out his money and found it to be the right amount
for fare to Aligarh. It is quite a long journey and he
was still without food or care. His usually immaculate
clothes were torn and he was dirty. At Aligarh, he found
his way to the Grand Trunk Road: a truck came by, and he
called to the driver who stopped and listened to the
story. In spite of his condition, the driver believed
him and brought him as far as Etah, about thirty miles
from Karimpur. When he left the truck and stood wonder-
ing what to do next, a bus came by. The driver was the
man they had hired for the Hardwar journey. He recognized Panditji at once, and of course knew of his

disappearance. He was not coming toward Karimpur, but he advanced the necessary bus fare.

Meanwhile, Panditji's sons, his wife, his grandchildren and most of the villagers were watching for his return. Panditain wept day and night. The men with him had searched every temple and bathing spot where he might be, but finally gave up and returned home. Fortunately, Panditji arrived just as his second son was setting out for Hardwar to follow his journey, step by step. Panditji could scarcely walk. At home he received every possible care. His family and the village rejoiced, and he was satisfied that he had made the right choice in returning. He could worship as well on his wide platform or in his courtyard beside the sacred tulsi plant as in a remote temple. He might retire to an ashram some day, but not now.

I cannot explain this tale. It had happened, that was clear. Later, as I revisited lanes and homes, I heard no word of skepticism when the story was mentioned. The people of the village had accepted it with open minds and regarded Panditji with even greater reverence than before. He had resumed his evening reading, and occasionally he went to villages nearby for a kirtan or a katha, though he had become quite weak. When he stopped to greet me in passing, he seemed to take pride in the fact that people still called on him rather than on a younger priest. He was too humble to realize that his presence had become a benediction which all sought.

All that time it was customary for men and women of the village to gather for a religious ceremony when it was deemed wise to placate one or more gods or goddesses. Anyone was free to attend and everyone was expected to contribute. This was not an annual affair, the date depended on circumstances rather than the Hindu calendar. Ordinarily it was conducted in the fall, but that year (1963), the panchayat voted to hold it in the spring. By so doing they would be providing urgently needed protection for their homes and fields, for they would be

petitioning that they be spared the disaster which was
expected to attend the imminent confluence of eight
planets. The ceremony was held in an open space beside
the district road, beneath a peepul tree shading stones
symbolizing the god Shiva. At one end was a low earth
platform for the officiating priests, who like the
observers, would be seated on the ground.

The panchayat asked Panditji to preside, assisted
by two babas. When the ceremony began he was there with
his Ramayan before him on its wooden stand, and a baba
on each side, all three prepared to read in turn. The
first purchase from the money contributed that year was
used for a complete outfit for Panditji. Although such
a gift is not exceptional Panditji was deeply touched.
Because it was to be a special occasion for him, he
chose to use my pump that morning for his ceremonial
bath. Then he put on the new white dhoti, shirt, and
cap, and limped over to the gathering. The whole of
the Ramayana was to be read without a break. The three
readers sat on a low platform with a hollow cement
square beside them for the sacred fire.

Panditji sat very straight and read with ease.
One of the babas was a husky young man of our village
and the other I did not recognize. While they read in
turn, ten young men of the village stood in a row near
them singing lustily while clanging cymbals and tongs
and beating oblong tambourines. They were replaced by
other performers every hour, as their contribution was
exhausting. Village men and women came and went when
they were free from other chores. The men came alone
or in groups; the women always in groups of four or
five. The ceremony was a time of relaxation and of
friendly visits during an hour or two, free from work.
With all this there was the assurance that they were
sharing in a ceremony that would safeguard them and
their families. As it grew dark and chilly many left.
The young village baba slept while the other baba read:
Panditji remained sitting upright with his coarse white

homespun cotton sheet wrapped around him.

The following day, after the reading and singing were finished, a crowd of boys led by one baba came trooping through the village. The baba carried a bucket of well water to which had been added Ganges water, some leaves of the tulsi plant, and buttermilk. This he doled out with a large spoon as he went from house to house. But Panditji was too weary to join in this final flourish, nor did he participate in any subsequent ceremony: his years of duty as pandit were over.

A few weeks later he had a stroke which left him helpless. His family called a doctor from Mainpuri twice, but he could only prescribe medicine that would bring slight relief. Panditji's wife and youngest daughter-in-law were beside him continually; his sons and nephews, his grandsons and grandnephews hovered near him; and his daughters came as often as possible from their husbands' homes. There was no lack of concern or affection. They gave him whatever herbs or treatment any relative or friend suggested; yet with only a ropestrung bed and a sheet, with a pile of torn quilts serving as pillows, they could do little to make him comfortable.

The attitude of his family toward him gradually deteriorated. Even Panditain, his wife, devoted to him as she was, began entertaining visitors in his presence by copying his almost incoherent speech and demonstrating how he called for his mother. She even mimicked his frantic, uncoordinated movements as he tried to scratch his arms where the scabies were worst. The ointment I brought required his soiled garments be removed and boiled and that he be bathed before it was applied. The women of the family thought it a good idea, but both steps would be difficult.

One afternoon when he had been more restless than usual, I asked if someone would read to him from his Ramayana. This seemed foolish and everyone in the courtyard laughed. He could not possibly understand what was read. However, his cheerful thirteen year old grandson brought

out the heavy volume, chose a page, and began to recite.
I had not realized that he could read such difficult
Hindi. At one point, he stumbled over a particularly
long word. Before he could go on, Panditji supplied the
word and went on to the next verse, repeating line after
line from memory. His voice was weak, but the words
were correct and clear enough to startle the whole circle.
From that day on someone read to him every afternoon.

The last months were a torment to him, both to his
frail, wasted body and to his spirit. Men who had pros-
pered, some of them with his help, shook their heads and
speculated as to what he must have done to merit such a
humiliating illness. Finally someone absolved him by
recalling the disgraceful conduct of a brother of his,
long dead. His suffering was expiated for his brother's
guilt. Everyone accepted this explanation gladly. Meanwhile Pandatji longed for death. When it finally came,
he and his whole family were relieved. From the moment
his funeral pyre was lighted, his long siege of helplessness was forgotten, and men spoke with affection and
reverence of his devotion to them and to the gods.

*   *   *

We saw little of Chander, Ramesh Lal's younger
brother, during our earlier years in the village. He
had no advisory or priestly functions but handled the
farming and the practical affairs of the family in order
to free his brother for his duties as mukhiya and Pandit.
It was Chander who assigned tasks day by day to the men
who worked under him. Some of them had succeeded their
fathers as retainers of Panditji's family, while others
were hired by the day during busy seasons. Chander worked beside them as they moved together from plot to plot,
ploughing, sowing, cultivating, irrigating and finally
harvesting. They raised the ordinary crops--wheat, barley, maize, millet and sorghum, several varities of legumes, sugar cane, cotton, peanuts and rice, mustard and
a small garden of vegetables. At harvest time, when

grain was threshed and winnowed, Chander turned over to
the women to dry and store the grain he estimated the
family would consume before the next harvest. The rest,
the portion intended for sale, he and his helpers stored,
protecting it as well as they could from rats and weevils.
Because he was equipped with a granary, larger and better
than those of most farmers, Chander was able to hold back
their grain while he waited for prices to rise. When the
market seemed favorable, he undertook cautious bargaining
with wholesale dealers. When the sale of grain was completed, Chander turned all cash received over to Panditji.

When he discovered that Panditji had loaned money to
some less fortunate villager, Chander took it upon himself
to see that the money was returned, with interest. He
felt justified in doing this to safegaurd the future of
the family, even though it gave him the reputation of being a hard man. Now, a generation later, members of the
family say that had he taken over all financial dealings
they would still be comparatively prosperous. At the
same time, poorer villagers continue to express gratitude
for Panditji's generosity.

Twice, to the best of our knowledge, Chander inter-
rupted his farming to make arrangements for weddings in
the family. Panditji participated in the long ceremonies,
but he left all negotiations with the bridegroom's party
and their entertainment in Chander's hands. We attended
the first wedding and were able to watch him in the role
of Uncle-of-the-Bride, the bride being Panditji's youngest daughter. In this role, he was at a disadvantage.
He was the host and master of ceremonies, whose duty was
to arrange for the comfort and pleasure of the bridegroom's party of 100 men for almost three days. They,
as wedding guests, were free to be rude to him. It was
their privilege. Chander struggled beforehand and during the days and nights of ceremonies to make sure that
every detail was so well handled that there would be no
room for criticism. He assigned duties to every man and
woman of the family as well as to relatives who had come

to assist. So busy were they with cooking and preparations for entertainment that they had very little share
in the ceremonies. When, in spite of this, the guests
scorned the food, the entertainment and the gifts offered, he became more and more irritated. It hurt his
pride; and we discovered how extremely proud he was, not
only as a Brahmin but of his standing and that of his
brother in the village. As the ceremonies and feasts
went on, the situation had become so acrimonious that we
wondered how the bride's in-laws might treat her when
she arrived in their home. Chander made an effort to
control his anger while his frightened niece was lifted
into the special wedding cart that would carry her to
her husband's home. But when the long line of carts
filled with wedding guests disappeared in the dust of
the district road, he exploded. From that moment on, he
refused to mention his joint in-laws. Three days later
he sent the bride's brother to bring her home, as is
customary. When she arrived, she was still frightened
and nervous, but to our relief she was pleased with the
kindness shown by her mother-in-law and sisters-in-law.
The men of the husband's family had paid no attention to
her. They had succeeded in embarrassing her uncle: that
was all that counted. As for Chander, he had staged a
wedding worthy of his and Panditji's position and their
fellow villagers had been impressed. The bridegroom's
family lived in a distant village and need not be seen
again except for the one man of the family who would
come later to take Panditji's daughter to his home to
live. Fortunately, his visit would, of necessity, be
brief and formal.

A few years later, when Chander's elder son, Raju,
was to be married, the story was quite different. Chander was now in the enviable position of Father-of-the-
Groom. He went into the wedding with enthusiasm and
with obvious intent to compensate for the way he had
been insulted during the wedding of his niece. Any village with a daughter to be married expects some form of

humiliation. But none I have known has received treatment such as Chander and Panditji subjected Raju's
bride's family to. Both brothers seemed to make a game
of finding ways to embarrass the emissaries who came from
her home during the preliminaries, and men who went
from here with Chander and Panditji in the wedding party
described it as highly amusing when telling about it
afterwards. Years later I heard the story from Chander's
daughter-in-law who was the unfortunate bride. She is
able to laugh about it now that she is well established
in her husband's home as the mother of two sons. Here
is the story, from the bride's point of view:

> My father was a farmer, and we were highly
> respected in our village as Brahmins. But
> we were poor, very poor compared with my
> father-in-law. He and Panditji were pros-
> perous then. My father gave them all that
> he could at the lagan ceremony when our
> marriage was contracted. Yet they com-
> plained that it was too little. A short
> time before the wedding, my father sent a
> message to my prospective father-in-law to
> say that he could entertain one hundred
> wedding guests. He did not have provision
> for more. Perhaps this was a mistake.
>
> Anyhow, on the day they were to arrive, we
> had a boy out on the main road to give us
> warning. He came running to our house to
> tell us that there were at least one hun-
> dred carts, with four or five men in each
> one. My father and mother were in a panic.
> While my father went out to greet the guests,
> my two uncles rushed through the village
> begging people to loan them grain and call-
> ing on the women of kahar caste to come
> quickly to help clean the grain and grind
> flour. They begged ghee for frying cakes
> from others and sent someone to the nearest
> town for more sweets. We had kaf plates
> and clay cups ready for all the meals we
> had expected to give, but we had to use
> them all for the first meal. My father
> quickly sent someone to the Potters and
> Platemakers to get more ready. It was a
> terrible time for all of us, especially
> for my parents.
>
> When I came here to live, I heard that
> after my father-in-law had invited the
> hundred guests he had intended to invite,

he sent out word to others of their caste
that they could share in the joke. Anyone
who had an ox-cart or could borrow one was
welcome to join the wedding party. It was
the season when the oxen were not needed
for field work, so many joined them.
Everyone enjoys being part of a wedding
party. He had promised the extra ones who
came at least one good feast and plenty of
fodder for their animals, all to be provided from my family. They could return home
on the following morning. It was about a
ten mile ride.

They had to wait until midnight for their
feast, but they were entertained with music
and dancing for which my father went into
debt. They laughed over the disturbance
they created. They all laughed even more
when my father bowed nearly to the ground
before Panditji and my father-in-law, begging them to keep only one hundred guests
with them for the remaining days. He did
not know this had already been planned.
Their joke was a success.

But more trouble followed. After midnight,
when they had feasted well and their oxen
fed, they finally came to the doorway of
my home for the door ceremony. My brothers
had arranged the brass water jars and brass
trays and utensils, part of my dowry, in
two neat towers, one on each side of the
wide door. They had also collected sheets
and mats from neighbors so that all the
wedding guests could be seated in front of
the door. The men of our village crowded
behind them. It was back in the darkness
of the room inside the door with my mother
and the other women. The bridegroom came
forward and sat in front of the priest who
waited in the doorway. Before the ceremony
could begin, my father-in-law stepped up;
with his long staff, he swung at the pile
of brass vessels on one side and then on
the other, sending them scattering with a
terrible crash. Then he shouted at my
father and uncles, asking them if this was
all they expected to give. Then he sat
down and waited. Everyone else sat and
waited. My poor father came rushing in to
us. He and my mother and brothers went
into the storerooms and brought out more
brass things. They had been kept there
in chests as part of our family treasure
and had not been taken out for years.

These my father offered in a humble attitude, although he was trembling with ner-
vousness and rage. My father-in-law acted
as though they might be acceptable. Then
the ceremony proceeded.

She knew little of what transpired after that. She
was kept with the women in the courtyard where cooking
was going on or seated in the wedding booth with her
young husband. She could only gather from discussions
around her that bitterness between her people and her
husband's people was seething. As a result, she was
thoroughly frightened when she arrived for her brief
visit in Chander's home after the wedding. Later when
she came to stay, she found her mother-in-law cheerful
and patient. They did not take advantage of her as newest daughter-in-law by giving her the heaviest or most
disagreeable tasks. They all worked as hard as she did.
However, she never recovered from her fear of Chander.
She discovered that the women around her, even the older
ones, were also nervous when he came into the courtyard.
He remained the strict overseer and disciplinarian.

The families of the two brothers shared one house
as long as Chander lived, with Chander carrying the burden of the farm work and financial dealings and Ramesh
Lal performing his duties as priest and mulchiya. The
wives of the brothers were congenial, and the children
took for granted that they would always live together.
The courtyard was not large, and part of it was occupied
by an open well so gradually it became uncomfortably
crowded. Storerooms that had once been adequate were
now overflowing with chests of clothing and containers
of food. So to alleviate the congestion the two branches
of the family separated. Panditji remained in the old
home and Chander's family took over part of the granary.
With the division of the family, the land was likewise
divided. Panditji and his three sons now had slightly
more than twelve acres, and Chander's two sons had the
same.

Not long after Chander's death, the family fortunes

rapidly declined. It was then that his brother, his
sons and his nephews realized how wise his stewardship
had been. Panditji had an ample store of silver and
gold hidden in walls or floors of his house and granary;
and like other prosperous villagers he feared attacks of
robber bands--dacoits. He considered tranferring some
of it to a bank, but again like others, he distrusted
the strangers in charge of an impersonal bank. When a
friend of long standing living in town offered to take
charge of his treasure, he was relieved and entrusted a
large amount to him. No papers were signed. When Panditji was in need of money, he went to his friend. The
latter denied having received anything from him. A few
years later, Panditji was persuaded to invest in a brick
kiln not far away. Brick kilns were prospering and this
one appeared to be a profitable venture, but either it
failed or the profits went into someone else's pocket.
Now, more than ever, they missed Chander's hardheaded,
decisive action. Comparatively little wealth remained,
and they were obliged to live more simply.

When I think of Panditain, I smile with pleasure.
Through years of prosperity and years of adversity and
sorrow, she never lost the roguish twinkle in her eyes.
There were times when the twinkle was discreetly veiled;
but it was still there, to reappear as soon as the disturbance had passed. She was the first woman of Karimpur to accept me as a normal person. She must have
thought me strange in the early days, just as others
did; but she quickly discovered that as wives and as
mothers of sons, we had much in common. It was hard to
believe that she had rarely been outside her door. During our first five years in the village she became, and
has remained, one of my best friends. It was I who gave
her the title of Panditain. She was known as "Mother of
Suresh." A husband's name is not used by his wife, nor
is his name associated with hers when someone speaks of
her. I never heard her referred to as Ramesh Lal's wife,
nor had anyone in Karimpur heard her own name, for only

in her home village was it used. She was always "Mother
of Suresh," This seemed a cumbersome name for so small
a person. At first the new title, "Panditain," amused
her and her family, but gradually it was accepted by
everyone.

Her parents were Brahmins of Jampur, a village almost thirty miles away. Two wives of Prakash's family
and the wife of Panditji's next-door neighbor had previously come to Karimpur as brides from Jampur. Since
Panditain's marriage there has been a succession of
brides from there to the Brahmin community of Karimpur.
When Panditain came here as a bride, she was still a
girl, just turned thirteen. When she left home and came
here to stay, she found herself in a household of strangers. She was no longer a child and no longer Rani, be-
loved daughter of her father. She did what she was told
to do by her strict mother-in-law. Often when she performed some task as her mother had taught her, she was
scolded and shown how it must be done in this courtyard.
She was expected to work throughout the day, with no
time to play and no one to play with.

There were moments of kindness on the part of her
husband's mother or father, but their chief concern was
her behavior. She must remember at all times that she
was the newest daughter-in-law of a proud and prosperous
Chaube Brahmin family. There were other women in the
courtyard, some still in their teens; others were almost
as old as her mother-in-law. They were her husband's
sisters or wives of his paternal uncles. He was eldest
son and she was the wife of this eldest son which demanded that her conduct be above reproach. There were
times when she wept bitterly, but quietly, her face
hidden by her head scarf while she struggled with the
heaving grinding stone or scoured greasy brass utensils
in a corner of the courtyard.

She was not allowed to leave the courtyard. When
the other women of the family went in the mornings, each
with a lota filled with water, to a field near the

12. Panditain

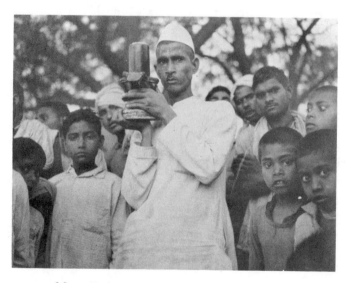

13. Indar at the temple opening

village which served as their toilet, she had to remain
at home. A crude latrine had been devised for her in a
corner of the courtyard, protected by a low wall. It was
cleaned daily by a sweeper woman. The one thought that
made life endurable was that she had been promised a trip
to Jampur to visit her people after she had been here for
several months. When the time finally arrived and her
uncle came to call for her, she tried to hide her excitement, but once she was safely in his ox-cart, she laughed
and cried during most of the long journey.

At home she was free again, pampered by her parents
and her brothers and sisters more than ever before. She
heard her own name, Rani, again. Her brothers' wives
watched her enviously. She was having her turn at sitting
idle, free to talk or to run out into the village lane.
She was given all the foods that she liked most. Her
mother questioned her anxiously about her life with her
in-laws, especially about the treatment she received from
her mother-in-law. Although her mother had just repri-
manded her own newest daughter-in-law for her awkwardness
in the shaping of flat wheat cakes, she expressed sympathy
for Rani when told of the scoldings she had received.
She did not at all approve of the mother-in-law's way of
preparing a particular gram dish, and she was shocked at
the combination of spices used by the mother-in-law in
bhujia, made of cabbage and potato. She was sure that
her daughter looked undernourished, especially when she
heard how little milk the child had. In a home as
prosperous as that one, there must be plenty.

Rani visited her friends, went out to the fields,
reclined on a charpai when she pleased. She wanted each
day to last forever, but her visit was soon over and her
husband's brother was there at the door with his ox-cart.
Her father persuaded him to rest with them for a day.
This gave her one more precious day and night at home.
But her departure could not be put off longer, and she
was on her tearful way. Her brother-in-law sat stiffly
at the front of the cart and she at the back, with large

jars of fried cakes and sweets and baskets of gifts for
her in-laws, between them. This time she knew just what
to expect on arrival, and under the mantle that covered
her completely she wept most of the way.

During those early years, she rarely saw her husband. No matter what she was doing when he came into
the courtyard, she quickly drew her head covering down
to hide her face. She did the same when any man of the
family older than herself entered. She could count on
her husband's coming in for his meals, but he seemed
more concerned with his ritual of bathing beside the
courtyard well and reading from one of his books and
counting his beads before eating than in communicating
with her. His mother or an aunt or one of the sisters
served him his food.

They were both carefully chaperoned and had no opportunity to meet until their elders decided that they
were old enough to have children. Then she was allowed
to place his tray of food before him, and she could give
him more food as he desired. It was while he was eating
his evening meal that he formed the habit of speaking to
her. At first he simply spoke to tell her that they
would meet that night and to designate where she should
be waiting. They met thus, seldom, and for only a short
time after dark in one of the storerooms or on the roof.
Then he would slip away to take his place among the men
of the family. After her first terror over these clandestine meetings, she looked forward to being with him
alone. It gave meaning to her presence here. She was
no longer a daughter-in-law, now she was a wife. Neither
at this time nor during the many years of their marriage
did she ever address her husband as Ramesh or Ramesh
Lal. She might refer to him as Panditji, but she could
never address him in that way.

When her first child was to be born, she was allowed to go home where her mother and the family midwife
could care for her. When her baby arrived, her hopes as
a wife were realized: she had a son. He would be the

the eldest son of the eldest son of the eldest son. As
soon as he was able to travel, she was prepared to take
him to his people without the dread she had known on
earlier returns. From then on, Ramesh's family recognized her in her new role as mother of the son they
wanted to carry on the family line and the priesthood.
Life became easier and less rigid for her.

By the time I met her, she was head of her courtyard.
Her mother-in-law had died, as had her aunts-in-law;
and her husband's sisters had long since been married
and were settled in the homes of their in-laws. Ramesh
Lal had only the one brother living, Chander. Chander's
wife looked up to Panditain as senior daughter-in-law,
and Panditain had become accustomed to her position and
the duties that were hers. She sometimes expressed the
hope that she could do as well for her own daughters-in-
law as her mother-in-law had done for her. Her husband
was free to talk with her now, but he rarely did except
to discuss special family needs for clothing or food. He
took for granted that she and Chander's wife would care
for the grain and pulses reserved for family consumption,
and he expected meals to be well prepared and ready whenever he or his brother or sons came into the courtyard
to eat.

She worked long hours to meet the demands of the men
of the family and the quite different demands of the
children. Food, whether to be processed and stored as
it came from the fields or to be cooked for each meal,
occupied the time of both women. They were spared the
burden of planning clothes for the family. Chander or
Panditji bought all material when on grain-selling trips
to the Mainpuri bazaar, and they turned it over to a village Tailor who did the fitting and the sewing. Once
each fortnight Panditain and her sister-in-law hurriedly
collected all soiled clothing which the children or men
had cast off and handed them to the Washerman's wife.
When she returned the clothes, unironed, a week later,
they stacked them on a chest in a storeroom where anyone

could pull out what he or she needed or wanted.

A kaharin, of serving caste, came to help when work was particularly heavy, as after each harvest. Her husband and two sons helped Chander in the fields, receiving their noonday meal as part of their pay. She received food after the others had been served on days when she was working. Once a year she was given a new skirt and blouse. Her help was invaluable to Panditain. She remained a faithful servant over the years, growing old along with her mistress. Now, with barely enough food for those in Panditji's household, she no longer serves but comes frequently to visit. When she comes, she spends her time massaging Panditain's arms and legs. This she once did when Panditain's body ached from heavy work, but now they are the aches and pains of age.

In spite of all her responsibility and work, Panditain was radiantly happy. She was no longer a submissive daughter-in-law, but mistress of her home, fulfilling her destiny as a wife and mother of sons. For several years her children were around her. Then her daughters were married and left home, one by one, before they were old enough to do much of the work of the courtyard or to be companionable. She saw little of Panditji, but knew that he was more dependent on her than he himself realized. Her sons left the courtyard and moved into the men's world as they reached their teens. They remained in the village and depended on her in many ways. I had taken for granted that the five boys growing up under her wing were her sons. She, as head of the courtyard, treated them as hers; and they regarded themselves as her children and as brothers. It was not until they were married and grown that I was able to sort them out: three were Panditji's sons and two were Chander's.

Despite problems and seclusion, the women found enjoyment in traditional ways. When Panditain first invited me to a dancing party in her courtyard, I wondered what kind of dancing there could be with a group of Brahmin women, most of them old or quite young--women

old enough to walk out of their doors and through the
lanes and daughters of the village not yet married or
married and home on a visit. The evening began like any
singing party, everyone sitting on the ground around the
one who was to play the harmonium. The older women huddled together in a group at one side where they could
gossip between and during the songs. The younger women
formed their own group and provided most of the music.
When someone felt the urge to dance, she stood up and
announced the song she wanted as her accompaniment; and
while she danced, the others sang. Nowadays, before
beginning to dance, a woman tucks the end of her dhoti
in at the waist to keep it out of the way. At that time
it was the long head scarf that had to be made secure.
The very full skirt then worn lent itself to the village
type of dancing very well. The person performing would
twirl her skirt and sway and wriggle her stomach and hips
as she had seen a professional dancer do at some wedding.
That was all, repeated again and again with pauses in
between, while the performer got her breath or finished
her dance and joined in the song. Then to my surprise,
several of the older ones, in turn, stepped into the open
circle and caricatured them. They were less self-conscious than their daughters and less inhibited. It was
the kind of fun in which everyone could share. Panditain
enjoyed these occasions, often being the one to start a
song, others joining in the chorus. She knew a good many,
some remembered from her childhood, others learned while
she sat in the background as a listener in her mother-in-
laws courtyard. The women sitting nearest to her kept
prodding her, urging her to dance. Finally when a love
song called for dramatizing, she stood up and turned herself into a parody of a lovesick young man. She drew up
her full skirt, tucked it in at the waist so that it resembled a man's dhoti and wound her scarf around her head
like a loosely bound turban. Then she took the hand of
one of the women in the group, pulled her up, and danced
and strutted around her. When another song followed, she

made herself into a town dandy like one she had seen in
her home village. With skirt drawn up tighter so that
it was more like trousers and with a cap on her head and
a stick as a cane, she was a clown. In the first dance
her partner had been startled and awkward, but Panditain's
gaiety infected her until she forgot herself in playing
her part. In the second dance she chose a cousin-in-law
equally good at acting. Their performance was hilarious.

It was during the period when her children were ad-
justing to life away from her that Panditain met her
first serious disappointment. Her eldest son had shown
a weakness for gambling even before he left the courtyard. Once outside, he wasted time and money on it and
added other misdemeanors that distressed her and Panditji. He who was to have been their pride was their misery. When they arranged his marriage to a girl belonging to a family of high standing, both parents hoped he
would settle down and prepare to succeed his father or
work on the land. He did neither. The girl, his wife,
had several miscarriages after coming to live here and
was weak and ailing most of the time. She became more
defiant and her voice grew harsh. Both she and Suresh
presented burdens and heartaches instead of the support
that parents count on from an eldest son and his wife.

A few years after Suresh's failure as their first-
born son, Panditain was again faced with disappointment.
Their second son was as gratifying in his ability and
his behavior as the eldest had been disheartening. When
Panditain heard of the marriage Panditji planned for
him, she was delighted. Not only was the family of the
girl of good social and economic standing, but she herself was to inherit property from a widowed aunt. However, instead of being an asset, the land proved to be
a detriment by cutting through the family ties. The
new daughter-in-law, a girl of fifteen, was more concerned with her land than with her obligations to her
husband's family. Before she had been here a year, she
was called to her home to claim her extensive property,

and her husband was invited to come to administer it. Panditji could not deny his son such an opportunity; moreover, the girl's home was in a small village only three miles away and the land might eventually belong to his, Panditji's family. For Panditain it meant the loss of both a promising son and a bahu.

The marriage of their youngest son, Shiv Lal, brought them a different type of bahu. She came with a modest dowry from a respectable family of Brahmin farmers in a distant village. She had learned to cook and help with whatever work was to be done, no matter how heavy. Best of all, she proved to be Panditain's mainstay. She was a plump, good-natured girl who was an antidote to the high-strung difficult senior bahu and a comfort after the departure of the second bahu. Control of the court-yard seemed to have passed from Panditain to the senior daughter-in-law. Yet it was still Panditain's courtyard, the only home she had. She had long since abandoned visits to her own old home, now in the keeping of women who were strangers to her, her brother's wives. Without this youngest bahu, her life would have been unbearable. Finally Shiv Lal found it impossible to come into the courtyard for his meals. The only escape was to build a house of his own. This he did and as soon as possible, he installed his mother and his wife and two children in it.

During the years known as "the Householder" period in the life of a Hindu, when Panditji and Panditain had become joint heads of the family, they were free to dis-cuss problems related to their children, clothing, or household affairs without a crowd of listeners. When Panditain reminisces, she expresses no regret over the infrequency of these husband-wife discussions. They embarrassed her, partly because she was not accustomed to talking to a man and because when she did talk with him she felt obliged to keep her face covered or care-fully averted. In their early years as husband and wife when they were together, it was as lovers. They

were young, free from all responsibility, romantic,
and spared from possible disagreements. Now, as heads
of the family they were older and more burdened. Each
accepted the judgment of the other. So why raise questions? She could see him every day and serve him his
meals or direct her bahu to serve him when he came into
the courtyard. This was sufficient. He never commented
on the food and ate whatever they placed before him. He
seemed absorbed in affairs outside of her world. She
knew that he shared his serious problems with Chander
or with a close friend while she could share hers with
Chander's wife or her favorite niece, Premi.

Then his illness made it difficult for him to artic-
ulate and his voice was weak, he preferred to express
his needs to one of his sons who might come in to visit
or one of his daughters who had come home for a fortnight
and was free to sit beside him. This relieved Panditain
of the strain of trying to understand him or of asking
him to repeat, for he quickly grew impatient with her.
Again, she did not feel rejected: it was her destiny.
He was her husband and she must always respect his desires, but as months passed and he could no longer speak,
the strain wearied her and she became less in awe of him.

Even though everyone knew that Panditji longed for
death to release him from his helplessness and suffering,
his own family, as well as every family in the village,
grieved when he died. Panditain, above all others, had
shared his longing to be released, but when the final
hour came and he was lifted from his charpai to the
ground so that he might die in the arms of Mother Earth,
she was overwhelmed by a loneliness she had never known
before. She was no longer a wife, but a widow.

Her sons met the men who came to the outer room to
express their sorrow at Panditji's death and the women
came flocking into the courtyard to mourn with her, each
one in turn patting her shoulder, urging her to be calm
while expecting her to weep the more. She was exhausted
from the months of nursing and from the effort of enter-

taining and feeding the relatives and others who came to
spend time watching and sympathizing with Panditji.

As soon as she was physically able to leave the
courtyard and visitations were fewer, she knew that she
must perform the painful duties attendant on the death
of one's husband. With her niece, Premi, she walked to
what is known as "the ceremonial pond," about a mile from
the village. Sitting on its banks, she removed her toe
rings and then broke her glass bangles and threw them
into the water. Toe rings indicate that the wearer is
married. Colored bangles may be worn by any girl or woman as long as her husband is living, but when he dies,
she must give them up. Not long after this ceremony,
Panditain's eldest living son presented her with a pair
of silver bracelets, for a widow may wear only two silver
or gold bracelets. The next step was difficult and more
tiring. She and Premi went to Fatehgarh, a city forty
miles away on the bank of the Ganges. Under the direction of a family priest there, Panditain first bathed in
the river, then bathed a second time wearing the new
dhoti given by her brother for this particular ceremony.
When she came out of the water, she draped herself in
one of her old, worn dhotis while removing the wet one.
The priest indicated a waiting untouchable woman to whom
she was to give the ceremonial dhoti. With the passing
of the dhoti from her hands to those of the untouchable,
the ritual ended. After paying the priest, she was free
to return home.

During the years following Panditji's death, she
spent most of her time on her charpai, small, frail and
aged in body, while youthful and brisk in spirit. She
still held court, almost as Panditji once had, but with
a difference. He guided and directed; she entertained.
There were days when she complained of her many ailments,
and those were the days when she wept and expressed her
longing to die. With Panditji gone and her children
grown, life for her was without purpose. Her eyes grew
dim and she could not hear unless the speaker was close

beside her. Her spells of dizziness increased during
her last years. With the aid of a cane, she continued
to visit her grandnieces and nephews and her grandchildren and great grandchildren across the lane, and when
they came to visit her and clamored for her monkey face
act, she became as gay as they. If they were too demanding, she drove them out, saying that they should
work off their energy in games and that she needed rest.
Rest to her meant no noisy children and no neighbors or
relatives waiting to be entertained. It was in these
intervals of calm while she was quiet and in repose that
her face revealed qualities that I have come to associ-
ate with village women like her. In her eyes and her
whole expression there is intelligence bordering on
sharp perception; and there is merriment too. The deep
furrows and lines on her forehead have been left by
times of anxiety, annoyance, and questioning or doubt.
There is a determination in the set of her chin, and the
wrinkles around her mouth might be those of resignation
or secretiveness or both. On her cheeks and temples the
lines of grief crisscross with others that could have
come only from laughter. Her whole attitude was one of
acceptance, acceptance of the good as well as the bad
that has come to her. It included acceptance of the
pleasant courtyard which was her own, the affectionate
concern of her youngest son and daughter-in-law, and
best of all her position of dignity which is never
questioned even though she possesses neither money nor
worldly goods.

During her long pilgrimage with Panditji she saw
more of people and places of the outside world than have
other women of her age. But that was long ago and since
then she rarely went beyond her own small circle. She
was never taught to read or write, and she had heard
little about women whose lives were different from hers.
Whatever knowledge she had was acquired from experience.
Her wisdom came unaided from her own inner resources.

Then the time came when she was too weak and too

prone to dizziness to leave her charpai. Her body seemed
to shrink and looked as frail as a small child's. She
was over ninety when she died during the winter rains
of 1970. It was the coldest, most desolate season of
the year, disastrous for the very old and the very young,
and wretched for everyone. For Panditain, it was the
first winter rainy season in many years when she was not
in misery.

The Second Generation

When we came to Karimpur in 1925, Panditji's eldest
son, Suresh, was about sixteen. The family had taken for
granted that he would follow his father's profession as
priest, but apparently no effort had been made to provide
him with training comparable to Panditji's. As for discipline, he learned early how to escape it. His grandfather was head of the household at that time and in a
position to pass judgment on any dispute within the family, and Suresh was his grandfather's favorite. If either of his parents dared to punish or even admonish him,
he knew that he could go to his grandfather for sympathy.
Suresh disliked school and left it early. He rebelled
against work in the fields. If anyone happened to be
going to town or to a fair by ox-cart, he was free to
go along. He had money to spend, either begged from his
grandfather or collected from the sale of grain. He began playing cards with a group of village men, older and
more experienced than himself. Soon his playing developed into gambling. He was an easy victim of old-timers
for he seemed unable to learn their tricks. Those who
remember Suresh as a youth report that it was his grandfather who encouraged him in his gambling.

By the time his grandfather died, Suresh was a con-
firmed gambler, but still not a winner. The more he lost,
the more desperate he became for money. When cash was
not forthcoming at home, he tried to borrow from neighbors. When he could not repay them, they collected from
his father. Soon he began carrying off large quantities

of wheat from the family granary. When this was discovered, the battle between father and son began. Panditji threatened, then beat Suresh. Thrice after such
punishment Suresh ran away, only to return when his money
was gone. Panditji tried sending the boy to relatives
with sons of Suresh's age with whom he might work and
who were not inclined to gamble. This helped, but only
temporarily. Suresh found his cousins congenial until
they expected him to share their work in the fields.
When he sat in the shade of a tree while they worked in
the hot sun, he was no longer welcome and was sent home.

Like other village weddings in prosperous families
Suresh's was elaborate. In addition to the feasting and
entertainment, the bride's parents gave a dowry that
even Chander could not criticize. Suresh apparently regarded her as a new diversion. She did not complain,
but suffered from his over-attention. Finally Panditain
begged me to take her to a doctor for advice. She had
had a series of miscarriages and was ailing most of the
time. I went with her to an experienced woman doctor
who was staying with friends in Mainpuri. The doctor's
diagnosis was, "to much husband." Her advice was, "as
soon as she becomes pregnant again, remove her to her
own home and keep her there until the child is born."
This the family agreed to do.

The baby, a son, was born, and there were no more
miscarriages. She had babies instead. She lost three
in infancy and had nine more children, all still living.
Her husband's persistent demands and the strain of bearing children in too rapid succession may explain her
change from a pleasant attractive girl to a bitter, worn
woman. Her features became sharper and her expression
grew hard: her hair was uncombed and her clothing soiled
and all but one of her teeth missing. When Suresh died
before he was forty, he left an embittered wife and nine
children whom he had neglected and parents who mourned
the loss of the their eldest son even while relieved of
the unremitting fear of some new disgrace. When Suresh's

wife finally died, one daughter had been married and had
gone to her in-laws. Two of her sons were married and
their wives had joined the household. In their mother's
place there were two bahus to look after the younger
children still at home. I heard no expression of regret
in the household beyond that imposed by tradition over
the death of the mother. Her hatred of Suresh and his
family and the violent expression of her bitterness had
estranged them.

*   *   *

Ishwar Das, Panditji's second son, received none of
the favors showered on his elder brother. By the time
he was twelve he was helping with chores under Chander's
supervision along with Chander's eldest son. He attrac-
ted little attention until it became known that his wife
was to inherit property. When the aunt died and the girl
became legal owner, Ishwar became official administrator.
Panditji had already divided his property. One half,
twelve and a half acres, went to Chander's two sons and
the other half to his own three sons. Ishwar's third
mounted to very little while his wife's acreage was
large. Living with a wife's family is regarded as a
step down for a husband, a step which is seldom taken.
He became an important and respected man in his wife's
village, but his parents felt abandoned and humiliated.

*   *   *

As a child, Shiv Lal, the youngest of Panditji's
sons, was overshadowed by his two brothers. He was given
the least encouragement and his training was negligible.
Even now he attracts little attention from relatives.
He is a farmer and aspires to be nothing more. At the
same time, he has proved the most steadfast of the three
sons. It was a relief to Panditji and Panditain to have
one son without ambition and with a firm arm on which
they could lean. Ashamed of their eldest son and torn
between pride and disappointment in their second, they

found comfort in Shiv Lal, free from emotional strain. The village was surprised that it was he who quietly took the initiative in planning and building the new home for his parents and his own family, and respect for him went up. He continued to defer to Panditji in all important decisions, but the house and land became known as his.

When I first knew Shiv's wife, she was still in the old family courtyard, always busy on the small verandah reserved for Panditain and herself or in the storeroom behind it. She stored the grain and pulse reserved for Panditji and Panditain and cooked their food, sometimes aided by Panditain. She served Panditji and Panditain as well as her busband and children as a faithful daughter-in-law. All around her was fighting and suspicion, but she worked quietly on, avoiding any entanglement with Suresh's wife: it is difficult to quarrel with a person who remains unruffled. Except to cross the courtyard to the well, she remained in her own corner, busy and silent.

It was only after the family was established in their new home that she felt free to move about the house and to speak without restraint. Slowly, as Panditain grew frailer, equal only to the slightest tasks, Shiv's wife became actual head of the courtyard. When Panditji became ill and helpless, most of the burden of his care was left to her. After Panditji's death, she and Shiv Lal were finally able to settle down to a quiet, routine life with their two sons and Panditain. Their only daughter had been married and was living far away, but her in-laws were kind enough to give her leave to return home for fairly long visits. Here she is her mother's companion and helper.

Following the wedding of Shiv's eldest son the women met the new daugher-in-law and were charmed with her. Six months later they called her here to stay as she was needed to help Shiv's wife who had just had a baby son, a happy surprise after years with no small child in the

house. A year after the bahu joined them, she too had a
baby son. From being a minor branch of Panditji's family
they now had their own extended family with Shiv as final
authority and his wife as undisputed head of the courtyard. Life had become easier and pleasanter, until,
without warning, tragedy came. Her chubby two year old
son died after a brief illness. For weeks she was in-
consolable and could think or speak of nothing else but
her grief. But her good nature and grandchildren eventually took over. Even without Panditain, the house is
a cheerful place to visit.

*   *   *

Across the lane from Shiv's house, the two sons of
Panditji's brother, Chander, live with their families.
Raju, elder of the two resembles his cousin-brother,
Ishwar with one striking difference: the air of pride
characteristic of Ishwar becomes arrogance in Raju. He
is the one member of Panditji's family who might be called a snob. His chosen profession was that of Pandit;
however, he did not limit himself to reading aloud from
the sacred books as Panditji did. He gave lectures based
on them. His clientele was different from Panditji's,
being more sophisticated and more widely scattered in
larger towns and cities. He gave me a demonstration of
his method one day in my courtyard, selecting two lines
from the Ramayana which depicted Rama wandering through
the forest in exile. Rama walked first and behind him
came Sita, his devoted wife. Lakshman, Rama's faithful
brother, came last. Rama represents God, Sita represents the world--worldliness, and Lakshman, man. Man's
weakness lies in his following after worldliness which
separates him from God. On this theme he was able to
speak for over an hour. His engagements were usually
for one or two weeks during which he gave a lecture every
evening. He wrote his lectures out by hand, word by word,
in a score of copy books like those used in the local
school. His script was beautiful and he illuminated a

184

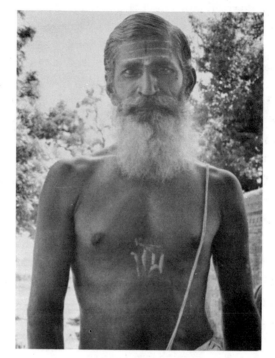

14. Raju

15. Ganesh and friend

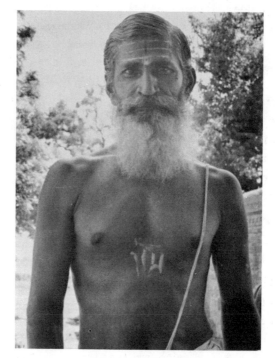

14. Raju

15. Ganesh and friend

number of the pages. It made an impressive collection.

He has always been scornful of his fellow villagers and the exuberance with which they observe holidays, believing that they have replaced authentic origins with popular legends. He contends that the way in which they celebrate Holi, with a large bonfire and the throwing of quantitites of colored dye on each other, is far removed from the real meaning of the holiday. To him it was originally a solemn occasion when men sought the blessing of the gods on the coming barley harvest. Barley is still a feature of the celebration although the religious significance of its place in the holiday is overshadowed by the riotous festivities.

Raju was even less concerned over his land and his family than Panditji; but with a difference. Panditji had an efficient administrator in his younger brother. Raju's younger brother could not be depended on for help of any kind as he was hardly able to manage his own land and his own family. Until Raju's eldest son was able to carry responsibility for their land, it was entrusted to hired men and sharecroppers: they kept more than their rightful share of each harvest, but Raju maintained that the income from his lectures compensated for the scant supply of produce. Yet all of the money that he earned was his to spend or withhold as he chose which kept his family in a constant state of uncertainty, and his wife found her position particularly difficult. For weeks she was responsible for the welfare of her children. Then without warning Raju would arrive and demand an accounting. She complained that when he was at home he handed her money at his pleasure and then ignored her. Except for the brief periods when she served him his food in the courtyard, he spent his time sitting on a charpai in the room reserved for him.

The Younger Generation

During Panditji's lifetime, the community took for granted that his family would provide a priestly successor. His father, Prem Chand, had served as priest to many families in the village and presided over the few ceremonies intended for the whole community. His duties demanded little of his time and he chose to devote his leisure to cards. Gambling not only provided him with entertainment, but also added property and money to his possessions. While thus engaged, he made sure that his eldest son, Ramesh Lal, was being prepared to succeed him. Ramesh accepted the assignment without question. His father did not encourage him to gamble, nor was he expected to work part-time in the fields as his brother, Chander, did. He was told to devote his days to his studies under Sanskrit scholars. When we met him, he had become a full-fledged pandit.

At that time he still hoped that his son, Suresh, would reform sufficiently to take his place. He was the logical successor. Suresh, however, rebelled, and Panditji was obliged to look to others in his family. His two younger sons, Ishwar, now living in his wife's village, and Shiv, satisfied with farming, were not interested. His eldest nephew, Raju, the lecturer, was well qualified, but his ambitions carried him far beyond our small community. Raju's younger brother Jagat, a farmer, was not even considered. Panditji's only hope lay in the next generation. Surely a son of one of his sons would be willing to prepare for the position which he himself regarded as an honor. Suresh's eldest son, Indar, finally volunteered; and Panditji went with him to Benares to make sure that he had the best possible instruction.

When I returned in 1961 and learned that Panditji had entrusted several duties to Indar, I wondered why. What I had observed of Indar had not inspired confidence in him. However, when he officiated at a ceremony for

Prakash, I was impressed. It was obvious that he had
been trained well. Most priests are familiar with the
details of routine ceremonies, but in our area only a few
have the facility to recite lines in Sanskrit which Indar
exhibited that day. His study in Benares had qualified
him formally as a priest; this training would have assured him prestige had he chosen to live as a mendicant,
moving from place to place. When a man remains within
the confines of one community, especially if it is his
home community, more is expected of him than ability to
repeat lines by rote. From reports that drifted into my
courtyard, I gathered that he was one of the least respected young men of the village. Like his father he
gambled and his behavior was regarded as unpriestlike,
and he was often ridiculed or deliberately shunned.

Indar's saving grace was his attitude toward his
wife. He was more considerate of her than his father had
been of his mother. She was very young when she first
came, and beautiful. She retained her charm even though
she had six babies and several miscarriages during her
twelve years as his wife. I never heard him abuse her
and he never struck her. When she became head of the
courtyard after his mother's death, she hushed the bedlam
and restored the cheerfulness that once had been there.

Then Indar's wife became more and more frail. When
the sixth child was born, she found it difficult to work.
She grew weaker and thinner so gradually that no one was
alarmed until she seemed to have wasted away and could
neither move nor speak. After a number of hakims and
physicians failed to help her, Indar finally agreed to
take her to a hospital in Fatehgarh, over forty miles
away. The journey was agony for her, but she was still
conscious when they arrived. Her illness was diagnosed
as pulmonary tuberculosis. She remained in the hospital
for months while Indar stayed with relatives in order to
provide her with food from a Brahmin kitchen. During
her absence Indar's sisters were substituting for her.

When she was able to come home, the whole family rejoiced. She had been discharged from the hospital with
the understanding that she return periodically for examination and treatment. Indar kept postponing such a
visit because of the strain on his wife and the expense.
When her baby was a year and a half old, she again had
warning symptoms, and suddenly she died.

Indar's grief was genuine and for a while he tried
to care for the children with the help of his ten year
old daughter. However, he gradually lost interest and
left the house. His daughter tried to cope with the
family alone. When not grinding or cooking, she ran out
to play with her baby sister on her hip. Her aunt-in-
law who shared the courtyard offered no help. Indar's
bereavement did not interfere with his gambling and soon
he was more deeply in debt than before and to escape
his creditors he left the village. His eldest son, then
twelve years old, gave up school to work for others to
earn the cash they needed. Indar had let out their own
land on shares. There was gossip about Indar's desertion of his children for a week or two, but no one attempted to trace him. It was later learned that he was
staying a short distance away.

The sequel to his desertion and his flight from
creditors was a surprise. Seven months after he left,
the first temple in the village was completed, the gift
of a humble kaharin, a woman of serving caste. Her husband and son had saved money for this particular purpose
during years spent as servants and messengers in Calcutta. The temple was dedicated to Shiva. The stone
lingam, symbol of Shiva, was stored in a Brahmin house
at the far end of the village waiting to be carried in
state to the temple where it was to be installed. Several canopied, four-wheeled ox-carts owned by wealthy
farmers formed a colorful procession, followed by a
crowd of men and boys. As they passed my house, a man,
obviously a priest, in the place of honor at the front
of the leading cart with the donor seated behind him,

gave the assembled household a smiling namaste, with the
gracious gesture of fingertips to forehead. It was Indar.
One had to admire his audacity and his insight. He had
timed his return perfectly, to make his first public appearance at a moment when he was serving in an important
role as priest. On such an occasion who would condemn
him for past misdeeds and his desertion of his children?

During the following days when there were speeches
and music as well as the usual elaborate ceremonies,
Indar was always in evidence on the dais or circulating
in the crowd. Other priests were there as speakers or
guests, but Indar was apparently master of ceremonies.
At the several feasts for visitors and the great feast
for all the village, he was among those who presided.
Shortly after the final ceremony, the kaharin left for
Calcutta, and no one in the village has expressed any
interest in the temple. A door of iron grating protects
Shiva and the small brightly dressed figure of his con-
sort, known in our locality as Parvati.

Indar's part in the installation ceremonies had set
him free. He remained in the village, indifferent to the
discomfiture of his creditors. Then suddenly he left
again, this time supposedly to search for his buffalo
which had been stolen. When he had been absent for over
a fortnight, villagers began to wonder. They knew from
experience that even the cleverest among them would not
try to locate a buffalo after such a long period. Was
this just another escape, perhaps from family, perhaps
from debts? He finally sent word that he was ill and
would remain with his great uncle Ishwar, the vaid, in
Ishwar's village just across the fields. Meanwhile, the
condition of his children became even worse than before.
Indar's brother and his wife, sharing the house, saw no
reason why they should give Indar's children the care
which their own father denied them. Other relatives fed
them occasionally but could not afford food and clothing
for all of them all of the time. When a joint family
breaks down as this one had, the children forfeit their

190

16. Panditain, her grandson's wife
    and a great-grandson

17. Usha and her daughter

security. Fortunately for the young daughter who had
done more than her share, her father's uncles arranged
for her marriage, including the wedding and dowry. When
barely a teenager she was carried away to her husband's
home leaving her brothers to fend for themselves, but
taking her baby sister with her.

When Indar returned to Karimpur, he decided to work
on his own land. As a farmer he did not get enough produce or money to meet the needs of his family, and the
families that called on him as priest contributed very
little. To add to his income he contracted for one-half
of the guava orchard of Janak's nephew, the other half
being contracted for by Dinesh the Oil Presser. To repeat briefly what happened: Dinesh fell ill during the
growing season and Indar took all of the fruit for himself making a generous profit from its sale.

Indar's younger brothers have added nothing to the
standing of the family. Soba, next in age to Indar,
showed no concern for priesthood or his family. He was
married but had no children. He refused to work on their
land. When pressed by relatives to find some occupation,
he decided to become a tailor. He could make a living
if only he had a machine, but the price of one was prohibitive. Consequently, he gave the village tailors no
peace until they allowed him to practice on one of
theirs. Soba monopolized one machine and treated it
roughly, they finally turned him out. They were low in
status but when their livelihood was jeopardized, they
asserted their rights, avoiding possible trouble by
offering to teach him their trade when he had a machine
of his own. He resorted to gambling.

The exploits of the third son, Depoo, were more
sensational. He began by making several attempts to kill
his cousin, Ganesh, Raju's son, of whom he had been jealous after dropping out of school while Ganesh continued
and received good grades. Later he came so near to mur-
dering a maternal cousin in another village that for
some weeks the cousin lay in a hospital wavering between

life and death while doctors and police waited. Depoo
had gone to his mother's home to claim jewelry which
she had understood was hers. When his request was denied one night, he tried to force open a chest in which
the jewelry was kept, using the heavy blade of a chopper.
When his young cousin came to the storeroom with a small
oil lamp to stop him, he attacked the boy with the chopper and cut his shoulder and head badly. Before he could
escape, he was caught and turned over to the police. Had
the cousin died, the sentence would have been severe.
Fortunately, he recovered, and Depoo's term in prison was
reduced to five years because of his age.

The other two brothers attempted to work their own
small parcels of land. They remained unmarried and like
their elders, were known for their bad habits and laziness,

*　　*　　*

I first met Ganesh, son of Raju and the most promising of the younger generation, on a raw, misty night
during my first winter in the new house. I was huddled
in one of the rooms at the back of the courtyard wearing
a sweater and a coat, trying to read by the light of a
lantern. I heard a quiet voice at the window beside me
which opens onto the courtyard, and I looked into large,
dark eyes that seemed sadder than any I had seen. He
began speaking in English, stilted and halting, but better than that used by schoolboys of the village. His
embarrassment and self-consciousness made his sentences
difficult to follow. But I caught the words, "I need
your help," At once I was on guard. He looked like
Indar. However, I listened while the mumbling voice
went on, "I need to learn more English. Could I practice it with you?" This was different.

He then introduced himself as Ganesh, grandnephew
of Panditji.

Ganesh was then seventeen and in second year of
inter-college at Mainpuri. He was not married.

Relatives had pressed his father to make the preliminary
arrangements, but Raju had decided that marriage should
wait. Ganesh liked his work in the inter-college, but
he had trouble with English. The assigned reading was
difficult: when he mentioned Burke's speeches, I understood. We agreed to practice conversational as well as
literary English whenever he should have a free evening.

He had not hoped to go on to college, but he had
done well in high school and his masters had persuaded
his father that he should study further. In the college
he attended, classes were held from seven to ten in the
morning and the same classes were repeated in the evening for students working in government offices during
the day. Ganesh had no one to help him get a clerkship
in a government office, and he had no pupils wanting to
be coached, so he studied or read in the college library
from ten o'clock until his cousin's high school hours
were over. Then they shared a bicycle on the return
trip to the village.

That evening's long conversation was the first of
many. There is a quietness, a stillness in Ganesh which
tempers his eagerness and makes it easy to communicate
with him. He lacks his father's positive views on Hindu-
ism, but he has a love of Hindi literature, both religious and secular, which his father lacks. He carries a
small homemade notebook filled with his favorite Hindi
poems in his shirt pocket to be read for his own pleasure or for that of his friends.

In contrast to this, English was just one more subject to be studied and one more examination to be passed.
All other subjects were taught in Hindi. He was told
that for a good government post some knowledge of English
was essential, particularly the spoken language. He read
Hindi classics from choice. English he read as a painful
duty. In spite of this he was sure that there were books
in English that he could enjoy if he knew where to find
them. And he was determined to be able to speak it without stumbling.

He was successful and when he completed the two year course and emerged successful from the ordeal of examinations, his father reluctantly undertook to send him on for another two years to prepare for the B.A. examinations.

Possibly because of his contact with the city, Ganesh seemed to feel himself less strictly bound by village tradition. A sense of independence which led him to one day announce to his father that if he were to meet a young woman he liked and wanted to marry, he would do so even though she were of lower caste, or even a Muslim or Christian. His father warned him that if he did this, there would be no more college for him and no home in Karimpur.

Ganesh did meet a girl whom he liked and admired while in his second year, and fortunately for him she was an acceptable Brahmin. She came from Agra and was much more sophisticated than Ganesh or his friends. Finally it was she, Premila, who proposed. Ganesh, who had been too shy to speak, accepted gratefully. The remainder of that college year was the happiest period of his life. Premila's father came to Mainpuri to meet Ganesh and approved. Ganesh's father went to town on his next home visit to meet Premila and he approved. The two fathers were negotiating a preliminary agreement when Premila fell ill. It was shortly before the final examinations and Ganesh was cramming and consequently was seeing little of her. During the coming summer holidays their wedding would take place, following which they would continue their studies together. No one seems to have realized the seriousness of Premila's illness, nor did she intimate to Ganesh that she was not able to attend the examinations. Their examinations were identical, but his were held in the inter-college that he attended while she was assigned with other young women to a school in a different part of town. The examinations continued for ten or more days with only short breaks. It seems strange that it was not until

Premila's father came to take her to Agra for treatment
that Ganesh was called to see her. He came the same
evening and spent some time with her, discussing the
examinations he now knew she had missed. She asked him
to come the next morning for a last visit together before
she left for Agra. He came, but the doctor present said
that her condition was so serious that she could not be
moved. Ganesh sat beside her, holding her hand, neither
of them speaking. Then, suddenly, she stopped breathing.
Premila's father, beside himself with grief, sent Ganesh
away. He was not wanted now. He could join them on the
journey to the burning <u>ghat</u> near Agra for her cremation
that afternoon if he cared to go. A friend found him
and went with him to the examination hall. Ganesh accepted the notebooks he was to fill and took the seat
assigned to him by the proctor. Too stunned to grasp
what had happened, he opened the question paper and
started to write. But before he was halfway through,
his thoughts turned to Premila on her last journey to
Agra. Suddenly he turned in his unfinished notebooks
and ran out of the hall. He went home rather than to
Agra. Premila had brought a new world and new life to
him, he was sure that he knew her better than her family
possibly could. But now they would claim her. Her father was the only member of her family he had ever met,
and he obviously regarded Ganesh as an outsider the moment Premila died. If they had been married, he would
have been needed and wanted, but not even the pre-
wedding ceremonies had been performed. He could not
bear to be treated as an intruder where Premila was concerned, so it was better to stay away and be forgotten.

Afterwards, he could not remember the bicycle ride
home. He went into the small room which served for worship and study, closed the door and sat alone with his
grief. His mother and other relatives had never seen
Premila and had heard very little about her from Ganesh.
Now they expressed no concern. The marriage that the
young couple had planned was too unconventional to be

taken seriously. Premila was as much an outsider to
them as he was to her people. His father, who had found
in her all that he could want in a <u>bahu</u>, was away. After
a few months of close, congenial companionship, Ganesh
was more alone than ever. Moreover, he had failed the
examination which was held on the day of Premila's death,
and as a result, he was obliged to repeat the whole
series of exams the following year.

Ganesh was distressed over his failure but was not
humiliated. It was his father who suffered from humiliation and was furious. Had he not made it possible for
his son to advance further in his education than any
other young man of the village? Instead of showing ap-
preciation by passing with good grades, he had failed.
No one could now expect him, Raju, to pay for the education of such a son. As he talked about it, he implied
that Ganesh had brought the failure on himself by his
stubborn insistence on arranging his own marriage. If
he had waited for his father to proceed in the correct
manner, he would have passed the examinations with
grades of which his father could be proud. Raju rarely
spoke to Ganesh, and when he did it was as a successful
man to an incompetent servant. When he spoke to others
about his son, it was with disgust.

After the vacation of May and June, Ganesh resumed
his studies. His one duty was to prepare himself to
pass all of the examinations for that year whether he
attended college or studied privately at home. The latter is permitted by certain universities, including the
one with which his college was associated. The procedure eliminated all expenses except for the examination
fees. So he settled down with his books in his small
room. Studying on one's own and going over subjects
already covered, however, is not demanding. He began
spending more time with friends who were free in the
evenings but were working in fields or workshops during
the day--all but one whose elder brother had driven him
off of their land to fend for himself. The brother had

argued that there was not enough work for two and not
enough food for both of them and their mother. The boy
found no employment and begged food from his mother
surreptiously. This left him with days of idleness,
and he encouraged Ganesh to idle with him. They wandered through the fields or bicycled to town to loiter
through the bazaar. Neither of them had money to spend,
but they found plenty to explore.

Often in the evenings they met with others to sing
and to rehearse for an ambitious dramatic performance.
By the end of the summer they were ready to present the
Ramlila drama regarded by people in our region as the
most important feature of Dashera, a popular autumn
festival. For ten nights, crowds sit on the ground
watching scene after scene from the epic of Rama, the
god-hero, and Sita, his wife. A polished performance is
put on in large cities, and a less spectacular one in
district town. A village like ours cannot afford to
hire a professional troupe every year, consequently only
once in five or six years is the drama professionally
presented in Karimpur. Otherwise, the performers are
men and boys of the village. In that particular year,
Ganesh and his friends volunteered. They all took part
as actors, prompters, musicians or collectors of donations and of costumes from household chests. Three pro-
fessionals were engaged to provide the dances and ribald
songs between scenes. Once when I questioned why these
were included in a religious drama, I was told that without them the people would not come. Everyone knows the
drama almost by heart, and thus they all expect slap-
stick dialogue and clowning as a diversion. Very little
financing was needed, and each evening the audience could
be counted on for donations. Ganesh was chosen to chant
the lines, and as he sang, verse by verse, others enacted
the scene in pantomime. His voice was quiet, yet every
line could be distinctly heard.

Raju came home for the Dashera festival, but fortunately for Ganesh he did not attend the performance

until the last night. He and Ganesh had felt no urge to
communicate. A father and his sons do not eat together
and they go different ways unless they are working in
the same field or at the same task. Members of the family and neighbors, knowing Raju's attitude toward Ganesh,
did not mention his son's role in the drama. When Raju
finally took his place in the audience and recognized
Ganesh's voice behind the screen, he was infuriated.
When one of the young actors approached him for a dona-
tion he refused and stalked out. This prepared Ganesh
for the scene which took place after the performance.
His ten days of sheer enjoyment were over. His father
reminded him once more of his failure. And now, fritter-
ing away his time as he was doing, he would fail again
and disgrace his family again. He was to get out and
get out at once. He was to stay in Mainpuri where he
could devote his time to his studies. Ganesh did leave,
but not until the next morning when his mother fed him
well and provided him with homeground flour, pulses, and
ghee for a week. From the morning he left for town he
appeared only briefly on weekends to collect more food
supplies. He roomed in an ashram near the town and
lived among priests, cooking his own food and studying.

When the examinations were over, he felt free to
come home assured that he had done well. He did not
know definitely that he had passed until six weeks later
when the list of candidates and their examination results was published in a daily newspaper. Long before
this, his father arrived with the announcement that he
had satisfactorily arranged a suitable husband for his
one daughter. The boy had prospects of property and a
naukri, understood to be a government post. From Raju's
description, he was all that Ganesh was not. Soon the
examination results were known and after Raju returned
from the first pre-wedding ceremony at the bridegroom's
home, he called Ganesh to his room. Ganesh anticipated
some word of approval on his passing. Everyone in their
neighborhood had been talking about it. Raju, too, must

surely have heard, but he made no mention of it. The impending marriage was more important. However his attitude toward his son had altered. He informed Ganesh that he was to make all of the arrangements for the wedding. He gave instructions that every detail of every step in the ceremonies must be carefully planned, that each feast must be more sumptuous than any within the memory of Karimpur or of the bridegroom's party, and that the entertainment must be lavish. He had just one daughter and he was prepared to spend up to three thousand rupees for her wedding. Ganesh was stunned and excited. Seldom had a village father entrusted such a large amount to an unmarried son. For the past year he had been obliged to consider well every paise that he spent and had to borrow money from friends to pay his examination fees. Now this fabulous sum was in his hands. His father would want an accounting of each item, but Ganesh was free to do the spending. And he did, with the enthusiastic help from his friends. That summer, life in the family centered around the wedding. Female relatives of all ages came flocking, most of them with children, eager to share in the excitement of preparing such enormous quantitites of rich food of which they themselves could eat their fill. Professional cooks were employed for the large scale frying of puris. Men, expert in making the fancy sweets not attempted at home, were also hired.

It is possible to stage a very ostentatious wedding in Karimpur for three thousand rupees. Plates of leaves made by local dhanuks (mat makers) were purchased by the hundred for very little. The Potter attached to the bride's family welcomes the meager amount offered for clay saucers for sweets or curds and tumblers for water, the only drink served. Tables and table coverings and decorations are not needed as guests sit on the ground to be served by men of the family and friends of the same caste. Puris and sweets are served from homemade baskets; legumes and vegetables are ladled directly from brass kettles to the leaf plates. Even the decorating

of the wedding booth and the courtyard in which it is
erected is inexpensive. Young relatives and friends
bind colored tissue paper around the four stout bamboo
poles that support the booth, weave strips of more colored paper to make the roof, and hang still other strips
from the sides as festoons, tipped with homemade paper
flowers. Small pennants are cut from colored paper,
glued to twine and strung wherever space can be found.
Ganesh hung large bright lithographs of four favorite
gods and their consorts high on the framework of the
booth, one picture on each of the four sides. Mango
leaves, a sheaf of barley, clay pots, a few accessories,
and a container for the sacred fire completed the setting. With so little spent on decorations, Ganesh was
able to spend most of the money on essentials--food and
entertainment.

The wedding passed smoothly and brilliantly. The
bride, frightened and weeping as she should be, was carried away. It was all that Raju or any other father-of-
the-bride could want, and he was given, and graciously
accepted, the credit. After all, it was his money.
Ganesh found his satisfaction in knowing that he had
spent the three thousand rupees effectively. I could
not resist asking later if he had been able to salvage
any of the money to be used towards the expenses of his
final year in college. Yes, he had saved one hundred
rupees. To me this seemed very little compared with
thirty times that amount spent within three days, but
he explained that the one hundred rupees would give him
a start during the first weeks for books and fees. After that he could manage, and he did. He returned to
the simple life of the ashram and secured two tutoring
jobs which brought him forty rupees a month. This made
him independent during his final year.

Ganesh had settled into his routine of classes and
study when a cousin unexpectedly appeared at the ashram
with word that he was to come home at once. He went
that evening: on the platform at the front of the

granary he met a stranger with his father. Raju introduced the man as Ganesh's father-in-law-to-be and informed Ganesh that he was there for the preliminary or tika
ceremony. Everything had been arranged: there was
nothing that Ganesh could say or do.

That evening Ganesh sat through the tika ceremony
as spectator rather than as a participant. Early the
next morning he returned to college and his studies. He
was called home once more for the lagan, the final pre-
wedding ceremony. By this time his astonishment had
changed to acceptance. When Raju sent for him later to
come join the wedding party, he came like an obedient
son. The wedding party was comparatively small, perhaps
twenty men, since railway fare to the bride's home in
Kanpur was expensive. Once there, they were entertained
in a rest house connected with a temple. The food did
not taste as though it has been prepared at home; and
when Ganesh entered the house for part of the ceremonies,
he understood why. "Home" was an unbelievably small
flat. He knew no one in the family nor any of the Kanpur
guests. But he did not particularly care because the one
person he wanted to see was the bride. Only late in the
ceremony, however, was he allowed to look at her with her
face uncovered.

He was pleased with what he saw, but there was no
opportunity for them to talk to each other. He returned
to Karimpur with his party. Usha, his bride, came too
and spent a few days in his home. Here, as in Kanpur
during the wedding, they were not able to communicate.
She was kept in the courtyard with her mother-in-law and
aunt-in-law. Apparently she was critical of their life
and customs, as Ganesh's mother told me in an offended
manner after Usha had left. Ganesh resumed his studies,
working long hours to make up for the classes he had
missed. After her return to Kanpur, Usha began sending
him letters asking for replies. He did not know what to
write without being better acquainted with her, so he
went to Kanpur. She was a town girl and was free to

talk to him. He liked her even better than when he had only looked at her. In her home as in his, however, they had no privacy. There were always children pressing around them in the two small rooms of the flat. Since he could spend only one day with her then, he planned to go again a few months later before his examinations began, and he urged me to go with him.

After a long trip in the heat of April, we found our way to Usha's house. By the time Usha appeared, I had cooled off and was prepared to meet her. To my surprise she came as any new village bahu might, with face completely covered with the end of her sari. She knelt down and touched my feet and remained there. I first spoke to her in English. When there was no response, I resorted to Hindi. I learned later that the only member of her family who converses in English is her father. I told Usha that I had come to get acquainted with her, the bride of Ganesh whom I considered a grandson. How could I communicate with a sari? Still, she waited, and I remembered that it was I who should uncover her face and present her with a gift in keeping with tradition. I drew aside her sari and uncovered an attractive face. Her eyes were shining with laughter and her lips were smiling. I placed in her hands the sari I had brought for her. The brief drama was over and now we were free to talk naturally.

I learned several things from her about which Ganesh had been vague. He had the impression that there were two or three children younger than Usha: actually there were six. Also, she told me that when her father had informed her that she was soon to be married, she dropped out of school and registered for a course in sewing: Ganesh had thought she was still studying. She impressed me as being more practical than Ganesh--the kind of wife he needs.

Then she showed me their flat. Behind the room where I had been sitting was a similar one stacked high on three sides with metal boxes; everything they owned

was stored in them. There were gunny sacks and various
garments hanging from a rope strung across the room, and
there was just one charpai on which Ganesh was sitting
at ease. Beyond this room a miniature verandah led to
the miniature courtyard. Off the verandah was the kitchen, so small that both Usha and her mother could not
work there at the same time. Their cooking, to my surprise, was done on a chula with a wood fire--exactly as
it is done in our village homes where people can afford
wood. The only improvement noticeable was a hood above
the chula to carry off some of the smoke. Off the courtyard was a latrine and beyond it, the bathing room.
That was all. The family had occupied this flat for over
a year and as yet had neither running water nor electric-
ity. Their furniture consisted of two charpais, one high
stool which served as my table, and an empty metal drum
which was Ganesh's table. In the front room stood Usha's
sewing machine, the family's one extravagance. The children did as all village children do--they ate anywhere
and slept on the floor or charpai wherever they could
find room. To Usha and her mother this flat was spacious
compared with the one they lived in before. There were
hundreds of families in this one housing project and other thousands were in more crowded sections of the city,
stifled in narrow back lanes with gutters as latrines.

The next day gave me an inkling of why the Sharmas
think themselves better off than their village relatives.
In the morning Mr. Sharma took Ganesh on the back of his
bicycle to a bazaar. When they returned, Ganesh was excited over the vast number of shops that he had seen;
and Mr. Sharma had told him that there were still other
similar bazaars in the city. If he had money, he could
buy anything. There were all kinds of fruit and vegetables, most of which are seen in the village only when
in season. There were cloth shops, brass shops, bak-
eries, and shops where a great variety of sweets were
sold. Mr. Sharma bought a loaf of white bread thinking
that I would prefer it to his wife's fresh puris. The

flour and dried legumes and vegetables which they bought
at the bazaar for the next few days' meals were ready
to be cooked. No grinding of flour, no drying or split-
ting or soaking of legumes was required of the women.
Mr. Sharma does all of the buying except for emergency
supplies which his son can get from a small shop a few
blocks away. Ganesh also reported having visited a large
and beautiful temple which added to the attractions of
Kanpur.

That evening in order to help Ganesh and Usha spend
time alone, I proposed taking them and Usha's brother to
a cinema. Inside the theater they were side by side, at
last. It seemed strange and not quite right that a husband and wife must go to a public theater to be alone.
The movie was tragic, the story of two young people,
married and deeply in love, but denied the consummation
of their marriage because of adverse circumstances. On
the way home Usha was silent and grave. Her marriage
was thus far very similar to that of the drama.

From that time onward, she made every effort to be
with Ganesh as his wife, but in her home it proved impossible. During our visit there Ganesh had enjoyed
talking with her and sharing his most cherished poems
with her. Apparently he was content with that for it
was more than any of his friends had experienced with
their brides, and more than he had hoped for. But Usha
dreamed of romance, having seen cinema pictures and
heard songs over the radio that told of a love far different from that of the married couples she knew. Her
concept of marriage was entirely different from that
held by villagers. Moreover she herself was very young,
sixteen at the time of her marriage. Ganesh's reiter-
ated statement that they resign themselves to waiting
irked her. If he really cared for her, he would give
up college as she had given up school. Then he could
begin earning at once for her father had offered to
use his influence to get him a job as guard on the railway. They could have railway quarters to live in where

they would be alone.

On our return to the village, Ganesh's friends scoffed at the idea of his working on the railway. They listed the reasons why he would be a complete failure as a guard. Any one of them would fit into that kind of routine, but not he. On the other hand, not one of them could hope to get a B.A. degree. Now he was on the last lap with the prospect of a teaching post just around the corner. They were all married, but marriage had not upset their lives. Wives were expected to serve and obey their mothers-in-law and their husbands. A wife who tied to push her husband into any kind of a job needed to be taught her place. His companions were curious about Usha. Did she actually talk to him in the presence of her parents? When would she come here to stay? They had no expectation of seeing her face, but they could not resist conjecturing, "How is a city girl different from our wives?" The answer would have to wait until Usha came and could be inspected by their mothers. Ganesh assured them that he would not send for her until his examinations were over.

To his surprise and consternation, however, he soon received a postcard from her. She wrote that she must see him and was awaiting him to bring her to Karimpur. Deep in his first examinations, he could not possibly leave, so he sent a cousin for her. Not until some time later did I learn the reason for such a precipitate visit. After Ganesh had left her, the days seemed long and lonely. She spent much of her time thinking about him, haunted by her fear that he might be injured, like the hero in the movie they had seen. Must their separation go on indefinitely? If Ganesh remained firm in his refusal of her father's offer of a job and if they could never be alone in her crowded flat, why not try his home? While she had been here for the few days following the wedding, she had been impressed by the size of the courtyard, at least ten times as large as hers, with several storerooms around it, containing a family smaller than hers. When she felt that she could not endure waiting any longer, she had sent the postcard.

She came with high hopes, only to find herself under the close supervision of his mother and aunt, like any other village bride. To her disappointment, Ganesh made no move to be alone with her. Perhaps because their marriage had been arranged in orthodox fashion, he expected it to continue in the traditional way. Especially here in his home he observed village customs and stayed outside the courtyard except for the meals that his mother served him. What he did not know was that Usha's comments on village women had antagonised his mother, and she had retaliated by ignoring Usha's evident desire to communicate with her son. Usha still had to learn that the sympathy of the head of the courtyard must be won if a young husband and wife are to be within speaking distance of each other. Meanwhile, because of the pressure of his examinations, Ganesh moved back to the ashram in town.

I saw Usha frequently, but just long enough to exchange a few sentences. Her mother-in-law, usually gentle and considerate, kept her young bahu occupied in the kitchen or sat near her on a charpai during her free time. During one of my visits Usha expressed a desire to have her picture taken. It so happened that a week later a friend arrived with a camera. Usha was not exactly a typical village subject, but Ganesh's sister and cousin were. All three girls were excited over the prospect of a photo. Other women whom my friend photographed went on with their work, but these three took it seriously. They were in ordinary dhotis when we entered the courtyard, but they insisted that we wait until they were properly dressed. Ganesh's mother and aunt were at first amused and then, after a long delay, irritated. My friend wanted a picture of Ganesh's mother and his wife together. When I proposed it, his mother looked down at her soiled dhoti and turned to show us a long rent in her blouse that exposed most of her back, and remarked caustically, "I am not going to look ridiculous. Let her put on airs. I am just a village woman." By the time Usha appeared in a silk sari with her head un- covered, her mother-in-law was tight lipped. The other two girls had followed Usha's example, wearing saris in- stead of dhotis, but Usha had outdone them. She carried a bright plastic handbag, the first I had seen in the village. The bag at once set her apart from the women around her, a symbol of the city life from which she had come and to which she intended to return. It. could be interpreted as a courageous declaration of independence or as a gesture of defiance made by a girl too immature and inexperienced to measure the consequences. She was young and alone, surrounded by women who did not and could not understand her attitude. Those who had gath- ered out of curiosity for the photographing ceremony were shocked at her uncovered head and the handbag, and said so with voices raised.

As the situation deteriorated, Usha was desperate so she wrote to her father begging him to send her broth- er to bring her home. Ganesh's sister, enjoying her se- cret mission, carried the card to the village post office. When Usha's brother arrived a week later to accompany her to Kanpur, her relief was unmistakable even while she feigned surprise. Her mother-in-law's surprise was gen- uine while she feigned regret at losing her only bahu. Ganesh was not informed of her departure until his next visit home.

When the results of the examinations were published, Ganesh's name did not appear. He had failed again. He concluded that where romance and examinations compete, examinations lose. However, as he had done after his failure two years earlier, he vowed to be successful the second time. To everyone's amazement, his father was not exasperated. He talked with Ganesh and took time to discuss plans with him for the first time in two years, offering no explanation for his change in attitude. He was to work in their fields during the day and study "privately" at night. There was to be no leisure for aimless wandering about or for Ramlila performances, and he was to stay away from the distractions of Kanpur.

Ganesh accepted his father's mandate, and turned to farming. By working along with an experienced hired man, he learned a good deal. He now acknowledged his laziness during the past four years. Moreover, he was so occupied with field work and studies that Usha's frequent letters from Kanpur did not disturb him. Their enforced separation was harder for her than for him, but finally he disobeyed his father's orders and went to Kanpur. Finding Usha ill, he took her to a government hospital where charges were low. Then he remained a week, spending each day with her. Reluctantly, he left as soon as she was back in her own home, returning to his fields and his studies. He had been impressed by her fortitude.

That year Raju made more frequent home visits and apparently noted his son's self-discipline. At the end of one visit, he invited Ganesh to go to Agra with him where Ganesh could purchase textbooks not available in Mainpuri. This was his first offer of financial help since Ganesh's failure over two years before. On the journey to Agra, Ganesh was introduced to a father he had not known. He had admired Raju's familiarity with Hindi literature and respected him as a lecturer but had been denied any opportunity to talk with him as an equal. He found in Raju an unexpected response to some of his own ideas. Ironically, it was Raju who changed the verses at the next Ramlila performance, while Ganesh stayed in his room with his books.

The 1966 examinations came and went with no emotional crisis. When they were over, Ganesh was free to look toward the future. His great desire was to teach. If he could complete one year of additional training he could teach in Mainpuri and live at home. He could bicycle back and forth and supervise his father's fields. He would be free to read Hindi literature and write poetry of his own. It sounded like an ideal arrangement for a bachelor. "But what about Usha?" I asked. I had known her disappointment on each of her visits. His confident reply was, "Where I am, she will be content. In the beginning at least, we shall live in my home. She will accept my judgment."

He went to Kanpur and brought Usha back with him. He knew that her desires for him conflicted with his own, but for the moment what he wanted most was to have her with him, and he was still optimistic about Usha's and his mother's ability to make a satisfactory adjustment. For his sake, Usha came, resolved to please his mother, but his mother was not inclined to respond. Apparently she still harbored resentment at Usha's earlier remarks, and she seemed bent on showing Usha that a city girl had much to learn as a village wife. She treated her as an ignorant bahu and assigned her heavy tasks to which she was not accustomed, like turning the heavy millstone every morning. Usha, tense, often bungled and was reduced to tears. Later I heard of her futile attempts to convey her misery to Ganesh. She was now allowed to serve him his meals. As she set the food before him, she could squat for a moment while waiting to make sure that he was satisfied. This was her one opportunity to speak to him. To avoid being overheard, she lowered her voice, already muffled by the dhoti drawn down over her face. As a result, Ganesh caught only a few words which he interpreted optimistically. He took for granted that she was accepting her new way of life as he was accepting responsibility for their fields. As yet, they were denied even a brief rendezvous at night.

Then one day without warning or explantion, Ganesh's mother announced that her brother had invited her to come to her old house for a long postponed visit. He would be calling for her any day, and she was entrusting the household and all food preparation to Usha. After all, Ganesh's aunt would be cooking at her chulha in the same courtyard and could make sure that Usha made no serious mistakes. Ganesh reacted with a mixture of perplexity and relief: Usha dared say nothing. After Ganesh's mother had left, it was a delight to be with them, especially as Raju was also away. Ganesh's small brother and his sister, who was here on a home visit, enjoyed the novelty of being cared for by a young sister-in-law. His aunt found Usha congenial, and the two talked and laughed as they worked together. When word came from Ganesh's mother that she was extending her absence for another fortnight or perhaps a month, no one expressed regret.

The two young people had what both of them wanted most--freedom to be together. Then to please Usha, Ganesh made a drastic innovation. Just beside the entryway leading from the triangular platform to the courtyard was a storeroom seldom used. Ganesh removed the few bags of grain still there, and he and Usha transformed the room into a retreat for themselves. He moved his own metal trunk and Usha's into it, brought in a charpai which Usha covered with a bright quilt, and together they hung lithographs of gods and goddesses on the walls. There was just one door and no windows, so the room seemed dark when one first walked into it. However, when the time came to prepare for Diwali, the Festival of Lights, and walls along every lane were being freshly plastered with clay or whitewashed, Ganesh not only whitewashed the whole front of their house, but also the walls of their room as well. At once it seemed lighter and more attractive.

The one flaw was the knowledge that their freedom would not last. As the time for the return of Ganesh's mother approached, Usha became restless. She pressed Ganesh to apply for a job that would take them anywhere outside of Karimpur, but he could not relinquish his hopes of teaching. With his mother's arrival, the old tensions were revived and he realized that he had been overly optimistic. Usha insisted on leaving, and Ganesh took her home. On his return he seemed forsaken and their room looked forlorn.

A few days later he brought four copies of an application to the Railway Board for the job of assistant
station master to be filled out on my typewriter. He
explained that this was better than being a guard. He
would become a permanent railway employee and could look
forward to promotion that would ultimately place him in
a responsible and remunerative position: he was obviously trying to generate enthusisam.

Then the examination results were announced: he
had passed! Immediately he abandoned the railway idea.
He could and would become a teacher; and he immediately
applied for admission to a training college. But he had
not reckoned on Raju who announced that he had decided
to give fewer lectures so as to devote more time to the
writing and publishing of his materials, thereby causing
a drastic reduction in income. If Ganesh had been working faithfully on their land, there must be enough to
provide for them until the next harvest. Ganesh asked
about the training Raju had encouraged him to take. His
father seemed to have forgotten his offer of help and
replied that there would be no training that year. When
the training course opened in August, he was still at
home. He consoled himself with the fact that next to
teaching, he liked farming, and if he could not be a
teacher, he would be a farmer, one of the most progressive in Karimpur. He joined forces with two young men
who, like himself, were determined to move ahead of the
older generation.

The three decided to learn all that they could from
the Village Level Worker associated with the community
development program. He followed the VLW's instructions
and counted on a good yield. Unfortunately, the rains
did not arrive that year and the fall harvest was a near
failure, not only for Karimpur but the whole of Uttar
Pradesh and the states to the east and south. Like his
two friends, however, Ganesh had invested in irrigation
and fertilizer and had a better crop of maize than that

of many experienced farmers. Moreover by cultivating
the fields himself with the minimum of hired help, he
was able to retain most of the harvest for the family.
He had twice as much as he would have, had he let the
land out on shares as his father used to do. When the
time came for the fall planting, the three agreed to
experiment with what was called "Mexican wheat," a new
high yielding variety. Older men shook their heads and
waited.

The spring of 1967 started out as a repetition of
1966. Ganesh brought Usha home and the familiar tensions revived, while he went steadily forward with his
farming. Outwardly, he was still an amateur farmer and
a dutiful son, but under the surface a high level of independence was developing. In spite of his father's
non-cooperation and Usha's tacit opposition, he determined to carry out his own plans, not in the dim future,
but this year if possible.

March brought him the first encouragement. The con-
vocation date for receiving his B.S. was set. When the
day came, he set out very early with his rented gown,
and immediately following the ceremony he brought his
diploma home for all to see. His was the first B.A.
degree in the village. When I went to his house a few
days later, Usha pointed to it, already framed and hung
high on the wall of their room.

Then his following of the VLW's instructions resulted in an abundant potato crop. The pea crop, a new variety, was excellent and plentiful with enough for the market and the family. After Holi, when he harvested his
barley, he had great stacks of it beside the threshing
floor. His yield compared favorably with that of men
with larger fields and more experience. But his triumph
was the wheat that he and his two friends had ventured
to try. Older men who had been watching the fields of
the three realized that the young men had gambled wisely.
Each one of the trio had produced five times as much per
acre as ordinary farmers had. But in spite of this, his

income could not cover the additional expense of training,
and he was obliged to accept one more postponement.

Then Raju took his wife with him to a conference at
his ashram: they were away for over a fortnight. Again
Ganesh and Usha were alone, he as temporary head of the
family and she as head of their half of the courtyard.
Last year the interlude granted them had been very exciting and intensely romantic. This year each was finding a deeper kind of care and affection in the other.
They were together as a normal married couple in a nuclear family. By the time Ganesh's parents returned, he and
Usha were so well established in the role of husband and
wife that irritations no longer upset them. Usha better
understood her mother-in-law's reactions and disciplined
herself to following seemingly unreasonable instructions,
although she still found it difficult to abide by village
custom, particularly what she regarded as the imprison-
ment of young wives like herself. Whenever we were alone,
she begged me to take her away to my house or any place
where she would be free to step outside the door. She
knew that neither of us could bring this about. She
learned to draw the end of her _dhoti_ down over her face
quickly when Ganesh or his father or uncle entered the
courtyard, but if anyone were near who might appreciate
the absurdity of it, she lifted the _dhoti_ just enough to
show her impish grin.

At the same time, Ganesh's mother was learning to
accept some of Usha's eccentricities. The one fault she
found hardest to condone was Usha's frank delight each
time her brother came and reported that her mother was
overburdened by her large family and needed Usha's help.
Usha would obediently express regret at being obliged to
leave again, but without asking permission to go, she
would hurry off to Kanpur. Other _bahus_ took for granted
that after the first year of marriage home for them was
with their in-laws. Usha's behavior was lacking in respect for village tradition and for Ganesh's family.
Ganesh's mother could not comprehend the loneliness from

which Usha was suffering.

But from the day Ganesh's mother told her friends with pride that Usha was pregnant, she treated Usha with greater consideration. Since her third child, Ganesh's younger brother, had chosen to spend his time in activities outside of the courtyard, she had felt lost and no longer needed. Now, at last, Usha would be bringing an infant into the courtyard for her to cherish as grandmother. To her relief, Usha seemed content to remain during her pregancy rather than go to her parents' home in Kanpur. She would be here for her confinement, which was as it should be: a son's first son should be born in his father's home.

Ganesh said little but was obviously gratified. All of his friends had children. He was glad for Usha's sake that he would not be leaving home shortly, as he had hoped. In the following fall the baby arrived. They had been confident that Usha would have a son, but when a tiny, frail daughter was born, she received more affection than a husky boy might have. The baby drew Ganesh's mother and Usha together in their common concern. Even Raju was touched by the baby's helplessness and was sometimes seen carrying her gently in his arms on the front platform. Ganesh could reconsider his training with the assurance that relationships with the family were favorable.

Financially the prospects for the year ahead were good. His harvest, like that of all the farmers, was excellent. With the money he had saved from the previous year's income added to the total from his harvest, the coveted training seemed within reach. But when he estimated expenses, the family's and his own, against the best possible profit from the sale of his grain, he found that he was still short of rupees. He was desperate. He had postponed the training for two successive years. Another year of waiting would be the end.

He knew from experience that Raju would not consider helping with finances, so there was no point in trying to talk to him. Usha was the only one with whom he could discuss the problem. Before he had finished his first few sentences, she amazed and embarrassed him by removing her gold earrings, a wedding gift, and laying them in his hand. Nor would she allow him to return them to her. They were to be sold for the cash that he still needed. It was the one way in which she could help him to realize his dream. These two gifts--the child and the earrings--drew Usha into the heart of the family. Never again would she be an outsider.

Now the only obstacle left in the way of Ganesh's training was his father's possible interference, and Raju lived up to expectations. When he returned from a brief lecture tour, he announced that he was leaving. He explained that his _guru_ had advised him to give up his lectures and renounce his duties as householder in order to retire to the _ashram_. Ganesh would now take his place as head of the family with all that the position demanded. Ganesh's startling reply was that it was not Raju but he himself who would be leaving. He had tried to comply with his father's wishes, but he refused to postpone his training any longer. Raju could accept his duties as householder or evade them. The responsibility was his, not Ganesh's. When Ganesh added that he had arranged for admission to a training college in Kanpur, Raju again did the unexpected. He agreed that this was wise. His retirement to the _ashram_ could wait. He himself had been exploring training institutions on Ganesh's behalf and had found that the one in Kanpur had the most to offer with the least expense. When Raju asked how Ganesh would solve the problem of finances and heard that he and Usha were handling this between them, it was his turn to be surprised. He had always seemed reluctant to commend anyone within his family, but on this occasion he did express approval with a tinge of respect.

It was during the spring harvest that Ganesh made his declaration, his commitment, but the college was not

due to open until August. During the months between he
was beset by uncertainties. First, there was the baby.
Instead of being a comfort to Usha during his absence
as he had hoped, she was ill and a cause for anxiety.
Would it be right for him to leave home unless she improved? Then there was Usha. Would she be willing to
stay here throughout the period of training? A year or
two earlier she would have insisted on going with him.
Her home was in Kanpur, and it was convenient for him
to visit her there although he would be living in a
college hostel. Only once did she intimate this, but he
quickly discouraged the idea. The baby had a better
chance of recovery here with fresh air and sunshine than
in a crowded flat. Also, his studies would demand all
of his time and he dared not risk any distraction. Finally, there remained the unpredictable Raju. He was at
home, but restless. Would he be satisfied marking time
here? If his guru were to call him again to the ashram,
would he be willing to delay the alluring retirement for
another year?

When the training center opened in August of 1968,
Ganesh was sitting at the desk assigned to him in one of
the classrooms, unbelievable as it seemed, he was actually there. During the months that followed, he concen-
trated on his studies in spite of disturbing news from
home. Usha's letters assured him that the baby was
thriving, but partition of the family seemed inevitable.
Trouble that had been simmering in the household had
boiled over during a quarrel between Raju's and Jagat's
wives. According to Raju's wife, it had been Jagat's
wife who started the quarrel. She had become jealous of
Raju's prosperity. Her husband was an ordinary farmer,
working day after day in his fields, while Raju sat comfortably in his room filling notebooks with lectures.
The money he was receiving from his lectures and from
Ganesh's improved type of farming had increased their
income until it was much larger than Jagat's and they
had not offered to share it. Raju had tried to explain

that his expenses were greater than Jagat's, especially with the cost of Ganesh's training, but Jagat and his wife argued that this was just an excuse on Raju's part to curtail his responsibilities as elder brother.

The only way to end the wrangling was for Raju to move out with his family. When he could afford it, he would build a new house. Meanwhile, Jagat could retain the larger portion of the house and he himself would manage with the smaller portion at the front. He sealed the door between them, making the division of the family final. To create a courtyard for his own family, he made use of the triangular platform where Panditji once sat surrounded by villagers. He marked off a section at the rear of the platform and hired workmen to build a mud wall around it. This made a courtyard that was protected but so small that it was barely sufficient, even without Ganesh. Enough of the open section of the platform remained for himself and his visitors. The entryway to their former courtyard where bicycles had been kept and the room beside it which Ganesh had reserved for himself and Usha became Raju's storerooms.

Raju's wife readily accepted the improvised court-yard. She greeted her friends with a smile when curiosity brought them trailing in through the narrow front door just completed by Raju's Carpenter. She assured them that she was better satisfied here with too little space than in the old imposing courtyard filled with harsh words and tension. She proudly demonstrated her new pump on the side of the courtyard opposite Raju's room. It was much more convenient than the well across the lane from the old courtyard.

For Usha, the move was just one more adjustment. She had already gone through the more difficult one--that of learning to live as a village wife. The new kitchen was small, but it was open to the courtyard and more pleasant than her mother's tiny kitchen in Kanpur. In leaving the large courtyard next door, she felt one loss in particular--the companionship of Jagat's wife. She was nearer Usha in age than her mother-in-law and had often helped Usha through difficult periods in her most rebellious days. She now learned to work alone or with her mother-in-law. The baby helped smooth out their relationship, both of them caring for her in moments between tasks and enjoying her when work was done. There was one unanticipated privilege for her in the location of their new courtyard. The door looked out on Panditji's platform and the lane leading to it. For his convenience Raju had hung a screen of slender reeds over the doorway so that the door could be left open. At times when she was free and unobserved, Usha could look out at activities in the lane through the minute slits between the reeds without herself being seen by passersby. It gave her a glimpse of life outside of the courtyard and helped to pass the months of waiting for Ganesh's return. He came just once during the year of training, at the time of the autumn festival.

The most surprising transformation to take place during Ganesh's absence was in Raju. The quarrel between his wife and Jagat's apparently shook him out of his absorption with lectures, and he turned his attention to the family. The changes in the house for which he was responsible were to his disadvantage, but he talked about them with enthusiasm, pleased with his ingenuity. As soon as the family was established in the new quarters, he began work on plans for a new house for himself and his wife, his children and for the next generation. There was space across the lane where relatives of an earlier generation had lived and died, the walls now heaps of mud. It was beside the new house Shiv Lal had built for Panditji and Panditain. There he would build a house of baked bricks.

When Ganesh returned to stay, he brought the training school certificate to be hung beside his college diploma in Raju's room. Usha was proud of it and so was Raju. Immediately Ganesh was swept into the spring harvest: soon the training course seemed unreal, less important than it had a year earlier. Grain had to be threshed, winnowed and marketed if the family were to have food and if the new house were to materialize.

But although house plans and harvesting occupied much of his time, he set out in search of a teaching post. He soon found two openings, one of which he chose for the first year. It was in a small school just three miles away where his classes were English grammar and Hindi and would give him the practice he needed. Before the beginning of his second year, he was offered a post he had applied for earlier: his subjects were, and still are, Hindi, Sanskrit, and English in a private school known to have the highest standards in Mainpuri. He has now been made a permanent member of the staff and is reported to be popular with the students.

Fellow masters are puzzled by his habit of departing for his village home as soon as classes are over. Several have commented on this and have asked why an otherwise sensible person like Ganesh choose to live in a village rather than in Mainpuri, the bustling headquarters of the district. Ganesh's friends on the college staff, most of whom have spent their lives in similar provincial towns, point out that if he were to build a house in town, he could spend his afternoons with other young teachers, playing badminton or tennis and participating in town social activities. This has not tempted him. He prefers the pleasure of a bicycle ride home along the quiet road bordered by fields and orchards When he arrives and has had a welcome meal, he supervises his fields and in slack seasons may have a game of volleyball with friends. Later he enjoys the time with Usha and their children--they now have two with the arrival of the hoped-for son. Still later there may be reading or music with friends.

During the year Ganesh spent in Kanpur, the young men gradually lost interest in getting together, either for singing or for fun. By the time he returned, every able-bodied man was called on for harvesting, but as work became lighter and days were longer, they reminded him of the singing parties they had missed. For them a singing party is more than singing. After a day of monotonous work in the fields or in a father's workshop, they find it relaxing just to be together. They count on the fun, the banter, the miming or the talk of local affairs. Before and after and in between these incidentals, there is music. They gather wherever it is convenient. Sometimes they sing on my verandah, and I am premitted to be the audience, listening and watching from my window. Some are eager as they come, some indifferent, led by more enthusiastic friends. Ganesh comes with his very old harmonium, and another young man has the dholak, an elongated drum, played at both ends. In the beginning they sit by twos or threes and talk while Ganesh quietly plays tunes at random. Then suddenly he straightens up and begins a song, playing his own accompaniment while the drummer beats the rhythm. It is a chant, a prayer, as is customary in all gatherings. Then follows a love song to which they listened tranced. Without deliberate shifting they gradually form a circle, coming closer. Then he starts a song most of them know. If it is less familiar, he sings one verse at a time and then they all join him on the second round. Many of the songs are long with what seems endless verses. Soon everyone is singing. There are gaps between songs when talking and laughing seem to come more easily. Ganesh leaves the talking to others while he plays on quietly, almost meditatively. Someone may interrupt him to ask for a favorite tale of some adventure or misadventure in Mainpuri or in the big city. He complies and loses himself as they do in the story. When the laughter dies down, he goes back to his music. If someone spontaneously starts a song, he and the drummer swing into the accompaniment; and so it goes, hour after hour. Sometimes they have a competition similar to a spelling bee. It adds excitement and fun. They laugh uproariously as one of them shouts,

"I am defeated." When it grows very late, they clamor
for a one last song, and then Ganesh's voice comes clearly over the courtyard wall in a closing song. Shortly
after this, they scatter, their voices fade, and no
sound breaks the stillness of a village night.

Among those who gather around Ganesh, a few have
begun to read books from his small collection. More of
them want to hear his reading of poetry, his own and
that of others. Others look forward to hearing about
his city experiences or about people he has met outside
of the village. All of them count on an evening of
music with him. They take more pride than he does in
his B.A., the first in the village. Nath, who was next
to receive the degree and Anand who recently became
M.Sc. have had ambitions that led them to large cities.
Ganesh, with his additional training, could be teaching
in a major city like Agra. Instead, he has chosen a
post in Mainpuri which makes it possible for him to live
here. He is not only a schoolmaster, but a farmer, like
themselves, and carries all of the responsibilities for
his land and his family without a father's supervision.
Field plans are made by their fathers, and they are
treated like day laborers with their only payment the
good they eat. They have no share in the harvest which
ordinary laborers are granted. Seldom do they have cash
in their hands to spend as they choose. They know Ganesh has plenty because some of them have been in the cooperative grain market in town helping their fathers
when he is there, and they know how much he has received.
They also know that he spends it for practical things as
their fathers do, not for sweets or in the movie house
in town as they would enjoy doing.

They do not appear to envy him, which is easily understood. They have been well aware of the obstacles he
has faced--frustration, disappointment and even failure.
They know that when he is in the fields he works as hard
as the best of them. When work is over, he seems as relaxed as the most free and easy. He lounges inside his

courtyard, or he sits outside on the platform which is his whenever Raju chooses to stay with his guru. At such times he can be found sitting there with three or four other young men, all laughing or talking together.

But beneath his casual manner, there is another more serious self which seldom comes to the surface. When it does however, Ganesh may discuss the implications some action taken at district headquarters or in the state capital might have on the farmers. At such times Ganesh expresses a deep concern for his village, and for villages all over India. He sees them as more vital to the life of the country than city-oriented leaders seem to comprehend. What would India do without them and the farmers living there? Why are they not given the same encouragement and respect as others? Politicians praise them while campaigning for their votes, but quickly forget them after the elections. In such ways does Ganesh express his regard for his fellow villagers, especially the farmers he works side by side with.

Quite a few men are leaving Karimpur to work and live in cities today. They are usually landless, belonging to the lowest strata of caste groups. They leave their families and send money by mail or bring it when they return for a visit. A few sons of landowners have left for work or study with the understanding that their homes are in Karimpur and with the assurance that if they fall ill or lose a job or complete their studies, they are free to return. More young men of all castes will be obliged to do this as their families increase and the land they own cannot provide for all of their needs. I have observed that the few who have left to work and reside in a city are in the city, but not of it. Each of them has found a few others like himself, alone, who have become his friends even though they know that the relationship is temporary. This gives them a place in a small, congenial community, surrounded but no longer overwhelmed by the crowds that surge around them.

Ganesh's friends are right when they say that he is here from choice while they are here from necessity. Actually, he is here from a choice to which he has held in spite of the problems involved. From the time he left the local school and began the bicycle rides to and from town, he felt that Karimpur was where he belonged. His marriage jeopardized his hopes until the day when he finally passed his college exams and set out to be a teacher. Now he is both teacher and farmer. As teacher he has the stimulating companionship of colleagues in town and as farmer he is among young friends who share his varied interests. They are vaguely aware that something has been released within him, perhaps through his adventures outside of the village or his books, his poetry, his music, or all of them. Whatever the reason they are sure that he has combined the best of two worlds.

ashram	A religious center of meditation and instruction.
baba	"Father" or "grandfather," often used as an honorific term for an older male. Sometimes used to refer to sadhus.
bahu	"Wife" or "daughter-in-law."
barhai	A member of the Carpenter caste.
basant	The spring season.
batsa	A puffed sugar candy, often used as an offering in religious ceremonies.
bhagya	One's fortune (or misfortune.
bhujia	A vegetable dish.
bigha	The traditional unit of land. In Karimpur there are five bighas to an acre.
biri	An Indian cigarette.
chapati	A flat, unleavened baked wheat bread; the staple food of the Karimpur diet.
charpai	A string cot, the most common type of bed in Karimpur.
chulha	An earthen fireplace; used as a cooking stove.
dacoit	A robber or bandit.
Dashera	A Hindu festival occurring in October-November celebrating Rama's victory over the demon Ravana.
dhanukin	A female member of the Midwife/Mat Maker caste.
dholak	An elongated, double-headed drum most commonly used as musical accompaniment in Karimpur.
dhoti	The principle article of dress, worn by both men and women. It is made of a length of cloth (5-6 yards long) which is wrapped around the wearer. Men's and women's styles vary.
Diwali	The Festival of Lights. Occurring in October-November, it welcomes the Goddess of Wealth, Lakshmi, into Hindu homes.
gali	A form of verbal abuse.
gauna	The marriage consummation ceremony, usually occurring six months or more after the actual marriage ceremony.
ghat	Literally meaning, "the edge or bank" it is most often used to mean the place where the dead are cremated.
ghee	Clarified butter.
guru	A spiritual preceptor.
hakim	A traditional doctor or medicine man.
Holi	The Hindu festival marking the spring harvest. It is often a riotous celebration.
jajman	The patron in a hereditary system of patron-client relationships.

kacchi	A member of the Farmer caste.
kahar	A member of the Water Carrier caste.
kamin	The client in the hereditary system of patron-client relationships.
karma	The results of one's actions; that which pre-determines the outlines of one's next life.
katha	A religious story.
Khera	The mound overlooking the village of Karimpur. According to legend, it is formed by the ruins of a fort which was destroyed in the eighteenth century. The word khera also refers to the section of the village at the foot of the mound where the Farmers live.
kirtan	A type of religious song, a hymn.
kismet	"Fate," interpreted as "luck,"
kshatriya	The second varna category, generally desig-nating a traditional occupation of warrior, king, or other guardian of the social order.
lagan	The second of the major wedding ceremonies. In it, the wedding date is set and the first installment of the dowry is presented to the groom's family.
lingam	A phallic symbol used to represent the god Shiva.
lota	A small brass pot used for carrying water.
maithil	A specific caste of Brahmins, common in eastern Uttar Pradesh and Bihar.
marusi	Tenancy rights to land.
mela	A fair.
mukhiya	The village headman appointed by the British Government prior to 1947.
namaste	The traditional Hindu greeting, it can be used to mean "hello" or "good-by."
nari	A leafy green vegetable.
naukri	A job, often used nowadays to imply a permanent service job. Government jobs carry the most prestige.
ojha	A specific caste of Brahmins. (Can also mean a curer.)
panchayat	Literally, "Council of Five." Prior to Inde-pendence, the panchayat was comprised of the village elders, informally chosen and without legal status. Now the members of the panchayat are elected and officially recognized.
pandit	A priest, a Brahmin by birth.

pradhan	The village headman; an elected official (the post did not exist prior to Independence).
punya	Religious merit.
puri	A fried wheat bread, an honorific food served on special occasions.
rabi	The spring growing season or harvest; from October to April.
raksha bandan	A Hindu festival taking place in July-August. On this day women seek the continuing protection of their brothers.
Ramayana	A Hindu epic which depicts the story of Rama, an incarnation of the god Vishnu.
rathor	A specific sub-caste of Oil Pressers.
rishi	A Hindu saint, holy man.
sadhu	A Hindu holy man who has renounced his family and all worldly possessions.
sangam	A meeting place.
sari	The modern form of dress worn by women.
sudra	The lowest category of varna rankings, generally designating a traditional service occupation (e.g., Carpenter, Tailor, Potter).
tel	Oil
telin	A female member of the Oil Presser caste.
thakur	A member of the kshatriya category, often a landlord or powerful person.
tika charan	A ceremony in which an auspicious mark (tika) is placed on the bridegroom's forehead. It marks an official betrothal.
tirth (pura tirth)	A place of pilgrimage, the "complete" pilgrimage.
tulsi	A basil (Ocimum Sanctum), a plant held sacred to the god Vishnu.
vaid	A practitioner of traditional medicine.

BIBLIOGRAPHY

Wadley, Susan S.

1975   Shakti: Power in the Conceptual Structure of Karimpur Religion. The University of Chicago Studies in Anthropology, series in Social, Cultural and Linguistic Anthropology, No. 2.

1975   "Folk Literature in Karimpur," Journal of South Asian Literature, vol. 11.

1976   "The Spirit 'Rides' or the Spirit 'Comes': Possession in a North Indian Village," in Rituals, Cults, and Shamanism: The Realm of the Extra Human, A. Bharati (ed.), Mouton.

1976   "Brothers, Husbands and Sometimes Sons: Kinsmen in North Indian Ritual," Eastern Anthropologist, Vol. 29.

1977   "Power in Hindu Ideology and Practice," in The New Wind: Changing Identities in South Asia, K. David (ed.), The Hague: Mouton.

in press   "Women's Calendrical Rites in a North Indian Village.: In R. Gross and N. Falk (eds.) Women and Religion: A Cross-Cultural Perspective.

           "Texts in Contexts: Oral Traditions and the Study of Religion." In S. Vatuk (ed.) AIIS Commemoration Volume.

Wiser, Charlotte Viall

1936   The Foods of a Hindu Village of North India. Allahabad: Superintendent, Printing and Stationery, United Provinces, India.

Wiser, William

1933   Social Institutions of a Hindu Village of North India. Unpublished Doctoral Dissertation, Cornell University.

1950   The Hindu Jajamani System. Lucknow: Lucknow Publishing House.

Wiser, William H. and Charlotte V.

1971   Behind Mud Walls: 1930-1960. With a Sequel -- The Village in 1970. Berkeley: The University of California Press.

AUDIO-VISUAL AIDS

Looking Behind Mud Walls. Narrated by Charlotte V. Wiser, Asian Studies Curriculum Center, 735 East Building, New York University.

JACKSON LIBRARY – LANDER UNIV.
HN690.K293 W57   CIRC
Four families of Karimpur /

3 6289 000864956

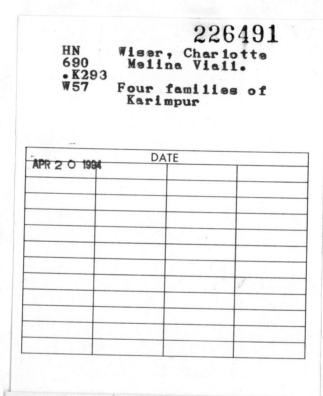

226491

HN   Wiser, Charlotte
690   Melina Viall.
.K293
W57   Four families of
          Karimpur

DATE		
APR 2 0 1994		

CARD REMOVED

© THE BAKER & TAYLOR CO.